In the Beginning
A Spiritualist's Bible

The Original Works of Rev. Eugene C. Larr
compiled by Rev. Donald R. Schwartz

Strategic Book Group

Strategic Book Group
P.O. Box 333
Durham CT 06422
www.StrategicBookClub.com

ISBN: 978-1-60976-691-7

Printed in the United States of America

Book Design: Suzanne Kelly

Table of Contents

BOOK II

BOOK III

BOOK IV

BOOK V

For the purpose of bringing forth the truth and universal knowledge that resides in all mankind.

Acknowledgements

Rev. Donald R. Schwartz recognizes and conveys his deepest and most sincere gratitude to the ministers, staff and students who brought Gene's legacy to print for the benefit of all mankind for generations to come…

Rev. Eric Berg
Rev. Sherry DeLoach
Rev. Don Miller
Rev. Bob Sisler
Rev. Nell Rose Smith
Debra Bernath
Marie Dardarian
Helene Dorian
Monica Hagen
Melissa Hall
Ernie Linkous
Wanda Olson
Dietmar Rothe
Suzanne Sisler
Drucilla Thiercof
Sheri Wachstetter

Precepts of the Philosophy

The following nine precepts make up the building blocks of our philosophy. They are not new; they are as old as time itself.

1. We affirm that there is an Infinite Intelligence in action through all time. Our definition of God is, simply, that "God is."
2. We affirm that there is a continuation of the individual beyond that change called "death."
3. We affirm that reincarnation is one of the major spiritual laws and that it IS the mechanism through which life evolves toward perfection.
4. We affirm that there is a general evolution, from simple to complex forms; both in life forms as well as inanimate matter, and that this same law is in effect in the physical universe as it is in the spiritual universe.
5. We affirm that heaven and hell are two states of living, here and now. They are not places "somewhere" but are the result of living in the now. We experience heaven when we live within the proper framework and hell when we live out of harmony with the universal laws.
6. We affirm that karma is simple causation; we as individuals are responsible for our actions in that we give out that which we wish to be returned to us.

   This is, of course, the "Golden Rule."

7. We affirm that there is communication with the so-called "departed individuals," under proper conditions, which can be used for the betterment of all mankind.
8. We affirm that the universe, both physical and spiritual, had no beginning. It has always been and will always be.
9. We affirm that the universal laws have been known by mankind since the earliest dawning of consciousness, and that it is these same laws which the great Masters of the past have tried to bring into man's active lives.

An Introduction to Rev. Eugene C. Larr

I arrived at the Chapel of Awareness in Encinitas, California, on a November night in 1973. I went there on the recommendation of Rev. Nancy Tappe, a brilliant teacher, psychic, and compassionate soul whose classes I was attending through the open university at San Diego State. Rev. Tappe is the most accurate aura reader and color theorist alive, in my opinion, and someone I trusted without reservation. So there was no doubt that the trip to Encinitas would help with my spiritual search.

I borrowed a friend's VW and went to a Sunday evening service. Several ministers helped out with the healings and messages, with Rev. Larr providing the lecture and guiding hand to the proceedings. This was the beginning of my many years of being a student of Rev. Larr, the Chapel, and its many gifted teachers and enlightened teachings. Through my efforts and with the help of many others, I would go on to become one of its teachers and ordained ministers.

One of the first lectures I heard Rev. Larr give, began as he stepped up to the podium in his usual suit and tie, as he was quite formal back in those early years. After a minute or so, he took off his suit coat and continued lecturing. A minute or so later, off came the tie, and he continued. Later, he removed his cufflinks. What was going on? Then he changed from the topic he was using as a distraction and addressed the real subject of the evening—Appearances! He asked if we were blind to the value, spirituality, and depth of individuals due to the way they dressed or the positions they might hold. Did we understand the difference between appearance and substance, humanity and spirituality? He was pointing out the need to develop our awareness in all ways to see the truth about people, ideas, philosophies, and psychic experiences if we are truly to advance. I entered a new realm. Here was a group that confirmed what my ideas on life and religion had always whispered to me. I became a student of this philosophy which meant becoming a student of all philosophies. The journey had to start by learning to look within, and committing to the lifework of self-understanding and controlling my mind.

The monograph you are about to embark on is called *In the Beginning, A Spiritualist's Bible*. It includes material from lectures and writings of Rev. Eugene C. Larr. My goal with this introduction is to give you an insight into his mind, purpose, and vision for the teachings that he shared with so many. It can be difficult, especially in transforming the spoken word, into its cold black-and-white representation on a page. What evokes the words is what we are hoping to grasp. I remember the comments of students many times saying they would come to hear Rev. Larr speak even if he read the phone book. As a candle flame provides both light and warmth, Rev. Larr conveyed not only the message, but that the listener was greatly valued and loved.

Rev. Larr was aware of the Holy Bible from a young age, as his grandparents insisted that he memorize passages. *A Spiritualist's Bible* presented here reflects more on Rev. Larr's insistence that a set of teachings should embrace the fullness of physical and spiritual reality. He believed that philosophy, biology, mathematics, archaeology, astronomy, physics, poetry, and religion were all avenues to discovering the whole truth about life and existence. Issues appearing to be contradictions or problems for mankind's knowledge and way of thinking are simply reflecting the limitations of human perception and awareness. In much the same way, the universe seems to get larger every time we make a bigger telescope.

We are immersed in the universe, but we don't always see how it operates. Rev. Larr taught that the necessary change was the perception and awareness within the human mind. Regardless as to whether the topic was sub-atomic particles or loving-kindness, we can and must open our minds to grasp the truth. His teachings and interactions with numerous students over the years carry his core belief from Buddhist tradition that each and every being can and will awaken the mental control and awareness potential within. From that affirmation, the spiritual awakening progresses. From a Christian perspective, it parallels the statement from Luke 17:21, "the Kingdom of Heaven is within you." The abilities which Rev. Larr discovered within himself, he saw residing in everyone else as well. To say it simply, we are all Spirit, individual, yet connected. He made the choice to help others find the universal spirituality and awareness residing within.

The keys to Rev. Larr's ability to teach and inspire so many people were his caring, acceptance, deep regard for each as they are, and diverse subject areas of interest. He was so curious about so many things in life that he was able to find common ground with practically everyone. Gene was equally comfortable discussing the Bible, hydrogen bomb explosions (which he observed and analyzed for the Defense Department), aliens, or the Muppets—he connected to students on so many levels. Again, we see his inclusive awareness that all of life is pieced together, and all things have their place.

Rev. Larr was a Renaissance man. He studied and researched many disciplines: paleontology, astronomy, Egyptology, woodcarving, orchids, classical music, fishing, Bible studies, making the perfect peanut brittle, as well as excelling with his psychic abilities. I believe this drive to understand so many fields of knowledge stems from a point of philosophy given to him by his spirit teacher Tau Sing: "I will become a master of all traits and ignorant of none."

Gene grew up in Oklahoma with a family that infused him with a philosophy that what came to you in life was caused by your hard work and efforts. No mystery there. As Gene grew, he never waited for others to push and motivate him. As he grew older, he did have the insight to place himself in situations to learn from some of the brightest lights of his day. Attending lectures by Albert Einstein and working under Edward Teller served to feed his knowledge—hungry mind. As deeply as his scientific curiosity ran, he always desired to understand spirituality and the meaning of life which mirrored that intensity. He studied and trained as a Buddhist in Hawaii toward the conclusion of WWII, and later studied Spiritualism upon his return to the mainland. He finally found his appropriate mentor in Rev. Jean Bradley in Pasadena, California, where she had founded St. Michael's Spiritualist Church. Under her direction, he learned to appreciate the many religious traditions, and how Spiritualism provided a door to a beautiful experience which encompassed his rich background.

Rev. Larr founded the Chapel of Awareness in order to share this beautiful philosophy and help others develop the psychic and healing abilities he worked hard to master. He pointed to a golden thread of truth running through all philosophies. An example is the Golden Rule which is stated in all teachings, ancient and modern, with only small changes in wording. The limitations and differences that arise in traditions can be explained through cultural traditions, human interpretation, recording of events, and the evolution of mankind's understanding of the world. The East Indian story of the blind men and the elephant illustrates this beautifully. Each man touches a different part of the elephant in the road, and each confidently claims to understand fully what an elephant truly is: like a tree trunk (leg), or a wall (the side), or a rope (tail). Of course everyone is missing a much bigger truth underlying these separate parts. Mankind likes to draw conclusions even when complete information is lacking.

Gene believed that with intense study, honest personal reflection, and learning to control the mind through the dual efforts of meditation and concentration, each student could break through his or her self-imposed shell of ignorance and fear. He believed that all traditions needed to be investigated for truth. He blended together, for the philosophy of the Chapel, the highest principles of Eastern and Western traditions. The outcome is the simple philosophy he set forth with the guidance of his spirit teachers. This way of viewing life, the universe, and our time in it, is what I am hoping to pass along to you as you read the writings and words of Rev. Larr. In this way of seeing, the universe is infinite, without beginning or end. It is constantly changing form and shape due to a structured order which Rev. Larr called Infinite Intelligence. He shied from quantifying or qualifying God, but simply affirmed that God is.

Like Buddha, Gene avoided trying to define this concept. He liked to refer to the notion from the story *Lost Horizon* which stated that there are times in people's lives when they touch the Infinite. When an individual develops awareness to a point, one will know, not guess, the nature of the Infinite. As with all matters of growth and development, he said things will happen for you "In time, and on time"—not before you have laid down the ground work required.

Rev. Larr's philosophy also taught there was no devil. He believed it was a human invention to explain undesired events or to relieve individuals of responsibility for their actions. Heaven and hell describe our experience of the here and now. It is our complete responsibility which side of the scale we experience. He spells out the keys for living life, and each moment, in a positive and spiritual manner with simple, yet profound guidelines. First, we are all responsible for our actions due to the working of karma, or cause and effect. As you sow, so shall you reap. Actions follow from thoughts and thus the guideline he repeated often, "Thoughts are things. So you think, so you are." We move our lives in the direction of how we think.

Life serves an opportunity to grow and advance along the greater pathway of spiritual development according to Rev. Larr's philosophy. The life we each live now is but one of many. The growth of one's awareness, both of what is within our being, and the universe outside, is the underlying drive for us as spiritual entities. Developing an appreciation, a caring, and wisdom of ourselves and others, is a gauge to judge one's own life. In addition, he extolled moderation in all things, not interfering in the lives of others, avoiding distractions, and finally, Jesus' command to love one another. These he pointed to as the highest virtues for our aspirations, and reflected true spirituality.

Rev. Larr taught psychic development and healing for many years. He always stressed the importance of grounding the psychic work within the greater spiritual framework that has given us individual existence, and of which we are a part. Being humble before the truth is a necessity. It isn't what you <u>can</u> do that is important, but what you <u>do</u> with your abilities. Rev. Larr embodied this philosophy to a high level. This made him someone with whom you wanted to study. Being around him, there was always something new to learn. He had the quality of sharing his abilities or thoughts, inspiring all his students to believe how much more each could be: a better person, professional, friend, medium, parent, whatever roles one chooses in life. Sometimes we all need role models to find the inspiration and strength to lift ourselves up to the highest levels of accomplishment. Rev. Larr served many students this way, all the while reminding all how hard they must work and invest in themselves to bring about something worthwhile.

So he shared his love of life, knowledge, and spiritualism. Whether it was a formal class on the Bible or a relaxed lesson at the local coffee shop on how to bend spoons with your mind, he was always sharing. Rev. Larr led trips to Egypt, Japan, Mexico, the mountains and deserts, to the beaches of southern California, to the rooms within our minds. He taught a simple way to open oneself to the abundance of life by teaching your mind to do two extraordinary things: 1) concentrate on a single thought, and 2) be silent to all thought in meditation. Learn to do these two things, and you will discover the greatest gift the Infinite has given to you: awareness.

I hope you enjoy *In the Beginning, A Spiritualist's Bible.* Remember, words are symbols that point toward reality and truth. Words fall short of actual experiences. We say the word "love," but it does not convey all we feel, think, remember, and hope. In the same vein, the words I've used to give a background of Rev. Larr, from my own experience, probably come up a little short. They should serve to open your mind to the core of his teachings on Spiritualism and his vision that we would experience life more abundantly. He worked tirelessly to bring these ideas to thousands of people over the years. I do hope what I've shared about this wonderful human being will help bring a depth and fullness to your understanding of what he was trying to share with all of us. One last thing to remember, the book isn't about Rev. Larr, it's about you!

By Rev. Bob Sisler

An Introduction to the Beginning Lecture Series

For more than thirty years, Rev. Larr refused to have his classes, lectures, and lessons published in print. He remained concerned that misinterpretation or misrepresentation would ensue. This is an issue we all worry about when discussing our spiritual beliefs with others. He referred to the classic reference of how the words of Jesus, Buddha, and Muhammad have been used, sometimes twisted from the original meaning, by their followers.

In the last years of his life, Gene was finally convinced, through the urging of some of the Chapel of Awareness ministers, to print and share his many teachings and lessons. The lessons and Truth presented are timeless, and may clarify for future generations the simple points about life that he worked so unceasingly to share. It really is a great gift. Gene may no longer be physically with us, but his teachings are preserved in the pages that follow.

The chapters herein are mostly transcriptions of classes given before a church full of students hanging on his every word. An honest representation of his educational background and Oklahoma straight-forward approach are reflected here. Some grammatical elements have been sacrificed in order to maintain the flavor of Rev. Larr's style of delivery. It may feel as if you are sitting with him, hearing his words in real time, for he was indeed a unique man.

One of the reasons Rev. Larr hesitated to present these lessons in print was because the reader would not have him available to answer their questions as they absorbed the information and worked with it. He touched many topics and considered each student important.

Rev. Larr harbored a commitment to each student that was as strong as his commitment to each lesson. As you read, perhaps he will be there in Spirit as you ask questions, just as he was for students sitting in Chapel when these lessons were given.

We invite you to find a seat. Welcome! Together we will explore a fascinating realm which has caused human beings to question and ponder since their very beginning. We will open a pathway which you can walk with ever-growing confidence, gaining with each step a new awareness of life, and most useful in your everyday activities. We will introduce you to this new realm and teach you how it can be used to bring about a fuller, more complete life. We will teach you by encouraging you do it YOURSELF!

General Introduction to the Beginning Lecture Series

(1972) Good evening everyone, my name is Reverend Gene C. Larr. I'm founder of the Chapel. I've been a clairvoyant clairaudient medium for about thirty-five years, and I've been teaching the development of psychic ability for about fifteen years.

We started the Chapel with that in mind, and I know all of you have this little outline, and we'll get to that in a little bit, but I wanted to cover some other things first, by way of a general introduction.

Our main point here at the Chapel is to develop your awareness. Okay, what is awareness? What is this thing we're talking about developing? It is easiest to see on a physical level. You all have five senses; most of you do not use them properly all the time, but nevertheless, you've had them for a long time and do know how to use them.

There is also, of course, an equivalent set of five psychic senses, plus two others we will get into as we go along. And to develop your awareness is to learn to use everything that you have in your mind, for that is where all the sensations are registered, to get the most out of the environment you are in. And there are two very unusual ways to practice and learn to do this.

And they are concentration and meditation.

Let's touch first on concentration. For those of you who are still in school, you know what concentration is. For those of you who have been out of school for a while, it is a very unusual thing to control, and a very unusual thing to learn to do when you have gotten out of the habit of doing it. The problem is that we generally try to do more than one thing at a time.

We will have five or six thoughts running through our mind at one time, and, unless you've had some very precise training, you will not do justice to any of them. So keep in mind that the thing we're literally teaching you to do is to gain control of your mind so that you can use your five physical senses, and by controlling your mind, learn to develop and use your psychic senses as well. That's very intriguing; when I talk about psychic activity, most people will mention one or two, and I will bump into some people who insist they have never had psychic experiences in their lives.

I can assure you, you all have. Maybe you didn't label it as that, but you've all had many psychic experiences. The spectacular ones you will remember.

Learning to concentrate is extremely important if you are going to learn anything. Have you ever noticed those things that you are best at are the things you like to do? If you try to read a dull, boring book, and many students make a mistake in this regard, and you play music in the background, you will not concentrate properly, because part of your mind is listening to that music instead of paying attention to the information your eyes are giving to your mind. And I think you can spot this very, very easily.

If you start reading a very, very dull book, and the radio is going, and suddenly your favorite love song comes on, you will go humming along and singing the song while your eyes continue to scan the page, then you wonder when you get to the bottom of the page why you don't remember what that whole page was about. Now we've all bumped into that.

Another beautiful example of it is for those of you like myself who like to read in bed, you are reading, and you are reading, and you are reading, and somewhere along the way you have really gone to sleep, and you are reading the same line over and over and over.

Lack of concentration. You can't do two things at once until you learn to control that thing upstairs—your mind. And once you get that in control, and can control your thoughts and thinking, then you actually can think and handle up to five or six things at the same time. It is not easy, and unless you have some very specific training to start out with, you will have trouble doing it.

Okay, I mentioned meditation. This is something that everybody is familiar with now, but it is normally looked upon with suspect by a lot of people. Some of you, I imagine, have explored or may be using other forms of meditation: Transcendental Meditation, Yoganandan, whatever it happens to be. Do not throw those out, but we are going to be teaching you a different kind of meditation, total silence. Your mind is to be totally still. This again is something that at first you may find difficult. In fact, some of you may find it awfully damned hard. But if you will persist and practice, you will gain that control, and that is the only way to develop and control your psychic sensitivity.

Transcendental Meditation, TM, is a beautiful form of meditation. I would recommend for those of you who now are using it or are familiar with it, to use it as a prelude to the kind of meditation you're going to be doing here; use it as a form of relaxation. But TM by itself will not open a single psychic center. No way, because it is on a different pathway and it is aimed at a different goal, so you can't expect it to do both.

When you want to silence your mind, sit down in a room with subdued light and as relatively free of sound as you can possibly find, and simply tell your mind to shut up. Now you have to talk to your mind like it is a three-year-old child, because for all your life, up to this point, unless you've already mastered control, your mind has been doing what it wanted to do.

Have you ever sat down and tried to relax, and noticed that thoughts ran through your mind like a whole row of freight trains? You're going to stop those trains. You're going to make them be quiet and get still. It's a very interesting thing. And it is the gateway to every psychic gift there is.

I learned my meditation—my silent-type meditation—when I was a Mahayana Buddhist. I was a Buddhist for eight years and practiced deep meditation every day for many hours. We will not ask you to do that, because that does not accomplish what we're after. You will start out by meditating five minutes in the morning and five minutes in the evening. A little further down the line we will go to ten minutes, but that's as far as we will go. I want to show you that if you hear people talking about, "Well, I sat down and meditated for four hours yesterday," you can almost bet they're deluding themselves. For someone to sit in total silent meditation, unless they are a Buddhist, is almost impossible. Because first of all the body gets tired, and you're thinking about how tired you are, and then, of course, you've lost that minor little point.

There are so many things that you will discover as you go along with this kind of meditation that will be a great help to you both mentally and physiologically. But I want you to all diligently try. You're going to get very sick and tired of hearing me say, "Practice makes perfect, try again." You're probably going to want to stone me or something. But it's true.

The analogy that I always use is that probably most of you in the audience could come up here and pick out a simple tune on this piano, "Chopsticks" or something like that, but if you were going to sit up here and play a piano concerto, you had better do some practicing first. And it's just as simple as that. Practice does make perfect.

I have a little thorn in my side about these things called "psychic gifts." They're related, of course, in the New Testament as psychic or spiritual gifts. They are not gifts at all. You will work like mad for every one of them. Believe me, you will. You may experience clairvoyance or clairaudience at odd times, but that is not a usable tool. I want you to get to the point that when I ask for a clairvoyant reading, bang, on command, you can do it. Practice, practice, practice.

Let me touch lightly on several things.

First of all, be careful of the so-called "mind-expanding" drugs. And I'm using "careful" there in two senses.

Biologically, they are not good for you, obviously. There's a big argument about whether or not marijuana is harder on you than the cigarette I just put out in my office; I won't argue that point with you.

I have tried most of them, grass, LSD, etc., under controlled conditions, while I was already a clairvoyant-clairaudient medium, and they did not do a thing for me. Those techniques of crawling out of your head, if you will, are cop outs. You can do so much better by getting control. You cannot control a trip induced by drugs. Your mind, part of it, at least, has stepped aside; therefore, you have no control over the images, the lights, the colors, the experience itself. So don't play that game.

A little further down the line, when we start getting into actual circles, I would ask you to avoid a couple other things. Please don't come to class expecting to sit in circle after you've had three or four joints. Those teachers in some of these circles will know it, and it will show up in your work. If you want to have a drink with dinner, great, I do. I enjoy it. But don't drink a fifth of Hill and Hill and come to class. Unless you can hold your liquor a lot better than I can.

The biggest thing I want you to remember is this thing of excess: avoiding excess in all things. We'll talk about that extensively when we get into spiritual law. Many times people will ask me, "What if I smoke a cigarette? Doesn't that harm my psychic ability?" No, of course not. They will also say, "Well, I also see you drink coffee. That doesn't bother you either?" There are very, very few things that will, with the exception of certain drugs, and I don't mean the hallucinogens.

The one that upsets me is Demerol. When I had to be on Demerol because I was in the hospital, a few times some years back, all my psychic senses turned off. And if you want to wake up thoroughly scared some morning, try that. Right now I can see all of your auras and your guides and teachers that are around you, and of course I can see all my teachers and everything else and talk with them, and I had been doing it for years and years and years, and woke up in the hospital, and nobody was there. I almost went bananas, and the poor nurse didn't know what was going on. I didn't dare tell her I was upset because I couldn't see my invisible companions. I'd have gone from intensive care to the padded cell in one bold step.

So some of those may affect you, and I would be suspicious of those that are the so-called pain suppressants. Aspirin, as far as I know, does not affect psychic senses, but I'm sure it's a very individual thing. I know of one medium who also had Demerol in surgery and it didn't bother her at all, but it turned me off like slamming lead doors.

Okay. One of the things I want you to start thinking about doing is using your psychic ability. Now I'm not going to give you any assignments as far as meditation is concerned, because we want to talk about that next time before we really get into it, but there's a thing called "psychometry." Don't bother to take notes about it because we'll have a lesson on this. Psychometry is the ability to hold something in your hand and receive information from it. In other words, if I took my ring off and handed it to one of you and you held it in your hand and gave the first impressions that came to mind, you would be startled how right some of them can be.

But notice what I said: the first impression. That's extremely important. So this week, when you get your mail, for instance, before you open it, hold it between your hands. Before you look at the address and see who it is from, put it between your hands. Get still for just a second, try to get just as still as you can, and say, "What's in it?" I won't expect you at this point to read the letter, word for word, but later on, some of you can do that. Believe me, you can. If it's a bill, see if you can pick up any numbers that are on the bill. What is the amount, etc.? Just as an exercise.

Some of you probably unconsciously play another form of psychic sensitivity. The phone rings, and you know who's calling before you pick up the receiver. It is very interesting to watch students here at the Chapel as they start to practice this.

I want you to notice something about it. When you are walking toward the phone, or the moment the phone rings, and suddenly you say, "Oh, yeah, that's John," it will be John. And the thing I want you to notice is that you were not guessing. Suddenly you knew it was John. And if you can separate early in the game that subtle difference between guessing and knowing, you'll be halfway home free. So practice those two little things. I think you'll find it a lot of fun, and it's an excellent practice for you.

Okay, psychic knowing, the kind of thing you're going to do by opening your psychic sensitivity, can do a great many things. As I say, all of you have it to some degree. And there are two that I think everybody has simply because they're alive.

Because you are a Homo sapiens and you've got that gray matter up between your ears, you all have hunches and intuitions. Now these are two very precise, different things. I want you to remember that a hunch is a short-term bit of psychic information, short-term in the sense of talking about time! Intuition is long-term, psychic information. Let me give you a couple examples.

Let's say you're playing poker and you're dealt a couple of cards face down, and you know that the card right there is a red card. You pick it up and it's a ten of diamonds. Okay. That's a hunch. This is a little trick that the mind can do by stepping ahead in time and seeing what that card is.

Intuitions, long-term psychic knowing, are a little more difficult to pin down. These are the kinds of things that happen when you're puttering around the house, or you are working at your job, and suddenly you feel that something's wrong. You don't know what, but suddenly the hair on the back of your neck wiggles and you get uneasy. If it is a really strong feeling you'll generally find yourself walking around wringing your hands, trying to figure out what's wrong, then days, or much later, you'll get a call and find that someone you think a great deal of was injured in an automobile accident at that time. Okay, these are the kind of things you can spot.

I think the one that bugs me is I can sense company coming. I might not know who it is, but quite often I will have a day all planned to perfection, when I was going to do just exactly what I wanted to do, and suddenly I get this funny feeling that something's wrong, and sure enough, at the wrong time, company arrives and upsets all the plans. These are, as I say, two traits that you all have, and if you learn to use them, you can really help yourself. The other kinds of psychic knowing, of course, are the ones I mentioned earlier: clairvoyance, clairaudience, clairsentience and all these things which we will discuss in detail later.

And the biggest thing is, these abilities allow you to know something outside of your present state or knowledge, or let you have knowledge of something coming up in the future. Now there's one side of clairvoyance that generally makes me very unhappy, and we have seen a lot of it recently. In several of the newspapers like *The Inquirer*, we see psychics predicting everything. And some of the predictions are horrendous and horrible. And I think that is wrong.

A good example of it is, I have a high teacher around me named Tao Sing who you will all get to know a little later on, and one afternoon I was talking to him about this problem of major earthquakes.

I said, "Is Los Angeles going to be devastated by a gigantic earthquake?" and he said "No." And I said, "A lot of little ones?" "Yes, a lot of little ones. And by the way, the next major one is going to be in a few months," and he gave me the date, "in a Central American country." And I asked him which one, and he said "Guatemala." And of course it occurred, as you well know, with a large loss of life. And then I did something I want all of you to do, as you get further along and get developed, when you get that kind of information; ask two important questions: Is there some way the event can be avoided? Can I do something to change the event so it does not come about, or can I warn them in some way that the event is going to come about? If the answer is no to both of those questions, then forget it, completely. Because I don't like that kind of publicity and I don't think you would either.

And as Tao Sing pointed out one night in class when this came up, "If you saw a natural disaster coming and knew you could do nothing about it, would you run down to the newspaper to make a name for yourself about the death of ten or fifteen thousand people?" I don't think so. Use your psychic gifts differently than that, and I think you will find them very, very beneficial.

As we go along here, we're going to discuss in these lectures many, many things that are going to rub some of you the wrong way. Let me take just one of them: we're going to be touching on reincarnation a little later. It's not going to break my heart if you don't believe in reincarnation. And it's really not going to make any difference as far as your own psychic development is concerned whether you believe in it or not. But I love the answer that Rev. Bradley gave one night after she'd given a lecture at church on that subject. A man very belligerently was muttering in the back and making all kinds of comments, and finally he asked her if she really expected him to believe in reincarnation? And she said, "Well, I really don't care, but one of these days you're going to wake up and find out I was right." So I'll put it right there. Those things that we touch on, in these lectures that you cannot fit into your present existence, into your present way of thinking, file them away. I can assure you that further down the line, most all of them will fit into place. We're going to tear up some pet myths. We're going to tear up some pet concepts. Let me get a couple of them out of the way, because they always come up in the question-and-answer session.

Atlantis never existed in the three-dimensional world. California is not going to fall off into the ocean.

Now let's see, what are some of the others? There is no such thing as "possession" in the classic word; in other words, "Exorcist" was a good, scary movie, and that's about all. Anyway, things like that we're going to get rid of one by one.

Years ago I had a spirit teacher who came to me; we were seated around a table giving each other messages like we do some evenings, and he popped in. I saw him standing there in a dark suit and tie, and he looked like a college professor type, so I greeted him and acknowledged his presence, as you should always do. He said, "I will be your teacher if you are ready to throw out some of your pet ideas." Well, I thought, wow, who in the hell do you think you are? I thought, then said, "Okay, I'll agree if you replace every idea you make me throw out with something of equal or greater validity." And he taught me a great deal. And he threw out a lot of things. I had a lot of gorgeous little pet ideas that I thought were very neat.

Following reincarnation, if we look at the three major teachers of the past, Buddha, Jesu Christi, and Muhammad, they are almost exactly five hundred years apart. And I thought, 'How neat. That's the same entity, hopping back to redo what he was trying to do.' And that was a real pet theory of mine. And the teacher's comment was, "Very interesting, but not at all correct." So out went that one.

So these are the kinds of things that if we rattle your cage, file it away. Ask questions. Let me touch on that for just a moment. Even though you're seated in a Chapel, and it's obviously a Chapel where we do hold services twice on Sunday, healing services and things like that, when you are here on a class night, this is a classroom. If you want to talk about anything, let's talk about it. Anything from sex to pineapple; I don't care what it is because you came here to get some knowledge. You came here to get some tools. And if we start drawing lines on a pseudo-religious basis about what should and should not be talked about, then we're in trouble. I think if there were more frank discussions in some of the churches today, the churches would be much better off. But that's their problem, not ours.

Okay, as we go along, another question I'm always asked is, what books would I recommend? Well, there are two; my own little book, which is around here somewhere, called *Your Dawning Awareness*, and the other one I would recommend is *Helping Yourself with ESP* by Al Manning. Now Dr. Manning has written several other books, and I will not recommend them to you. He goes off on some interesting tangents, and I will not debate the philosophical correctness of some of those tangents. But those two are interesting.

The biggest problem with books is the proliferation of things simply to make money. When I was first studying with Rev. Bradley in 1948, you could count on one hand the books on psychic information, and they were almost all British books. I think one that I enjoyed the greatest was Carrington and Muldoon's book on astral projection.

I loved that little volume because astral projection has always been very easy for me, and it was fascinating to study. But if you go down to the bookstore today and look at the shelf on whatever term you want to use: psychic ability, ESP, witchcraft, all of those things, good heavens, there must be several hundred volumes stacked up on the shelves. Some of you, I'm certain, have done a lot of reading, and I hope you will do much, much more.

But one of the biggest things I want you to be careful about in your reading is some of the authors are not coming from a solid space. They're either writing from hearsay or they're copying someone else's book. Consequently, we have many, many books that are out today that are, to my estimation, not worth reading.

Now you will know, if you haven't guessed already, that I am very opinionated when we get into this particular subject, because it happens to be my life's work, and has been for a long time. So there are several things I've got little sticklers in my head about. That's one of them. I can't use my old cliché anymore; I used to say, "People who do, do; people who can't, write books." But since I wrote my little pamphlet, I can't say that anymore. But I can do what's in that pamphlet, and that's one of the things I want you to remember. As you go along and read some of these books, if you can't make the author's experience fit your experience, don't throw your experience out; the author may be in error.

Just because it's printed does not make it the truth, and I think one of the shining examples of that is *Chariots of the Gods*. A gorgeous book, which I'm sure probably made millions of dollars, and it did more to destroy anthropology and archaeology than any other single book ever written, in my estimation. It is wrong; all the stuff in it is wrong, but it makes fascinating reading.

But don't get swallowed up in it. The planet Earth is the only planet in this solar system that has highly evolved, intelligent life on it. There's life on Mars, and we're going to find it in, I hope, this last landing of Viking. But anyway, when you bump into situations of people coming from Jupiter, or Venus, or wherever they might happen to come from, and are telling you all kinds of things, just stop and think. Look at what is going on. The truth is always simple. Simple relationships are absolute.

I met, not too many months ago, a woman who insisted she was from Venus—and she looked like many of you—and I don't mean that as a slam—I mean she looked like an ordinary female Homo sapiens. She couldn't possibly be from Venus and have a body like that. (That was the wrong thought!) No, I'm referring simply to the biological process that made you a hydrocarbon creature living here on Earth. It was a very special little thing that occurred that made you like you are, as a live human being. So as you explore these books, or see the movies that have been made after them, don't get swallowed up in something too strenuous, because simplicity always is the essence, and it's always the case with the truth.

Okay, the books we will be drawing on here. I will refer to them but not assign them. I've divided them roughly into sacred books and textbooks.

The sacred books I'm referring to would be the New Testament, the Sanskrit writings of Buddha, and some of the Hindu concepts having to do with mind control.

Now we won't ask you to read the original Greek of the New Testament, nor the Sanskrit of Buddha, or the altered form of Sanskrit of the Bhagavad Gita, because it would be a chore, a real chore. But we will be drawing from them.

As far as modern books are concerned, most of them are ordinary textbooks having to do with all kinds of phenomena around you. When we get into reincarnation, for instance, there are many beautiful books and I may recommend some for those who simply like to read. Some of them are very, very beautiful, but I don't want you to look upon the concept of evolution, for instance, and think that you all must become paleontologists to understand it. Not at all. I want you to get the overall view of what is going on.

Okay, let's look at our outline for a brief minute. We will teach you by making you do it yourself. I want you to remember that. Here at the Chapel you will never be asked to do anything that cannot be demonstrated for you. I would never ask you to use psychokinesis unless I showed you it could be done. And here is one of those areas where we have an advantage, because I'm very, very proud of our teachers; they are fine people, both as ordinary individuals, and especially in their abilities. So even though you are going to get bored and you're going to get tired of guessing wrong, please stick with it, because one of the times you will stop guessing and you will be right. And that's what I want you to do. So let's just go down through these.

'General Introduction'—well, we just got that one out of the way. 'Right & Wrong, Spiritual Law and Karma.' Now there's a good handful. And we're going to cover some of these basic things: What is right? What is wrong? First of all, you'll find that there are very few things that are totally right or totally wrong. There is not a whole list of things, like the Ten Commandments and all the rest of the commandments given by Moses in the Old Testament. That's simply not true.

Many people have asked me, "Well, how do I know when I'm doing something right or wrong?" Well, basically, you all know it automatically. If you start to do something wrong, you know it inside. There's a funny little thing Jesus called the "wee small voice" that lets you know that's not the best thing to do.

One of the biggest problems with it is oftentimes, because we're humans, we'll say, "Well, that's wrong, but I'm going to do it anyway." Then karma comes into play.

Karma, as some of you probably know, is a Sanskrit word. It simply means causation; cause and effect. Here is one of those areas where most books really foul up. Karma does not step across lifetimes. You are not being condemned this lifetime for something you did your last lifetime or the one before. That clever little thing came from some Hindu reinterpretations of the original writings and has been picked up by some of today's modern churches as a way of punishing you for sins. Let me ask you, though, just a very simple analogy: would you punish your twenty-one-year-old son because he spilled milk when he was two years old? No, of course not. You punish someone when they know what they are being punished for. And that is karma. It does not step across lifetimes. Remember that.

'Spiritual Law'—as I say, we will talk about that—I think that will be a very fascinating evening for you.

Number III is going to be the lulu of the sequence—'Evolution: Physical and Spiritual, Reincarnation.' They lock tightly together. And remember, I want you to have the overall picture. I don't expect you to remember all the scientific names and this kind of thing, because that's not what you're here to learn. I want you to get the overall picture of what's going on. Evolution is the tool by which reincarnation works, and we will find out more about that as we go along.

'The Duality of Man.' I'm sure all of you are aware that you're more than just a physical body. There's a whole set of electronic fields or electrostatic fields around you which psychically we call the aura. There is also a part of you that we call the etheric; that is the real you that continues through all your lifetimes, and these are the things we will discuss.

'The Aura' is a fascinating thing. Some of you may be able to see auras now, and as we go along a little further, the rest of you will be able to learn to see them.

Rev. Bradley, who's standing beside me, for those of you who are psychic, just reminded me to comment right there on this thing of evaluating where you are. She reminded me of an argument that a husband and wife had in one of our advanced classes when I was with her. He could see auras and she could not, and it almost broke up the family, believe me. But later on, the ability was learned and the marriage was saved. So as we go along, we'll hammer away at that.

'The Mind of Man and Its Power'—if you've ever been afraid of anything in your life, you should be afraid of the mind. The mind is the most powerful thing in the universe. Under proper control, it can do incredible things. Under proper control, it can do almost anything. I said almost, because there are some things you cannot interfere with. But in almost all other categories, it can do almost anything. It's a fascinating thing.

Number VII, 'Meditation.' Stilling of mind. Of course, by this time you're all going to be doing meditation. Or you'd better be doing meditation. And at this point we'll talk about the different kinds of meditation. Those kinds of meditation that can be used for other things, as I mentioned before, like Transcendental, as a technique to relax.

Number VIII, 'Spirit Evolution and Communication.' In this one we will discuss the evolution on the spirit side. In other words, you are a physical animal, and you've also got a spiritual side of you, or soul, if you want to use the Hebraic form. This evolves as well, and it grows, and it learns, and it develops different techniques, and it does so very beautifully.

Number IX is 'Healing, Basic Concepts.' This lecture will relate to colors and how they affect you psychically and scientifically, on a purely psychological basis. Why do certain colors make you feel better? Why do certain colors upset you?

Healing is one of the greatest of the psychic abilities. This is something we hammer away at very heavily here, and in the Al Manning book, the section on healing is slightly different than you will get here at the Chapel, but it doesn't deviate too far from what we will be doing here.

Some of you are fine healers already. Some of you need to learn little controls to enhance the ability that you already have, and it is in these areas that we will explore.

'Mediumship'—all the funny things that mediums do. I think the one that actually blew my mind the furthest was when we had a visiting medium at Rev. Bradley's class. We had a candle going, and she gave everybody little 4x5 cards. We were to walk up and pass the card through the flame so smoke got on the card, then go back and sit down. Then she came around and took each card, and she picked up mine and gave me a fabulous reading. She told me what I'd been doing for the last several years and told me what I was going to be doing for the next couple years. And when she handed the card back to me all I could find on it was a little Scottie dog. But the card had nothing to do with it. It was simply a point of concentration. It was something for her to concentrate her mind on while she touched into the entire psychic realm that was around her and around me at that time. This is the same thing with amulets, crystal balls, these kinds of things, and we will go into those in detail, and see which ones mean something and which ones really do not.

I see I skipped one. 'Concept of Vibrations,' number VI. For those of you who have had some college experience, this will be old hat to you. But for some of you not aware of the physical matter in the universe, it might be amazing for you to find that this podium is not solid at all; it is mostly empty space, and especially if you get down to an atomic level, it is gross empty space; it just simply looks solid.

'Materializations, Aports and Teleports.' This is a fascinating realm, and this is what many people visualize a circle or a séance to be, materialization, so you can see a ghost or what have you. It takes some special things to do that. Special things up here (pointing to mind). And we'll be learning which ones to practice, what states of mind to get into, so that when you actually do get into circles, these kinds of things can occur.

Aports and teleports are devices that are given to you by Spirit as a gift, as you would give anybody else a gift. They are quite rare. I know in some areas or some organizations you can go into a circle and get a handful of teleports. These are not true aports and teleports, and I've broken some lovely hearts. A woman came up to me once with a handful of little gems and asked which one was a real aport or teleport. And I had to tell that none of them were real.

Case in point: don't ever ask me a question unless you want an answer. I'm one of those who has decided that if you came in and asked a question, by gosh I should answer it as truthfully as I can, or to the best ability that my teachers or your teachers can answer.

That holds true with all of the teachers here at the Chapel. If you ask a question, make sure you are ready for what the answer might be, because it might not be the answer you want. In fact, quite often it is not. But that is neither here nor there.

'Dark Circles,' 'Why,' and 'Your Next Steps.' 'Dark Circles' and 'Why,' explain frameworks of the mind, things you must do in order to properly enjoy a dark circle.

Well, I believe I have touched on each item in your little outline, maybe not in the exact order but sufficiently enough I imagine.

And your next steps, well, your next steps are things like here and now. If you want to go that direction and become a minister, great. We can do just that. If you want to become a healer, good. You can do that as well. But you've got plenty of time to make up your mind, so pick and choose, and as you go along, you will find your direction.

You will be required to keep two notebooks. One is for class notes, questions and activities, and the second one acts as a personal diary, recording your psychic experiences and dreams on a daily basis, which will allow you to compare and realize your progress. These are very important. The first one from the standpoint of questions, because all during the week you're going to think of questions you want to ask someone here, and then when you get here, you're going to forget the question. So jot it down; it's the only way to remember. And this other one: Psychic Experiences and Dreams.

If you see a little blue spot in your receptor, write it down. Next time you might see a blue spot with wings on it, so that's an advantage. Jot these things down so you can compare what you did a month ago with what you might be doing later.

Dreams are something else again. Your dreams of course also fall into two categories. One is a purely psychological dream that is working out things in your subconscious mind. For instance, if you come to me and tell me that you dreamed you ran over your mother-in-law, okay, it might happen, but I would bet it's a psychological dream. So don't worry about it. Dream dreams, the kind of dreams we have that are like nightmares, are generally triggered by physical upsets.

You're sleeping too warmly, you had cantaloupe and beer before you went to bed—any of those things are almost guaranteed to do it. But learn to write them down. Again, it's another training of the mind. Making the mind remember. That's extremely important. I'm not going to check those notebooks, incidentally, so don't faint if you think so—I'm not going to do that. Rev. Bradley did that to us; every three months we had to turn them in and she read every word. Oh, did I get bawled out a few times before I learned what NOT to write down.

Right & Wrong, Spiritual Law and Karma

Guideline: AVOIDING EXCESS IN ALL THINGS!

I. Right & Wrong, Spiritual Law
   A. The Three "R"s
      1. Positive thought
      2. Affirmations
   B. Wrong (Sin)
      1. A negative thought or action
         a. You attract, to and around you, the thoughts you entertain
         b. Mind your own business
            1. Judge not others, only yourself
            2. Be not deluded
      2. Suicide
         a. You are responsible for your actions, this cannot be avoided
   C. Spiritual Law
      1. Love
      2. Life
      3. Progression
         a. There is no backsliding
      4. Enlightenment
         a. Everyone can and will attain the Ultimate

II. Karma (causation—the law of cause and effect)
   A. The Eastern Concept
      1. You are not the same
      2. Punishment
   B. The Christian Variation
      1. A vengeful God, you pay a debt
      2. Life to life with problems
   C. The Spiritual Concept
      1. No condemnation
      2. Your choice
      3. Victory is yours

D. Thoughts are Things—Thoughts are Real
   1. So you think, so you are
   2. So you think you will be, so you will be

********** WORK FOR THE WEEK **********

Concentration: a flower, fifteen minutes on Wednesday, Friday and Sunday

Meditation: five minutes each morning and evening

Good evening. I'd be lying if I said I'm sorry it's crowded but I'm very pleased to see you all here. I would prefer to sit over here on the floor cross-legged along with the rest of you, but if I did that, I wouldn't be able to see any of you. So at least for now, I'll stay up here.

Tonight we are going to start getting into some of the first parts of what we talked about last week. For those of you who might not have been here last week, we talked about generalities and answered a few questions and that kind of thing. But tonight we want to settle down and really start doing something. And it is one of these things that you will have to do yourself. I and the assistant teachers here at the Chapel will help you in any way that we can, but we cannot give you any of the so-called psychic gifts. We cannot make you better than you are. You've simply got to do that yourself. But we will try every way we know how to bring about desirable changes.

Each evening you're here, you will get one of these outlines. I've scribbled a few little pencil notes on mine to remember what I've said before in these classes. You can do likewise.

There will be some things I would recommend that you write down because, for those of you who are going to go farther into these studies, we will have a test for you somewhere along the way. Don't worry about that now. But one important thing I want you to do is to get into the habit of study. And this is a habit.

All of you, who are still in school or have been in school or can remember when you were in school, as the case may be, will know that you succeeded in those subjects that you liked simply because you liked to study them. It's just as simple as that.

I can make this subject, I think, interesting to you. I could also make it almost impossible for you to study, because I've spent a number of years studying it in very detailed ways and it is not my point to teach that kind of detail. Where you're motivated to do the kind of study I have done, you will be motivated to do those detailed investigations yourself. But the thing that we are after here is a general overall feeling for what we are talking about.

A few of these things are extremely important, and you will hear me hammering away at them evening after evening. And as I said last week, the thing that is going to impress all of you, I'm certain, is that it all sounds too easy.

If it were something really complex, I mean if I told you that you had to stand on your head in a corner and drink milk upside down or something like this and it would make you spiritual, you would all try it, I'm sure of that. And you might even think you were accomplishing something. But you really would not. Because what we're talking about is control of that little block of matter up between your ears. And that is important. So let's dive into this. And we'll simply call this class two, even though last week was not really a class. We were just kind of chitter-chattering.

At the top of the outline each evening you will find a guideline. These are little things that I think are important. I hope as time goes on you will see their importance. And this first one is probably one of the most important of all: avoiding excess in all things.

This is not only an extremely important statement, but it is one of the prime spiritual laws. It is one of these things you do not break. And when I say avoiding excess in all things I mean literally all things: work, play, food, sex, drink, anything you can think of doing. When something becomes the total motivating force in your life, it is wrong. I'm sure some of you, in your own lifetime, have reached points where a single drive, a single desire is occupying almost all of your waking hours. Also during that period of time you probably saw your life being made quite unhappy and generally unstable. And this is one of these points. So avoid excess in all things.

A little later this evening, we're going to be talking about meditation. And this applies to meditation maybe even more strongly than to the others I mentioned. I mean, after you've worked long enough, you get tired and stop working. The same, I guess, applies to sex, or to drinking, or food. But the main thing is that meditation is something that must be understood, not simply practiced. You'll bump into people who say they can meditate all day long, but if they say they can go into total meditation for twenty minutes, if they are not a priest, they are kidding themselves.

So remember, regardless of what it is, avoid excess in all things.

Our major topics for tonight, number I, 'Right, Wrong, Spiritual Law,' and number II, 'Karma.'

I'd like to put them in that order instead of putting karma along with reincarnation and evolution because it really stands all by itself. And when we get down to karma, you will see what I'm talking about.

First of all, under 'Right & Wrong and Spiritual Law,' let's look at those things that would be considered right. Surprisingly enough, there are very few things that are totally right to everyone all the time.

What is right for me tonight, at this particular time, might not be right for me tomorrow night at this same time. And this is very difficult to understand mainly because we are not talking about civil law. We're not talking about the laws made by ourselves or a generation prior to us that govern how we should drive along the street, or how we should conduct ourselves in public, because those things are superficial.

It is easy to go around the world and pick out those things that are right and proper to do in one country that can be absolutely out of the question here in the United States and probably particularly in Encinitas. But what can you do? What is right? What are those things that approach being right all the time?

And here are three I want you to write down and remember because they are the three R's of our philosophy. They are not reading, writing, and arithmetic, of course, even though those are probably important. But the three R's that are a must for your spiritual development and your psychic development are number one, right meditation; number two, right thought; number three, right action. Remember those three things: meditation, thought, and action.

If those are kept in line, everything else will fall in place behind it. If you can master meditation, master the control of your thinking, you will automatically master every action that you take or even think of taking. And, thereby, you will hold the world in the palm of your hand. I mean that literally.

What about positive thoughts? You've all heard this so many times and yet it is so very important. There have been books, of course, written on it. Several very famous authors have written on it. But positive thoughts are an absolute must in your development because if you cannot train your thoughts in a positive way, you cannot control them.

One of the topics we often discuss is about positive words. You may be a little surprised at how difficult it is to make a series of positive statements. And surprisingly enough, most all religions have their basic doctrine scattered by negative words and thoughts, not positive ones at all.

One of the classics, of course, from the Bible, is faith, hope, and charity. Of course, as you know, charity in that case is not charity but love. Love is the only word there that is positive.

Hope is always negative. It cannot be used in a positive way. If you hope something is going to come about, it means that you are subconsciously or consciously admitting that it might not or that you feel it might not. Therefore, it is to be thrown out. Let us not use that word.

Faith is another magnificent negative word. By definition it is the acceptance of something unknown and unknowable. How negative can you get? So watch in your ordinary conversation, and especially in the way that you are thinking, that you phrase things in positive ways. And one of the easiest techniques one can develop to maintain a positive approach is our little number 2, 'Affirmations.'

Some of you might not know what that word means. An affirmation is simply a statement that is totally positive. It is something that you affirm to be so. In other words, that you know to be true. And I have three of them here that are extremely important to your individual development:

Number 1: I am teachable.
Number 2: I am open.
Number 3: I am receptive to spiritual truth and development.

The first one is quite obvious. I am teachable. I hear this so often and I'm so pleased to see that we have a broad spectrum of ages in the audience. This is beautiful, because so often I hear older people say, "I am too old to learn." That is utter stupidity. You are never too old to learn. I don't care how old you are, if you were given a hammer for the first time and tried to drive nails with it, and even if you were 99 years old and you smashed your thumb, after a while you would learn how to use the hammer. So you are never too old to learn. It is one of these classic cop-outs that you bump into. We see it disappearing because all you have to do is visit some of the college campuses today and you will notice that they are not totally overrun by our young whippersnappers. There are some mature people there seeking enlightenment as well.

But remember, you are teachable; you can learn. I had a big fight with a boss of mine one time. I was head of the optical division of Howe and Co. He was an older gentleman and I had designed a new way to do a particular piece of optics. I did it and it worked. Thank God it worked.

I mean, you know, prove your point first. Don't yell. And he made some smart crack and of course I smarted off right back at him. And he said, "You can't teach an old dog new tricks." I said, "No, but you can teach an old dog simple tricks." And we didn't talk for about two weeks.

I got my raise and everything went along accordingly. But remember, never cut yourself short. If you want to memorize a poem, okay, someone might be able to memorize it quicker than you can. Some people are simply built that way. Their mind works that way. It might take you a little longer but you can do it, too.

And all the things that we're going to be talking about here you can do, too. And you can do them for a different reason, because they are not new to you. You have done them before. And as we get into some of these really careful studies of psychic activities, you will suddenly notice things feel familiar.

You will hear me say something that you consciously know you have not heard before, yet for some reason it will ring a bell. You've heard it before and very likely you've practiced it before. So remember, you are always teachable.

You are open. The statement, "I am open." A simple statement. Many of the things I am going to say, either at Sunday lecture or sitting here, are going to seem strange to you. I would never expect you to accept all of them at face value. Anything I say that does not fit into your philosophy, file it away. You've got a lot of room in your mind so file it away. And I will bet as time goes on, you'll pull that card out and put it in your active file. Because we have a lot of interesting things from a lot of interesting people both on this side of the spiritual plane and on the other as well that make things look very, very true.

'I am receptive to spiritual truth and development.' Okay, that's why you're here. The proof of that statement will come from your own ability. The proof of that statement will come as you start doing those things.

So those are the major things that are right.

Isn't that ridiculous? I've told you almost nothing that is right. So what will I do with 'wrong'?

For instance, sin. It's a gorgeous word. I mean, I love some of my other minister cohorts, but there are so many places in the Bible that, if you substituted the word 'wrong' for 'sin,' the context would sound so different.

Okay, wrong. What is wrong? It is quite obvious that the opposite of the things we've been talking about are wrong. A negative thought or action is obviously wrong.

And under that little subheading "A." You attract to and around you the thoughts you entertain. That's a rather simple statement but it is a devastating one. And you see it all the time if you really stop to analyze it.

If you hate someone, hate them to the point of hitting them on the head with a club or something, they are not going to give you the opposite. They are not going to turn around and hug and kiss you. They are going to hate you back.

When was the last time you were really scared, I mean scared right out of your shoes? If you were with someone else, they probably got frightened as well. And if there are three or four of you, it can build and grow until finally all three or four of you are running around screaming, hiding and who knows what.

Love, of course, is one of the most delicate ones. One of those lovely little four-letter words that everybody talks about all the time and almost no one knows a darn thing about. But it is one of those things. If you love, you will attract love. You will not attract the opposite.

This is, incidentally, another little point you hear so often. Opposites attract. That only holds true in physics. The north pole of a magnet will pick up the south role of a magnet. But if you are going to be in a fit of anger and hatred, you're not going to attract someone around you full of love. You are going to attract around you someone full of anger and hatred so you can both get together and hate and get madder all the time.

If you fill your life and activities with love, you will surround yourself with those who are full of love and express love, not the opposite. So remember, this is simply not true. Opposites do not attract.

Many times you will hear people say, "I was attracted to my husband and/or my wife because we were opposites." Phooey. Maybe you were opposites on the surface, but underneath you were alike. If you were not alike, you would simply not have been attracted to each other. It would never work. Stop and think for a second. If you're going to go out hunting for a wife or a husband, what are you going to pick? You're going to try to find someone who is at least equal to you. That's better than saying better than I am. Although I've heard many people say she's got to be less than I am so I can dominate. But that's ridiculous.

Only when you find someone that is an equal, emotionally, intellectually, from all the other physical sides of love and attraction, only then will you feel comfortable. If you were to pick a mate that was a direct opposite, I will guarantee you it would not last. And I've married some and they don't. Believe me. Look for something you are comfortable with, and you are comfortable with the same things and not opposites.

Okay. "B" under our little subheading is one of the most difficult things to do. 'Mind your own business.'

Maybe this would be a good point to tell you that we are going to be talking about a lot of things. And I want all of you to feel totally relaxed at using words or concepts that you want to talk about. I don't care what it is. We are all adult enough to discuss things openly and rationally or we are just kidding ourselves; we are playing a game to which there is no solution.

So when we get into our question-and-answer period, if you have some question that embarrasses you, cover yourself up with a shawl and ask it anyway. Further down the line, when I'm working in trance and one of the teachers is working through me, believe me you cannot shock them. Any question that comes into your mind that is upsetting to you, demand an answer.

Stop and think for a second. If we cannot help each other as human beings on a level of human beings, then let's give up and go play with toy boats or something. So please, if anything like that comes up, don't you people be shocked by your neighbor. And you won't shock me, I assure you. And as I say, when it comes to the high teachers that will be working through me or one of the other mediums, you will not shock them either. They have lived and done things you would not dream of. So they have a vast experience to call from.

Mind your own business. You all know that. Everybody tells you that. And it's the one thing that you would rather not discuss.

You always mind your own business, of course. And the neighbor's and the person down the block. There is nothing more fun than minding someone else's morals. 'Leave mine alone but let me tell you what's wrong with yours.' This is one of those things that is wrong, and in a very direct way because it hurts other people. One of the major ways that you can tell if you are doing something wrong is this word, 'harmony.' If what you do causes harmony, it is okay. If what you do causes disharmony, then be careful. You did something wrong.

Minding your own business. I've heard a lot of people gossip. Men are as good at gossip as any woman ever dreamed of being. I've been in circles of both kinds and I can assure you the level and kind of gossip is not relative to sex or position. And it is incredible how it can multiply.

You've all played the parlor game. If I whisper something to this young lady and she whispers it, by the time it gets back to me, we could probably write an x-rated novel. But that's the whole point. Don't talk about something that is someone else's business. You can get me on a real tirade about that because this is one of the things that I get very upset about with some of our famous mediums, some of our famous so-called seers. I'm a fairly good clairvoyant, clairaudient medium. I can see what's going to happen to Liz Taylor or Richard Burton or whomever, but it's none of my business. And it's certainly none of your business. So when I see some of these fine mediums using their abilities to give you a good tidbit of gossip that's going to happen on June 4, well phooey. That's wrong. That is invasion of privacy. That is interference. It is certainly not causing harmony, except maybe for the medium, so she can stand by and say, "See, I was right." No way. Watch those things. They are wrong.

It is one of these things that is very easy to talk about but, as I say, gossip is so much fun. But mind your own business. If someone starts to tell you something that is not your own business, tell them so. You might lose a friend but are they your friend? Question, do they share good thoughts? And there's one form of gossip that is so insidious: "I am telling you this for your own good." First of all, you don't know what is best for that person. So be very careful. If someone comes up to me, for instance, and says, "Rev. Larr, I know you don't know anything about this but I've got to tell you about so and so."

If someone's going to talk about me, they ought to talk to ME, not to someone else, knowing full well that another person's going to tell me what they said. But what a ridiculous circle. I'm going to tell A, A's going to tell B, B's going to tell C, C's going to tell D, and then D will find out. Well, phooey. Come to me and tell me. If it is a business and a problem between the two of us, let's solve it between the two of us. Apply this to your everyday life. It is hard. It is one of these situations where more little white lies are told than anywhere else I know. For instance, if you want to be absolutely right, what do you do when your wife comes in with a new hat and says, "Honey, don't you love my new hat?" And you think it's the most horrible thing you have ever seen. At that point, remember that what you're doing to bring harmony is right, whether it is the truth or not.

You must keep harmony so you will say, "Yes, dear." And let it go at that.

But watch these other things. They are very important and we get in the trap of doing them. And they are a waste of energy. If I'm telling you about someone else's business, it's ridiculous. I can't do anything about it. You can't do anything about it. It doesn't involve you or me. Therefore, we're wasting energy. It's something Mr. or Mrs. X has to work out. That's their problem. Leave it alone.

There's one other thing that is wrong, and that's number 2. I don't want to talk about suicide extensively tonight. We will talk about it in the more advanced work. If there is a so-called unforgivable sin, several forms of suicide would be examples. And the reason is given by a statement here. 'You are responsible for your actions, and this cannot be avoided.' The kind of suicide I'm talking about here is when you would, through deliberate effort, build around yourself such an impossible set of conditions that you decided you could not live, and therefore killed yourself to avoid it. Okay. Somewhere along the way you are going to build about yourself that same condition because it is something you have to learn about or you would not have done it. So regardless of how black and how ugly the situation around you might appear, don't give up. You can change it. Believe me, you can. And most of the time when I have bumped into suicide victims who come from the other side to talk to me, it has been appalling at how simply the solution really would have been if they had just taken the time to stop and think. And we could get into a long one there.

The main thing to remember is that you are responsible for your actions. We'll get into that a little bit further when we talk about karma.

Let's talk about 'Spiritual Law.' This goes without saying; love in its absolute and pure form is one of the major laws of the universe. Love can be totally interchanged with the word harmony. And much of the time when you hear me lecture or talk about love and/or harmony, you will hear me using the term harmony instead of love.

We have sex and love completely mixed up. Believe me, there can be sex without love and there can be love without sex. I know that second one seems almost impossible to a lot of you. And yet, it is very true. In fact the highest form of love, another Sanskrit word called *kiwadine*, is one that is totally independent of any physical contact of any kind. And it is one of those exalted states that is almost unimaginable. But love and/or harmony is one of the major spiritual laws because this is what governs the universe.

You know stars don't go bumping into each other. Everything is doing what it's supposed to be doing in harmony with everything else. And this is what I'm talking about here.

You are living creatures. You must live the life you are involved in right now, because you brought it about. You set about to do something, or maybe several things, this time. And you've got to follow through with it.

And follow it to its logical conclusion and enjoy it. And again, here is our same thing. When you are living your life right and properly, you'll be surrounded with harmony.

We see so much of the opposite side of that coin. The world itself is in such a silly state of affairs. The only way it looks in harmony at all is when viewed from the moon, so that you can't see people. Humans seem to be the fly in the ointment. And yet, there is within each one of us the capability of making a change. We're not going to do it by praying for all of the nations to stop fighting. We're not going to do it in that sense. We're going to do it in the sense of making ourselves better and therefore those we come in contact with better. And then it will spread. And that's the only way it will spread.

This is what Buddha was talking about. This is what Christ was talking about. This is what Muhammad was talking about. The same thing. You can't expect anyone to do what you are not willing to do. Think about it.

'Progression'; there is no backsliding.' This is an interesting one. Progression, of course, is one we will be talking about next time because of the concept of evolution. Everything is moving forward.

The only constant thing in the universe is change, and the change is always forward. It is never backward. One of the interesting things in reincarnation is the concept, "Am I going to come back as a dog or a cat next time?" No, you're not. But it is one of these things that, once you gain a step in your spirituality, once you gain a step in being a better, more beautiful and perfect person, you will not lose it. You cannot lose it. It is a gift you have gained and no one can take it away from you—surprisingly enough not even yourself. Because if you did something right you know you did it right. And that is extremely important.

'Enlightenment,' this of course is the abstract sense. Enlightenment in our philosophy would be very, very closely akin to the Buddhistic concept of total knowing. Merging with the universal. The Christian interpretation is to become one with God, to join Godhead. All these concepts essentially say the same thing.

And regardless of what you want to call it, heaven, perfection, Nirvana, whatever, the most important thing is that everyone can and will obtain the ultimate. Regardless of what pathway you are on, regardless of what pathway all the other people are on, that pathway is going to lead to perfection. Some are more direct, obviously. Some are a little more circular. But everyone, every life form, is going to make it—because it has to. You are advancing forward whether you want to or not. Like I often say, be very, very proud of who you are. You've come an awful long way. Good grief! Not too many billion years ago you were amoebas. And not too many hundreds of thousands of years ago, if you had stayed there, you'd still be monkeys sitting in a tree eating fruit. Now you are a human, the highest form of life in this planetary system. And that's an awful big responsibility.

You are getting close to perfect, and you've come a long way to get here. Go ahead, take those other steps. They're worthwhile.

Okay, let's look at karma. And here we're going to cause some upset.

As you go along in these lectures, you'll notice that I sometimes enjoy upsetting people. But again, karma is Sanskrit. Its simple, direct meaning, if you translate it into Latin, then into English, is causation. It's called the law of cause and effect. And that is all there is to it. Causation. Cause and effect. And boy has it been screwed up. An Eastern concept started it. In its original pure form, it is referred to in some of the Brahman things from the Bhagavad Gita, given in pure form. But it gets very mixed up in some of the Eastern concepts. And then the Christians picked it up and very neatly fit it into their scheme. But let's look at this Eastern concept first.

Buddha was implying and telling you that you are not the same moment by moment by moment. Remember I said a moment ago, the only constant thing in the universe is change. You are always changing. If you don't think you are, watch as you go a little further in these classes, you will see your abilities changing. You will see your way of thinking changing. It can be brought down to a much more physical position, however.

Because you are a complex animal, and a warm-blooded animal at that, cells in your body are dying at the rate of 3 or 4 billion an hour and replaced with new cells that did not exist before. So when you go to sleep tonight and let eight hours go by, when you wake up in the morning you certainly are not the same one that laid down and went to sleep. An enormous part of you is now new material. Buddha, of course, was not referring to this biological concept because he didn't know about it, unless he gleaned it from some spiritual source.

What he was referring to is that he would make no distinction between you going to sleep tonight and waking up in the morning, or you dying tonight and being reborn in the morning. Exactly the same thing. The entity that is you is always there. If you died tonight and were reborn tomorrow, okay, you'd be shaped a little differently. Maybe you'd have different coloring of your eyes and so forth, but the little spark that is you is there. And so you are not the same. You are always changing.

However, some of the Eastern religions decided that karma, because of cause and effect, is a good way to punish you. It teaches you that if you don't do things right, something is going to happen to you. And one of the classic ones, of course, is all the sacred cows and the sacred monkeys. I personally favor sacred monkeys. I like monkeys better than cows. But they are around the temple and are taken care of. If you mistreat them, they seriously believe that you will die and come back as a cow so that you can be mistreated. This might keep certain Indian children, at least, from throwing rocks at cows, but it's not true. Once you are a person you are always going to be a person through your incarnations.

You are not going to backslide. Although I'll admit sometimes I think I would rather spend a little more time as some pet in the ideal household than this world. But it's not true. There is no punishment.

The Christian variation picked up the same thing. And it was a perfect one because of the Hebrew concept of a vengeful God.

You pay a debt. This leads to many of the concepts that I hear all the time.

You have gone through life full of problems. People come to me, and I'm sure some of you have tried to say it too, "I can't do anything right this time. It's my karmic debt. I must have done something last time that was a lulu." Well, I'm sorry, but if you're having trouble, you've got no one to blame but yourself, right now. Not what you did last time, or the time before, or the time before that, because it does not carry over. Why doesn't it carry over? Because you do not have a vengeful God sitting there with a book on his lap giving you black marks or gold stars for the things you do. Your punishment and your reward is here and now and a direct effect of karma. A direct effect of cause and effect. And I think it was beautifully pointed out. At one of her lectures, Rev. Tappe gave an example of karma that I think will make it more meaningful to you, especially those of you who are mothers with grown-up children. If your son had dropped a glass at the age of three and broke it and you said nothing, but at the age of twenty you suddenly hauled him in the room and slapped him and beat him thoroughly for breaking the glass when he was three years old, do you think he would learn anything? He would not remember breaking the glass. He would not know why he was being punished. So with the questions of karma, if you do not remember your last lifetime in detail, then why are you being punished for something that you do not know you did wrong? It's just as simple as that.

So please don't use it as a classic cop-out. For many people, if they fail, they say it's because of this or that or it's a karmic debt. It isn't. If you think it is, you can make it one in your own mind. But remember that is not the case, not the case at all.

And, of course, this leads us directly into the spiritual concepts we have been talking about. There is no condemnation. You are your own worst enemy. It is one of these things that you must pick and choose for yourself. You will be condemned by things that you feel you have done wrong, but that's where it stops, with yourself and no place else.

Some of the problems we bump into in a lifetime may be preset by your choice.

Now this sounds kind of harsh. We will talk about it in a more detailed way further along. And it is beautifully brought out in the Bible where one of the disciples asked Jesus about a baby who was born blind. The question was asked, who sinned, the parents or the child, as the blindness must have been a punishment for something. Jesus gave a simple answer: neither has sinned. But analyze that question and the situation a little more closely. When did the baby sin if it was born blind? What were they thinking? They were thinking of reincarnation, that he had sinned in a previous lifetime and was therefore born blind.

And Jesus said no, none had sinned. Even today, many, many cultures feel that the sins of the parents are passed on to the children. In fact, there are probably some people in this room who have heard that statement even in our Western culture. And it's ridiculous. It is not true at all, but sometimes they think it is. If the individual was born blind, it could have been because he wanted, in this lifetime, to work out a particular kind of problem that being blind would allow him to experience. That is one possible cause. It is one of these things we cannot talk about in generalities because it involves individuals, and we have to wait and see what the problem is. This reminds me of the Helen Keller story. Here is an entity who came in with an almost impossible combination of events to prove a magnificent point and to rise to fantastic heights.

Regardless of what the condition is, victory is yours. You can always say no. I don't care what the situation, what the karmic condition is, be it good or bad. Incidentally, of course, karma can be good just as it can be bad because it is just causation, nothing more. But you can get over any hurdle, any one of them. Use karma like a tool. If you want tomorrow to be full of love, plant some love today. If you want tomorrow to be full of hell, raise hell today. Do what you want and you will get what you do. And you will get what you do because of your actions.

Here's something I want you to catch in your mind: thoughts are things. Thoughts are real. And the two little things that follow, always keep in mind: So you think, so you are. So you think you will be, so you will be.

And if you remember nothing else from tonight, remember that karma is simply causation. And so you think, so you are. So you think you will be, so you will be. Those last two little statements are so important. If you go for a job interview tomorrow and you think, "Well, I'm probably not going to get that job," don't waste your time. Of course you won't get it. But if you go knowing, and I said 'knowing,' not 'hoping,' knowing that you will get it, the job is already yours if it is for your highest and best good.

Anything you start, make certain you don't kill yourself first by declaring to yourself that it's not going to work, because if you fill that as a thought form, it will not work. It's as simple as that.

Unfortunately, as I say, some of these concepts are way too simple.

'Thoughts are things.' I mean that in every sense of the word. There's not a thing in this room that you can look at that was not a thought before it was a thing. This pencil, this watch, anything. Someone thought about it, someone designed it, someone drew a picture of it, and finally someone made it. But it was a thought first. The same goes with everything in the universe.

It's absolutely abstract for our talk tonight. Remember, thoughts are things.

Thoughts are real. Up here at the top we were talking about negative thinking and positive thinking. How do we get rid of bad thoughts? We all think of bad things. I don't think anybody in this room is a saint. I don't see any saintly halos. Ah! Yes I do. There's one at the back. Saint David is sitting way in the back.

But no. Every once in a while; I mean, really. You've gone down and bought a new car. You pull into a parking lot. Someone backs into the side of it and scratches it. The next thought you have is not going to be neither positive nor necessarily spiritual. It's going to be negative, it's going to be ugly, and it's going to be a bad thought. How do you get rid of it?

By not thinking about it, you leave it alone. All thoughts are just like seeds in a garden. If you have a little pile of dirt and you put a seed in it and don't water it, it won't grow. If you water it, it will grow. It you fertilize it and take care of it, it will grow beautifully. The same thing is true with good thinking and bad thinking. If I take an ugly thought and it goes zipping through my mind, 'Oh I hate him,' leave it alone. Let it go. But if you pull it back every ten minutes and say, 'Boy, I really do hate him,' and then about ten minutes later you go back, 'I just HATE him,' pretty soon you've really grown this little seed into a weed of gigantic proportions. Don't do it. Let it go. And you know what's right and wrong. So don't let those enter your mind. Don't let them grow and they won't bother you at all.

Evolution: Physical and Spiritual, Reincarnation

Guideline: I AM IN COMPLETE CONTROL

I. Evolution
   A. Physical
      1. Non-living
         a. Dust clouds
         b. Stars and planets
      2. Living
         a. Molecular replication
         b. Plants
         c. Animals
   B. Master plan (the main line)
      1. Direction and evidence (seen in fetal form)
      2. Random variation in all directions
         a. Nitch concept
         b. Competition (survival of the fittest)
   C. Spiritual
      1. Mainline
         a. Plants (do they think?)
         b. Animals (circle of awareness)
      2. Master plan (God)
         a. Etheric mold (the tool of evolution)
         b. Physical shell

II. Reincarnation
   A. The tool of mastery
      1. Know the way
      2. Your choice
   B. Only upward
      1. One step at a time
      2. No backsliding
   C. Perfection
      1. Godhead
      2. Nirvana

********** WORK FOR THE WEEK **********

Concentration: Image a flower for fifteen minutes on Wednesday, Friday and Sunday

Meditation: five minutes each morning and evening

We have a lot of material to cover as you can see on your outline, but we're going to go through it fairly fast. Please keep in mind what I mentioned before, that the thing we are after here is not necessarily specific knowledge concerning evolution and reincarnation, but an overall view of the whole system.

Your guideline for tonight is quite an obvious one, most of the time. 'I am in complete control.'

Okay, this is a statement that one can tell themselves and aim toward because it is a key to your success in anything you do. If you are at the whim of someone else, then you are not in control, and things will not go the way you want them to go.

As I mentioned, you will notice tonight we are going to discuss evolution and reincarnation, mainly. We're going to hammer away solidly at evolution because it is extremely important to you as individuals as you advance up the pathway toward perfection. I'm certain that some of you remember the movies or have read some of the excerpts from the famous monkey trials back east. Some time ago, a biology teacher tried to teach evolution to his students. As you know, it turned into one of the classic courtroom battles of all time. And the battle was never really laid to rest because this Sunday you can turn on television or radio and you can hear this same problem being argued today—the argument over fundamentalism, or the creation concept, and evolution.

One must ask oneself very, very seriously, what are they fighting about? What are they *really* arguing about? The main things they are arguing about are two verses from the first chapter of Genesis in the Bible.

This section, of course, is from the original Hebrew and has been a little altered, but the two little passages that have caused all the fury is Genesis 1:26, "And God said let us make man in our own image. After our own likeness." A little further down, in fact the next verse, is "So God created man in his own image. In the image of God created he him." Okay. Fine.

The problem is, what was the image? What does God look like? If an evolutionist was to insist that the predecessor to man was a great hairy beast running around with knuckles on the floor, it would be hard to recognize that as God because of the interpretations we have put on the meaning of that word. So let's stay right within the Bible itself. Go into the New Testament where Jesus has answered a question point blank on that very exact statement. St. John, 4:24, "And Jesus said, God is spirit. And they that would worship him, must worship him in Spirit and in truth." With those two exceptions, there is certainly nothing that the scientist is going to fight about. Man is a very peculiar animal, a very advanced animal, but an animal, nevertheless. And certainly we do have a side of us that represents any concept of an abstract God you want to imagine. So the fundamentalists are arguing furiously over a Bible truth while the scientists, who are studying the paleontological evidence for evolution, don't really care one way or the other, because they are finding a different answer. People, who would accept the Bible verbatim, word for word, are in a great deal of trouble. You will never find a single Bible scholar of any organized religion who will accept every single word because there are too many snags that would prevent them from living the life they want to live, even under the guise of their own religion.

So let us take just one of the other sections of Genesis that has caused the scientists and students so much trouble. Much of the trouble was caused through ignorance and arrogance. Of course I am referring to the flood in the latter part of Genesis. As you know, right after the flood occurred, all of Noah's offspring and the offspring of his offspring are listed and named and their ages are named. Therefore, you can simply take those numbers, add them all up backwards and you can date the flood.

Archbishop Usher, a very strong gentleman in the guise of the Church, did so and proclaimed that the flood occurred in 2348 B.C. This was well and good because it occurred before a lot of archeological work was done. And then suddenly they started finding a number of cities that predated 2348 B.C. that did not show evidence of a flood. He and his group were challenged, so they decided, well, maybe they had looked at the Scriptures wrong. They went back to the same data, the same raw material, and recalculated—this time with maybe a little help from their imaginations—that the flood started on a certain Sunday in October 4004 B.C. That's well and good, but we know it didn't happen then either. We know the Nile valley and we know the history of the Nile valley at that point. We're finding more and more about the civilizations of Earth and they predate 4004 B.C. So, if we are to take the flood theory as fact, we have to look at it very skeptically.

First of all, the boat itself was not very big and you can get all kinds of arguments from scholars about what kind of wood it was made out of—cedar or lemon or oak or whatever. But that's irrelevant because the ship was not large enough to hold a pair of animals of every species on the face of the Earth. They won't fit. And stop and think for a second. We're talking about a flood somewhere in the land of the Hebrews. What did they do with all the animals that lived in South America at the time? Nobody even knew South America was there.

So if you even assume, by some miraculous feat, they got all the animals aboard in pairs with enough food to feed them, you then have another big problem that the dumb Bible scholars simply refuse to talk about—the flood itself. It rained, as you know, for forty days and forty nights, but the important thing is that the Earth was covered by a thousand feet of water for one hundred fifty days. That would have killed every land plant on the face of the Earth. Are we also to assume Noah took aboard seeds or cuttings from every plant on the face of the Earth? We're still finding new ones. And what about some of the trees that appear to be older than that? Why are they still there? So something's wrong. It doesn't take a great deal of research to see what is wrong. The story of the flood is lifted directly from some of the early Biblical or early Babylonian tales of creation. The Hebrews simply borrowed it. They made it more grandiose. A flood did occur in the Babylonian times in the Tigris-Euphrates valley, and it did drown and destroy almost all of their known civilization; but when the Hebrews picked it up and converted it to be part of an intimate episode of the creation of the Earth, they made it larger in scope to cover the whole world. Unfortunately, in so doing, they made it absolutely impossible to accept.

So that's what the arguments are. What about some of these other things? If you study carefully, you will notice that evolution can be proven many, many ways. As you know, I have a degree in invertebrate paleontology so I'm familiar with some of those ways. But let's look at some of them again in a general way because what we're after here is something extremely important to the philosophy, not in technical detail, but in its concept.

First of all let us look at evolution. You will notice that I've broken it down into 'physical' and 'living' because there is evolution in all things. The only thing that is constant in the universe is change. So let us look at a few of them. For instance, the non-living things. As you know, our Milky Way system is a galaxy comprised of many billions of stars. If you could look at it sideways, it would look like this if you could get far out into space. This is the Sombrero Galaxy photographed with the 100-inch on Mt. Wilson. This band across here is dust and gas. It glows because of stars. If you had a real super-spaceship and could fly away from that rim and fly up on top and look down, it would look something like this. This is M81 in Ursa Major taken with the 200-inch at Palomar. Here again, we see dust in between the spiral arms and all these stars, billions of stars. If this were the Milky Way system, we would find the Sun situated right here, about two thirds out from the center, running around the galaxy, because this thing is spinning just like it appears. And we're running around it like a little spark on a great big pinwheel.

Where did all this come from? Did God snap his fingers and say, "Let there be light?" No, because it's been going forever. There is no beginning, there is no end. It is not a closed universe. The second side of the Einsteinian concept is correct. It is an ever-replenishing supply. How?

One of the biggest problems an ancient man faced was that the stars were always there. Then he noticed a few of them moved and he called them wanderers or planets. And then as time went on he decided the Earth was the center of the universe. It took us hundreds of years to get over that. But after we got over that, we began to really start studying on all levels this problem of stars. The Sun, of course, being one.

The Sun is going to burn out. It's using fuel. It's giving off energy. It's got to burn out. Where did the Sun come from? What is it going to do after it burns out? Forget what it's going to do to us when it burns out, that's a minor point, but finally they began to extrapolate and bring out some beautiful theories: that stars were being born all the time, that stars are nothing more than the product and collapse of a giant cloud of dust and gas that has enough mass to become a star by sheer heat and pressure, until the atomic energy forces take over and turn it into a real star.

This plate of M16, again taken with the 200-inch, will show you some of these things in process. This is a star cluster involved with a huge cloud of dust and gas. This stuff is not dirt on the negative, believe me. Even though some of the early astronomers thought it was. But they said, "Okay, here are dust clouds that are huge." Something the size of this one, which you probably cannot see from the back of the room, is hundreds of millions of miles across. But the dust clouds are collapsing because of mutual attraction and because of light pressure. Probably the most astounding discovery to happen in certainly our lifetime happened in 1961 when survey plates of these kinds of areas were done again. Specifically, they redid a plate with a 100-inch that was done in 1954 and in which all the stars were measured with both spectroscopic analysis and as to their position. In 1961, less than ten years after the first plate was taken, there were two new stars that were not there before. So in less than ten years a cloud had collapsed to form two new stars and, for the first time, evolution could be proven in the formation of the whole universe.

Now what happened when the cloud collapsed? You'll notice here on your outline we're talking about dust clouds. They collapsed to form stars. They collapse to form stars and planets. Let's look at the Sun for a second.

There's a huge cloud of gas and dust several hundred million miles across, and it starts collapsing. It starts falling in on itself. And some chunks were left over. One of those chunks is the Earth. Other chunks were Mercury, Venus, Mars, Jupiter, Saturn, Uranus, Neptune, Pluto, and maybe other planets beyond that. If there is one it would be very hard to detect. But the whole key is that just as the Sun heated up to become a star, the Earth heated up as it was collapsing. It would be just as though you take a ball of clay and start squeezing; the ball of clay will heat up from friction alone. The Earth wasn't a big enough ball of material to turn into a star and so it started to cool off. As it cooled off, it formed a little hard round ball and was surrounded by a huge atmosphere with all kinds of stuff. And then it began to rain. It rained for millions of years. And for the first few million years, not a single drop of water got to the surface because it vaporized and turned back into steam before the drops could get there.

But finally water did get to the surface and this acted as a heat exchange and started cooling the surface of the Earth. Then a very interesting series of things began to happen. Puddles of water began to form, at first, of course, too hot for anything. But in some of those pools of water, ery complex semi-organic molecules began to get together. And this is our number 2.

Living molecules began to learn to duplicate themselves, to replicate their own shape as I've mentioned here. It was a giant step. As this started to occur in this so-called primeval soup, many of these little piles of molecules found it was easier to steal molecules from their neighbor instead of going to find their own, and so they became animals. Another little group of them found that if they floated higher in the little puddle where the sunlight was reaching them, they could absorb energy from the Sun. And suddenly here are plants. Now there's a constant argument as to which came first, animals or plants. Since light was abundant, one school will say plants. Because in some of

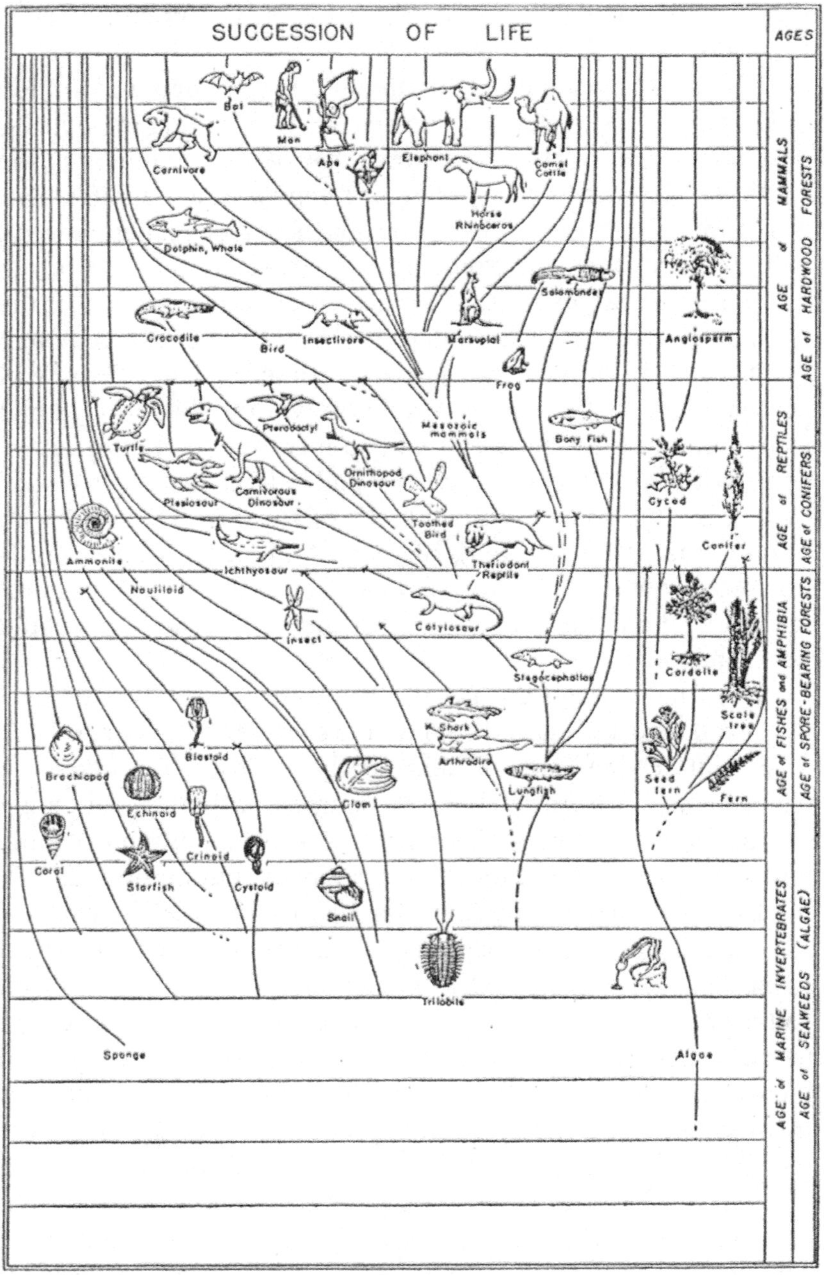
SUCCESSION OF LIFE
AGES
Bat
Man
Ape
Elephant
Camel
Cattle
Carnivore
Horse
Rhinoceros
Dolphin, Whale
Salamander
Crocodile
Bird
Insectivore
Marsupial
Angiosperm
Frog
Mesozoic mammals
Bony Fish
Turtle
Pterodactyl
Ornithopod Dinosaur
Carnivorous Dinosaur
Plesiosaur
Cycad
Toothed Bird
Conifer
Ammonite
Theriodont Reptile
Ichthyosaur
Nautiloid
Insect
Cotylosaur
Cordaite
Stegocephalia
Shark
Scale tree
Arthrodire
Blastoid
Brachiopod
Echinoid
Clam
Seed fern
Lungfish
Fern
Crinoid
Coral
Starfish
Cystoid
Snail
Trilobite
Sponge
Algae
AGE of MAMMALS
AGE of HARDWOOD FORESTS
AGE of REPTILES
AGE of CONIFERS
AGE of FISHES and AMPHIBIA
AGE of SPORE-BEARING FORESTS
AGE of MARINE INVERTEBRATES
AGE of SEAWEEDS (ALGAE)

Time Chart.

the studies of viruses, one group insists that animals came first, calling a virus an animal.

Then we got ready for some real big activity on a grand scale. On the back of your little papers tonight you've got a chart. This was taken from just a simple historical geology text I taught out of at City College, showing the so-called time chart of how animal and plant life appeared and disappeared on the Earth as time went along.

You might like to make some footnotes. If you take your pencil, up at the top of the page we have succession of life, go over to the right side and come down. You will find the life line running horizontally across it. Draw a pencil line through that line and label it 1,000,000 years ago.

First line from the top. This line goes through the back of the camel and through the stomach of the elephant, chops our poor old man in half. Label that one 1,000,000.

Now if you come down on the right side of the picture you'll see a tree standing there, or what's supposed to be a tree, with a name underneath it. The line immediately below that tree that is going horizontally, write 60,000,000 years opposite it.

Let's keep on going right on down the right side. We come to a thing that looks kind of like an arrowhead but is supposed to be a conifer, some kind of a pine tree. Below that is also a little line that goes clear across the chart. Label it 200,000,000 years ago.

Then come on down past the thing that looks like a bunch of asparagus to the little fern. Draw a line from that fern, not from any of the horizontal lines, but from the fern itself, and label that 290,000,000 years ago.

And then one of the most interesting things. Right in the middle of this chart is a little critter that looks like a fancy sow bug with whiskers and extra feet all around the edges. And he's labeled a trilobite. The line that touches his name label 500,000,000 years. And then this is going to be hard for you to conceive but draw another line to that same line and write that the width of that line represents 500,000,000 years of time.

Then if you'll go clear to the bottom of our chart and come up two lines, right where the little line from algae stops or

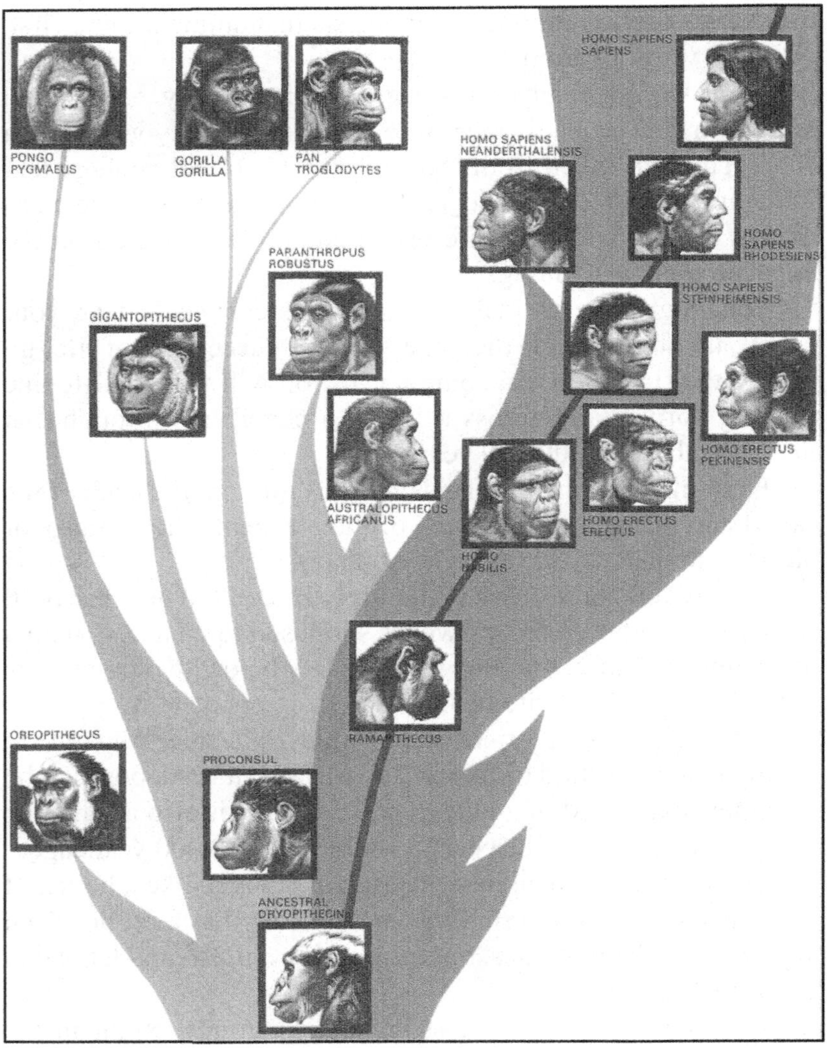

becomes at least dotted but stops near a line, opposite that line write 2,000,000,000 years ago.

And at the bottom of your chart label that bottom line 4,500,000,000 to 5,000,000,000 years ago.

Now this is roughly the time scale we're dealing with when we're talking about the Earth. Keep in mind what I just glibly mentioned about the universe—ageless, timeless, has always been, will always be. But the Earth is only about 5,000,000,000 years old.

One of the big problems with our evolution, you can see right here on the chart. See up there at the top where we put that first line with 1,000,000 years? Over near the middle is a cave man with a club standing there looking frightfully dumb. And off to the right slightly and down is an ape hanging partly from a limb of a tree. And again slightly to the right and down is a little monkey sitting on a branch. And the thing I want you to notice here is that there is not a line connecting the monkey to the ape or the ape to the man. If you trace them back down the chart, you will notice that they are heading for a common point.

And this is where Darwin got into trouble. No one believed what he said. They changed his wording to be what they wanted. Darwin did not say that man ascended or descended from apes and monkeys. Not at all. He said man, apes, and monkeys had a common ancestor. And there's a big difference in those two statements. And the common ancestor you can't see is going to be back down there below the monkey. So all those little lines finally come together.

Surprisingly enough, the critter at that point looked like a fat mouse with kind of nice fingers. So he did not look like a monkey at all. He didn't look like an ape either. But that's where they were common. He was an insectivore and he was warm-blooded and he did bring about the evolutionary traits that ended up with you and me.

So let us look at this chart in general for a minute. You'll notice that some of the lines end in small X's. This means that the animal became extinct at that point in time. It no longer exists. You will notice that man, however, has a line out the top of his head going to the top of the chart because he's still here, at least partially. The apes are still here. The monkeys are still here, and so on and so forth across the board. But you'll notice some interesting things occurred. Down there on that line that we labeled 60,000,000 years, run across it and past the center where we're talking of lines of man and apes corning down, notice there's an x, another x, another x, another x, another x, past the turtle, another x.

And notice the animals that are x-ed out there. The dinosaurs. They became extinct 60,000,000 years ago. They became extinct because they could not fill the nitch, because it required them to think and they couldn't do it. So let's go back a little further. Or go down a little further. Not a great deal happened as far as extinction of animals at our 200,000,000-year point. But it was an extremely critical point because it developed that funny, fat-looking little dinosaur with the fat tail that happened to have been a warm-blooded reptile. And from him came all the mammals.

And as we go down, the next most interesting point is our fern down here at 290,000,000 years ago. Let's not argue whether it is 290,000,000 or 300,000,000. I mean, when you are working on these terms, who cares? But there a very important thing occurred. You will notice if you go straight across from there, the funny little fish-looking thing called a lungfish. And you'll notice something that looks kind of like a warped clam. And on over, a funny little thing called echinoid.

But the intriguing thing is it was at this point that plants began to come out onto the land from the sea, and they did it by growing in the inner tidal area. As the tide went out, they learned to spend more and more time on the ground. At this period of time, and for the next 90,000,000 years, huge forests grew all over the Earth. They were not trees like we see today but a couple of the trees that are shown there. Some of them were fantastic gigantic ferns—tree ferns a hundred feet tall. The temperature was 85° and the humidity probably ninety percent. It was a fantastic place, but nobody was there to look at it. Why? Because notice as we went across our little line there, who did we find? A lungfish, a little above him a shark, or really a dog-fish. But no one was crawling around on the ground. That didn't happen for quite a while. Finally, who crawled out? An amphibian. Probably something like our little salamander. And some of them are still alive today.

So let's go on back down even further. Below that line immediately below the fern, there was nothing on the ground at all. It was bare rock—no moss, no twigs, and no leaves. Probably not even beer cans because there was no one to make the aluminum to build them.

But the ocean was something else. The ocean was full of life. All those little critters below that line with the fern are marine creatures. They lived in the ocean. But notice where I had you draw that line at 500,000,000 years, because that's where the trilobite started, where the snail started, where the crinoids started, and so on right across our chart. But you will notice two lines go below it and only two. Sponges and algae. And the algae goes clear down to 2,000,000,000 years. And the sponge somewhere above that.

The most intriguing thing to me about that line that I had you label carefully was that the width of that line was 500,000,000 years. Stop and think for a second how much time that is. We have just roughly gone from a little trilobite to man. And it took us 500,000,000 years to do it. And I'm telling you now that the line in between represents the same span of time during which everything else developed. And the reason that line is so important, not to you as students of awareness, but to scientists, is because it is a Lipalian interval. But the intriguing thing about it is that's when the moon and all of our solar system passed through one of these big bands of dust and rock, and the surface of the Earth was destroyed—rocks probably a mile to two miles deep were pulverized. And the fossil record is gone.

What's in its place? The major iron deposits of the world are right there. For instance, the Mesabi Iron Range back east surprisingly has all the same trace elements as nickel iron meteors. So during that period of time the record was erased. And for 500,000,000 years all that was left was the ocean. And it was probably in pretty bad shape. But some life survived.

If the Earth were to pass through that kind of cloud again, along with the solar system, all life would simply stop. It would be a glorious way to go; if you think a meteor is great, imagine a hundred million of them slamming clear to the surface of the ground. But you don't have to worry about it. We have gone around our little galaxy about every hundred thousand years or so. We passed those critical points of the arms. So if we were going to do it, we would have done it a long time ago. Probably the last time we did it was then, and very likely it was because we had gone once around and came right back through the same cloud of dust and gas that created the Sun to start with. Now we've gone through it several times and it has not been repeated. So you don't have to worry when you go home tonight—if you see a meteor, it is not announcing the end of the world.

So rest assured, the next major threat is in about 4,500,000,000 years when the sun burns out. And we'll worry about that when we get there.

Okay, now what is this thing I've been talking about and making fun of? Back on the other side of your paper is what we've been talking about—the Master Plan. This main line that runs up through that chart and ends up with man. Man is the highest-developed animal on the face of the Earth. No question about it.

But if you don't want to use the fossil record, we can look at it different ways. For instance, I think one of the greatest excitements of my younger life was when I learned a statement and had the professor tell me what it meant. I could mention it to people and most of them would look at me as if I had gone completely crazy. There's a beautiful statement, 'Ontogeny recapitulates phylogeny.' Now how's that? For a young boy of about twelve, I could really hold my own with that statement, but what does it mean? It simply means that you, in your embryonic development, go through every single step that animal life went through that brought you up to the level of man. Stop and think about it a second.

The male and female gamete sections are haploid in number, genetically. So only when we get a sperm and egg together do we have a single cell. In a very few hours that cell starts dividing and very quickly goes through all of these lower stages on our chart. If you were to look at a human embryo during its first four weeks, you could find its counterpart all the way up the chart.

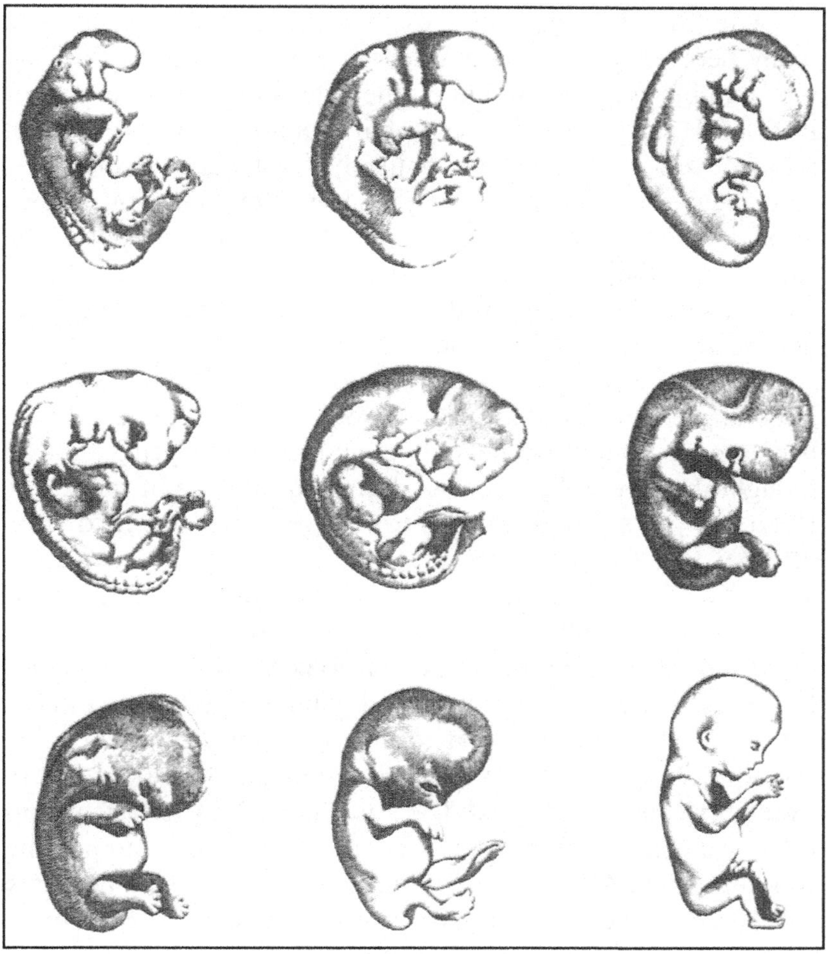

One of the first ones will be a little blastula stage that looks exactly like a sponge. In fact, if you took him at that time and preserved him and put him under a microscope, took the same little cell section from a sponge and put them together, there is not a biologist on the face of the Earth that could tell which is which. The only way he could do it would be to make a smear of it and see how many chromosomes were in each set of cells. Then he would know, but it looks the same.

After that little embryo goes on a little further, and much to many people's horror, he develops a tail and webbed feet and gills and his eyes are around on the sides of his head instead of in front. He gets over that stage fairly quickly because he's got a lot of work to do in nine months, but as he goes along, he is showing every single step along the way. Next time you happen to be down at the museum in Balboa Park, go in and look at the exhibit that they have on reproduction. It is one of the finest I've seen in a long time. And you can see all of these stages I'm talking about right up the line.

So that master plan is the why of the whole thing. We've got one problem and that's plants. You'll notice they might have been the first on the scene and yet up until a few years ago, we thought they were the dumbest things on the face of the Earth. But a few years ago, that began to change, partially due to some of the work of Baxter when he found that plants do have emotions. They're still arguing as to whether or not plants think, certainly as to whether plants think abstractly.

I have one of the little units that Baxter used on his plants. I also had a nice little experimental plant at home that couldn't run away from me, so I captured it and put electrodes on it. For several days, as I would touch the plant, it would get very excited because it simply didn't know me. But after a few days it knew me and I could reach over and caress a leaf and nothing would happen. All the needles and diodes would stay perfectly still. Then I asked myself, what can I do to show this to someone? I mean, how can I really depict it?

Baxter, of course, as you know, thought the same thing. And he thought, 'I'll get in my desk and get a match and light it and burn one of the leaves.' All the needles went off scale before he had picked up the match. The plant had caught his thoughts that he was going to burn the plant. Well, I didn't want to burn my plant because it had very pretty leaves. So I thought, 'I'll go over there, get a newspaper, roll it up, and I will just beat that plant flat!' All the needles pinned themselves. Not only did it catch my thought, but I'm sure it caught my visualization of it laying there in the flower pot. And this was thrilling because finally I had found some way that I could, by pure mental thought, make the plant react.

This went on three or four times and I got real thrilled with it. Then some friends came over to the house and I wanted to show them what you could do. I explained out in the yard what I was going to do, so they walked into the house and I walked over to the plant and stood there visualizing rolling up a newspaper and just beating the hell out of it. And it just sat there. And so I thought, Oh boy what a flop. And then it dawned on me why. The plant knew I wasn't going to do it because I had threatened to do it about four or five times and not followed through. So it knew I wasn't going to hurt it. Now I don't know if that proves thought or reason or logic or what, but it made me trim bushes and pick flowers much more gingerly for the next several months.

For those of you who might be interested in testing for yourself, the circuitry for the unit is quite simple. I think I tried it on every living plant around our place. English Ivy is the dumbest thing alive. It's weird. Without a doubt, it is almost zero on the list. You could hook it up and light a match to a leaf and the needle will do very little. The only way you could really get it to react is to hook up the leaf and then take a pair of pruning shears and trim the branch off. Then it faints. The intriguing thing about it is the plant faints, then if you stand the cutting in a glass of water, as you know, it will start forming roots and eventually grow. And the cutting stays fainted until the roots start to come out. And then it reacts again.

So maybe it's not dumb, it's just a lot slower than anything else. But I had a lot of good ideas. Hook these up to bushes by your door. Pretty soon your bush is going to know all your good friends, and it's going to let them come in without making all the alarms go off. But if a stranger came up and it didn't know the vibration, then all the alarms went off. I forgot one darn thing. Most prowlers prowl at night and the plant was asleep. So scrap one more idea.

The point is we are beginning to find out there is a common thread of life in all forms—through the animal kingdom, through the plant kingdom, and they apparently interweave very, very nicely.

Next one. 'Animals,' the circle of awareness. Okay, that's what we were talking about here on the other side of our paper about the changes of our physical structure as we evolved upward. You can do exactly the same thing about your awareness. What do you think an amoeba is aware of? Something he touches. He'll run around in a drop of water and if he touches food, he will eat it. If he touches a rock, he will back away from it. So his awareness is only at his surface.

Let's go another couple of steps up to one of the early worms. He can swim around. He's got little feelers. He can sense the pressure of the water. So he's aware of things that come close to him. Not much better than the amoeba, but a little farther away from him.

Okay, let's go another step, what about insects? Let's take an ant, one of our little friends out in the middle of the vacant lot. How much is he aware of? Many yards? He can go a great many yards away from the nest to pick up a seed and take it home. So his awareness covers quite an area.

Let's go another step up. What about birds, local birds? Let's not get into confusion about some of the migratory species. Birds are generally found in the same area. They are aware of maybe a city block, or something like this. And that's where they stay.

Let's go the next step up—a big step, of course, to mammals. Let's pick something we know about, let's say the howler monkeys of South America. How much is he aware of? Somewhere between fifty and sixty miles, because he can range over the forest and he knows where things are.

What's the next step? You and me. What are we aware of? We're aware of the Earth, an eight thousand mile ball. We're aware of space, the stars, the Sun; all these things we've been talking about, but most importantly, we are aware of ourselves and that is very critical.

One monkey in a tribe of monkeys does not call the other monkeys by name. They aren't Joe or Billy or Diane or Agnes or anything like that. They are aware of themselves as individuals, but even when you get into the high primates, the lowland gorilla, chimpanzee, even in the wild, they don't have names. They don't recognize themselves as individuals. They are part of the group. And a vital part. They communicate well in that respect. But one monkey doesn't go to the other one and say, 'Hey Bill, bring me that banana,' because he doesn't know that the guy's name is Bill.

Somewhere early in the game, primitive man went through the same thing. He didn't have names. But then finally, especially as language developed, he wanted to warn maybe one person. Let's have a row of people marching along and here comes a big snake. So instead of warning the whole group, let's have Joe know there's a snake and maybe he started out calling 'Hey you with the flat head, look out for the snake.' And he became Flathead. And maybe the guy that hollered became Snake Warner, and on and on and on until we have things you're more familiar with. Someone who hammers on iron all day becomes a blacksmith. Pretty soon you've got Mr. Blacksmith and suddenly man starts using names. It is extremely important to be aware of yourself, that's the top of the ladder.

What is this master plan? I've put it right here. If you want to, you can call it God, certainly if you want to attribute a God-like quality to a force because it makes the whole universe run in harmony, including plants and animals everywhere. The key to the master plan are those next two comments. We will talk about them extensively further down the line.

The etheric mold is the tool of evolution, and the physical shell is your organic you that fits into that etheric mold. What is this tool of evolution? Again, we can go back to Darwin. It is such things as survival of the fittest. Variations in an infinite number of directions. Let's look at survival of the fittest. Oh, that little comment met all kinds of static from people, but stop and think for a second. Forget evolution. Look at your own life. Who gets the best money in the job? The one who does the best work.

Survival of the fittest. Who wins the gold medal at the Olympic races? The one who runs the fastest. Survival of the fittest, pure and simple. If you go out in the middle of the street and decide you are not going to cope with anything else, and sit down and insist that the cars are going to miss you, your survival rate's going to be lower. But you have intelligence. You wouldn't do that. Most of us wouldn't do that.

This physical shell you're in is a direct by-product of this whole evolutionary scheme. The whole thing. One of the classic examples is the horse. Back in time, the little horse line started up and it goes clear to today because we've got wild horses alive today. But the first little creature called eohippus ran around on all five toes. As time went on, he migrated from the forests to the plains and found it easier to run when he didn't get all the sticks and stuff between his toes. Then a few minor foot variations occurred when the two outer toe bones pulled up off the ground. You can find them today sheathed in part of the horse's hoof. And the animals with three toes were doing better. A few more million years went by and some more variations. Two more toe bones withdrew and now he's running around on his middle fingernail. If you look at the anatomy of a modern horse today, you will find these four bones pulled back up into the body and you can label the toe bones one through five. And he's running around on toe number three.

Here is a perfect unbroken example. Some people say, "Oh, you can't prove evolution because you don't have a master plan." Phooey! There's a beautiful one—the elegant example of the horse. There are many of them, but just take that one. And that's how you are what you are. You have eyes in front of your face and developed stereoscopic vision because you lived in trees, and you jumped from branch to branch. Did you ever close one eye and try to jump and grab a branch? It doesn't work worth a darn. So until you get your eyes around in front of your face so you can focus on the branch you're going to land on, you're not going to be a successful tree dweller because you're going to miss that branch too many times and land flat on your whatever and that's going to be the end of the game. Perhaps there would be a big carnivore there. But as your eyes get more around the front of your face, you get better and better and better at it. That's why your eyes are where they are.

Did you ever stop to think about that thumb? Extremely critical. Opposed thumbs are characteristic of man. Very few creatures have it, only the high primates. Did you ever try to do anything without your thumb? Just imagine your thumb was not there. Can you imagine picking things up or writing or using tools? If that thumb was not there, you'd be in trouble. Another little variation that was successful.

Okay, what's coming up? People are going to tell us we're going to lose our little toe because we're wearing shoes. Well, that doesn't make any difference. We don't need five toes anyway because we're no longer hanging onto branches with our toes. That's why you had them that way in the first place. What other changes? Well, we're going to lose our appendix. That's not exciting for our development. Maybe it will save a hospital trip, but other than that, it's not going to make any difference to you. But what is? Get serious for a second. What's going to make a real difference to you? Your ability to control your spiritual awareness now. For the first time, you are in a position to do something about evolution yourself instead of being at the whim of all the other creatures. Let us run quickly through what makes you what you are. Again, don't worry about some of these names. If you want to read a beautiful book, the first half of the book called *The Emergence of Man* by John Pfeiffer is, I think, one of the most well-written and beautifully-written books I have read in a long time. It is this thing we're going to cover here very quickly.

As you know, Leaky was working in Africa (and incidentally under some spiritual guidance) in the Olduvai Gorge and found in strata roughly 15,000,000 years old a little animal called Ramapithecus. This was a little four-footed creature that ran around bow-legged, a little hump-backed, arms fairly long, probably frowning most of the time. In very similar beds of about 4,500,000 - 5,000,000 years ago, Leaky found an Australopithecus. Now here is really something. Here's a creature about five or six inches shorter than I am, heavier built than I am, and who walked upright. Some of them seemed to have maybe walked with their knuckles on the ground, but they were mostly upright. And if you dressed one up in modern clothes and put him out here on the street, probably anyone who is kind would say 'Good morning," because you could not tell him from modern man. Sure he had a beetle brow—but I've seen some pretty beetle-browed people. He had a weak chin—and we've seen some weak chins, too. I don't know if his face was all covered with hair, but I can prove to you that in man's case, if you don't shave, you'll be covered with hair. So that's kind of irrelevant anyway, isn't it? But this one section of the African plain seems to have been where man developed. Olduvai Gorge in Africa. There seems to be another pocket of them in Ethiopia. But 4,000,000 years ago, we had a pretty decent-looking man. He knew how to make tools. He used rocks to smash things. We're arguing whether or not he had fire. Leaky insists he did. A few other anthropologists don't think he did. We'll find out shortly. But then some very startling things happened. In beds approximately 750,000 years old, they found Homo erectus, you and me.

The man who walked upright. He had this s-curve in his spine. I mean, if you cut me in half, I'm bent like an "S" clear to here. That's Homo erectus, the man who walked upright. And you could not tell him from anyone on the street. In fact, I've seen some people I think probably are Homo erectus, but that's beside the point. Then finally, a giant step at 250,000 years ago, Homo sapiens appeared on the scene, people just like you and me. At about the same time, there was an offshoot, Homo neanderthalensis, in Europe. And there's every bit of good evidence that Homo sapiens, you and me, either killed Homo neanderthalensis off outright or bred him out of existence by dominant genes. I suspect it was a combination of the two. Then finally in very modern times, in the time scale we've been talking about, some 40,000 years ago, they find modern man with very, very thin skulls just like ours. And, in fact, in many locations, the only way they can tell that they are fossils is because the bones have been mineralized. They look so much like us, and they had all the same problems, arthritis, bad feet, and all these kinds of things.

So the question comes back. Let's go back to what we were talking about when we first started. 'And God said, "Let us make man."' When did he do it? On a spiritualist level, when did he make that difference? Was it Ramapithecus? He was very much like an ordinary animal running around and not doing anything outstanding. Was he Australopithecus at the time? No, probably not, because his brain was not that developed. Was he Homo erectus? Maybe, and there comes the interesting question. Was he Homo sapiens? Absolutely. And do you know what the magic thing was? One of them, as we were discussing before, began to recognize himself as an individual and started recognizing his friends as people and giving them names. And then the BIG step, when he walked out one night and looked up and saw the moon and said, "I wonder what that is?"

For the first time, an animal thought abstractly, and from that time on, we have been doing it and we have been developing. If you want to mark when creation appeared on a spiritual level, to be on the safe side, let's put it 250,000 years ago when Homo sapiens came on the scene and was a dominant animal.

You'll notice the last part of your paper, 'reincarnation.' We have already talked about it in detail this last hour. Reincarnation is the tool. Reincarnation is what we have been talking about—this inevitable climb up the ladder to man IS reincarnation.

These are tools of mastery, to help you know your way, and it is always your choice. And as I say, for the first time, you are a creature who has a capability of thinking and doing something about your evolutionary steps. What can you do to advance? Sharpen your awareness now. Don't wait for ordinary changes to make you more aware. Do it now. You can do it by learning.

And we're going to learn how, that's why you're here.

A lot of people resent being told that we evolved from the same stock as apes and monkeys.

You've been playing around as Homo sapiens for roughly 250,000 years. You could still be a monkey sitting in a tree. Be proud of where you are—you've come a long way. You probably spent a long time as an amoeba.

This is reincarnation in a nutshell. You were an amoeba. Pretty soon you learned to do everything an amoeba could do. And one time when you were on the spirit side you decided, 'I'm sick and tired of being an amoeba. Isn't there something else I can do?' And so you find a paramecium. Hey, that looks kind of neat because it can swim. So you jump into a paramecium. Maybe five thousand times you cross over and come back as a paramecium and then the same thing happens.

Pretty soon you're on the other side and you say, 'Well, I know I've got the amoeba act and I've got the paramecium thing down; there must be something else.' As you're looking around, evolution is going on and making all new shells for you to play with. So you picked a flatworm—which happens to be a worm I'm in love with anyway. I'm sure you've seen him. The little triangle head and he's cross-eyed. Okay, so you decide he looks like a good one. So you jump in. Now you've got to be careful because he's got a nervous system and a circulatory system. He can crawl around and he's got the rudiments of a brain. So instead of this taking you a few thousand times, let's say you're going to spend 1,000,000 years being a flatworm. But in those million years of being a flatworm, you're going to know everything that a flatworm can possibly know.

And you jump onto the spirit side again and say, 'I've got that one sewed up. Let's look for something better.' Maybe you pop into the body of an insect as he's forming in his little egg. You live out his lifetime and you learn a lot because of his complex nervous system and because he can really think. Ants are really smart critters and so are bees.

So you go through that and say you spend a few million years being ants and spiders and centipedes and all those kinds of lovely creatures. And then you pop back on the spirit side and say, 'Okay, what's next?' I know I was a Tyrannosaurus rex once, so okay, let's pop into a big lizard. I mean, that's great, running around biting things, make lots of noise. But he wasn't a good animal. He didn't perform well. And he became extinct in a few million years because he could not compete. So you pop back on the spirit side and say, 'Hey that was a bum trip, let's find something else.' And then you know what you're going to do? You're going to find an offshoot of this funny little fat creature here because he was warm-blooded. And he had a real brain and he could really think. And you might have spent a couple hundred million years playing that game. And we're using up time at a pitiful rate.

As you go on up, finally you get to a point where you know what all those little critters can do and you stand at the edge of mankind. You're going to get the biggest shock of your life as you become a man for the first time, because he is different than any other creature. He can think abstractly. And you're going to spend a long time being a primitive man until you can really hold it down. Now you have gotten very selective after 500,000,000 years of reincarnating along the evolutionary chain.

And so you waited until you found parents. Ah, hmm, that's going to be a red-headed baby; it's going to be a red-headed baby girl. Great. Bang! And so you were born, a red-headed baby girl. Or you can be more careful like Mozart, who on the spirit side knew there was something he wanted to do in the quickest possible way. So he chose parents that were very ambidextrous. He chose parents that had all the latent musical talents. And he appeared on the scene. Bang! like a skyrocket. At the age of four, he was composing at the piano, writing symphonies at the age of six, writing concertos at ten. You think he did that maybe in ten years? No way. Who was Mozart before? We don't know. He won't tell us. He's still on the spirit plane. I know one woman who talked to him a number of times because he still loves music. But you will notice what he did. He came on the scene; he did what he wanted to do, and disappeared in a little over thirty years. He knew what he wanted to do that time.

So as you go along this little thing of reincarnation, you will take one step at a time because that's all you can do. I know some of us might like to be way back when we started, let's say an amoeba, a paramecium and a flatworm all at the same time. Get all this out of the way. Well you can see that wouldn't work, just as it really wouldn't work today for you to be three people.

We have a hard enough time controlling ourselves as individuals, but you will take one step at a time.

This next little statement is extremely important. 'No backsliding.' I've been an amoeba, a paramecium, and now I'm a flatworm. If I fail dismally as a flatworm, I'll simply die and come back again as a flatworm. No one's going to take me back and make me be a paramecium again. Not at all. I've mastered that one. So now I'm a flatworm. I might have an awful time until I get over the flatworm bit, but I'll make it. I'm just like you. You've all been primates of one form or another. And now you're a human.

You're always going to be human, nothing else, until we get to the next level— Homo Novus. We will talk about him quite a ways further down the line.

What is the goal? If we could extend this chart, I mean good grief, it is very badly telescoped. If you could squash this thing all out in some other way, we know that further along the line, the Sun is going to go nova, or burn out, one way or the other.

And all life on Earth is going to stop. It's either going to get cooked or it's going to freeze to death, and the Sun hasn't made up its mind which way it's going to be. What's going to happen to you and me? I don't know if we should worry about that this evening because, after all, 5,000,000,000 years is a little ways away. But what are you going to do in between? What is the next step up here? What's the end of this thing? What are we aiming for? We're aiming at that little thing listed there as C, 'Perfection.'

And I mean that in absolute terms—to be perfect in every way. And I've simply used the two terms here that you have normally heard. The Christian concept would be to merge at one with the Godhead, to be part of the universal all. And number 2 is the one, of course, from my background of Buddhistic concepts, Nirvana, to merge with the universe, to have mastered everything and to have become perfect so there are no more lessons to learn and you can do anything you think of just by the act of thinking. That's where you're going. How fast you're going to get there, well, that's up to you.

Because only you can do it and only you can decide how fast you're going to take the steps. A little further down, we'll have some tests and we will experiment with some of these things of controlling energy. You'll be surprised what you can do with your mind.

Duality of Man, Etheric Mold, and Man's Concept of God

Guideline: THERE IS NOTHING BEYOND MY REACH

I. Duality of Man
   A. Physical
      1. Chemical energy
      2. Electrical energy
   B. Spiritual
      1. Energy
      2. Alterable

II. Etheric Mold
   A. Master Blueprint
   B. Thought Control

III. Man's Concept of God
   A. Prehistoric Man
      1. Nature spirits
      2. Gods in the form of man
   B. Egyptian
      1. Formalization of worship
      2. A God for everything
      3. One God
   C. Modern Concepts
      1. Christian—Hebrew
      2. Abstract
         a. In all things through all time
         b. GOD IS!!

********** WORK FOR THE WEEK **********

Concentration—Abstract spot in the minds' eye

Meditation: Five to ten minutes each morning and evening

The lecture tonight is shorter and quicker than the last two. We hammered through that one on evolution and reincarnation because I guess I'm an old fuddy-duddy and I think they should be given together because they are absolutely inseparable. Anyway, now we've got that out of the way, let's examine what we've got to chatter about tonight.

As you can see, this evening will be divided into three major categories: 'Duality of Man,' 'Etheric Mold,' and 'Man's Concept of God.' So let's dive into this.

Your guideline for the week: 'There is nothing beyond my reach.

Here again is one of these little statements that I want you to tell yourself every single morning. Stand in front of a mirror and repeat it and know that it is an absolute truth: anything you can visualize possessing is yours. Anything you cannot visualize yourself possessing, there is not a way in the world you can get it. So as we go along, we will be hammering away at some of these "how to" and "how not to" kind of things. They are all tied very tightly to positive thinking.

Okay, Duality of Man. You are two people, obviously. And I don't want to get into the academic argument of these various degrees of consciousness that psychiatrists love to play with. Let's see, you've got a conscious mind, an unconscious mind, a super conscious, an over conscious, a collective conscious, and on and on and on. Let them play their games. It's not important to us what's there. You are essentially, however, two creatures. One of you is a physical one and one of you is a spiritual one.

Let's look at the physical one first. You will notice here on your outline it says chemical energy. Chemical energy makes you live, literally. I assure you that if you stop eating long enough, you will die. So that's a foregone conclusion.

The system itself runs on electrical energy. You might want to visualize the two systems as working harmoniously like a power plant. Let's assume that you were the head foreman of the big power plant along the Colorado River somewhere. All the turbines were running and you were turning out all the electricity for the lights and everything else in Los Angeles. And then one afternoon, you decided, well, phooey, I'm tired of working and walked away. What happens? Pretty soon part of the physical mechanism starts falling apart.

And that's exactly what happens to you and me. It can either happen quickly or it can happen slowly. And this brings about one of the most critical parts that is causing real problems today. In other words, it was discovered many, many years ago that if you take a frog and chop off its legs and skin them and take silver and a copper wire and run them from one leg to another and touch them, the frog's legs will kick. It was also found that if you do the same thing with frog legs and drop them in a hot skillet, they will kick. Okay, now they've been away from the body for quite a while; yet at the moment, they act as if they are alive.

Are they alive? This is a very, very touchy question. In the case of the frog legs, we're not too concerned other than that we would rather eat them after they were cooked. But other than that, it gets very, very tricky when it comes down to the problem of you as a living individual and your point of death.

When are you clinically dead? The reason this has become such a critical point is this business of donation of parts, of kidneys, of almost every part of the body. When is the body really dead?

This ties in with the electrical energy part of your system. Your mind, of course, your brain functions on electrical impulses. And they say that if something happens and all electrical impulses in your brain stop, you are clinically dead. If something were to stop all of my electrical activity in my brain right now, I would be clinically dead. Parts of my organs would continue to live: oh gosh, major nerve trunks three or four minutes, isolated organs that are complete in themselves up to maybe 20 minutes.

Do they have a soul? A part of me has an entity called Gene. If I drop dead and someone hacked out my kidney and gave it to you, do you have part of Gene? No, not at all, because I inhabit this whole body, and there is no way to separate it. No way at all.

The only reason they use the electrical energy to determine if you are dead is because it is the easiest to measure. There are many cases on record of people being buried alive without, of course, embalming.

If you were not dead when you arrived at the embalming table, you shortly would be. But there are many cases with some of the semi-exotic diseases, various forms of catalepsy and this kind of thing in which, without monitoring equipment, there is no way you could tell if that body was dead or alive. Its heartbeat might only be twice a minute. It might breathe only once every good many minutes. Of course, that's a very dangerous state to be in because your whole system requires more energy than that.

So they have decided that when all electrical activity in the brain stops, the person is clinically dead. There are exceptions to it, and I don't know how they're ever going to get around this until we let a medium come in and check. A competent medium can see the aura around a body and if the entity that was inhabiting that body has stepped away, you can tell it at a glance. But that's further down the line.

Okay, you are another person besides the physical. You are the spiritual you. You are energy. We don't know exactly what kind. There is a big debate going on about that subject. We know that the physical body, the organic part of us, operates both on DC and on AC, and there is also apparently some static electricity. But we don't know if it is a combination of all of the energies or which one is playing the most important part. When we get to the spiritual you, that etheric part of you that we will be discussing in a moment, this energy is even more difficult to understand. It is difficult to disrupt. You can't tear it apart. So it seems almost as if it is an electrostatic field being held together by something we do not understand. It can be measured. I'm sure all of you have seen photographs from Kirlian cameras. Those are not showing the aura in its absolute sense. They are simply showing the effect of the aura, which, indirectly at least, is the same thing.

This whole thing boils down to the question, what is the spiritual part of you?

There are two words that have caused tremendous confusion: soul and spirit. They have come to mean quite different things, when in reality; if you trace them back the words are exactly the same. The only difference is that one comes from Latin and the other from Hebrew. So if you want a definition that will keep those straight in your mind, remember that a soul is the spark of life [in this body] and the spirit is the never-ending you, the entity that is you.

Imagine that I stretched a rope across here. We're going to call that rope your spirit, the entity that is you, that is going from some kind of beginning to perfection. At various places along this rope we will tie knots. So here is a length of rope and a knot, and a length of rope and a knot, and a length of rope and a knot, and so forth. Each knot represents an incarnation where you inhabited a body and thereby gave it life. In other words, you are only one spirit but you are the sum total of all your souls. You see what I'm saying? The spirit in this particular shell at this particular time I call Gene, and in the other shell last time I might have called Joe or Jack. It's still the same me if I'm talking in terms of spirit or entity, but it's a whole new soul that I'm standing in here. So remember, the soul is nothing but the manifestation of an entity that allows life to occur. The soul is a spark of life. The spirit is the non-ending entity that is you, the rope.

These are a lot of fun to play with because as you get a little further on you will notice the number two factor coming into effect here. Not only is the spiritual side of you made of energy, but it is also alterable. And it is alterable because you have a mind and can control it.

We will be teaching you how to feel things by extending your aura and touching something. You might want to try that, in fact, this week. For those of you who can see auras or anything of that nature, you can see me simply sit here, get still for a second, and let my etheric hand touch those flowers. And the intriguing thing about it is that the etheric hand will go through them but can feel that they are cool, they're moist and that one has a spider in it. But this is something you can practice.

Walk up to the edge of something and simply stand there, don't look at it, just imagine you are extending an invisible part of your arm. You stand there and say, Right there's the edge. Then you look and you're right, there's the edge because you can feel it. We will get into more detailed work on that in a few weeks.

The most fascinating part of this thing being alterable is that it is alterable because you can think. And it is altering itself automatically all the time on a grand scale because you are getting better and better all the time. Each incarnation and each individual lifetime, you are getting better and better and better as you go along.

What keeps this spiritual you in shape? That's our number two, the Etheric Mold, a fascinating thing. It is the master blueprint. You look like you do because that is the shape of your etheric mold. The shape of the etheric field is controlled genetically, but it can be controlled by thought as well. Probably the negative side of that is the easiest to see.

When someone has a foot or arm amputated, you will very often hear them say, "My big toe itches." Well, there's no big toe there. In fact, there's nothing physically there, but the etheric mold is still present. The etheric mold is sitting there saying, Hey, I'm empty, fill me. And if you have the proper thought control, you can do just that. Because stop and think about some of our little lower animals. If you take a little salamander or a little California newt, chop his foot off (for those of you who are sadistic), in six or eight months he will have a new foot. It will be exactly like the old foot because the etheric mold was still there and as the cells grew, they matched that etheric mold and made it just exactly like it was before. You all do this many, many times. How often have you worn a fingerprint off, or cut your finger? Let it grow completely back, check your fingerprint again, and they're exactly alike.

The geneticist, of course, would say that's because the genetics have the coded information to duplicate that fingerprint. I agree a thousand percent, but it did it by filling the etheric mold. The cells could grow into nothing else but the shape dictated by the etheric mold.

Genetics is a beautiful field and one that I've worked in quite a bit. It's fascinating to play with genetics. There's only one catch to this thing of duplicating the etheric mold and that is scar tissue. If you cut your finger bad enough and run around and keep it open and pour salt in it every day (which in itself is an interesting experiment) the cells will finally give up trying to match the etheric mold and scar tissue will form. And then when you take a fingerprint of that finger, you will have a line through it that does not match.

Scar tissue is the culprit, and it's very interesting because the only place we find that particular kind of scar tissue is in animals that die of old age. No animal that has the capability of rejuvenating dies of old age because nothing wears out, it gets replaced as fast as it wears out. Of course, in most cases they're small, simple little animals, crazy things like jellyfish and some of the sharks. Probably some of the sharks would be the highest form and there are a couple of the so-called newts that look very suspicious along that route. I know there's one in Mexico City that's been alive for something like 110 or 115 years. So he's not doing badly for a crazy little wet lizard.

But the whole point is that scientists are finding more and more that, if they can prevent scar tissue from forming, the combination of your genetic coded information and your etheric mold will faithfully reproduce exactly what was there before—much to the horror, I might add, of some plastic surgeons. If someone has decided their nose doesn't look right, so they trim it or bob it, it is surprising how with time those cells try desperately to get back to where they were. If I've cut my nose off and my etheric is out even further, each time a little skin cell flakes off and a new little epidermal cell is made, it says, Hey, I'm too far from the etheric, and it keeps going, keeps going. If you could live long enough, you'd be right back where you started from.

Most of the time that doesn't happen. The other thing is that, after the brain stops paying attention to an error in the etheric mold, the etheric mold will start to match the new tissue. In other words, I mentioned the man with the leg cut off. The bottom of his foot itches, but after enough time (and sometimes it takes years) the etheric will come back up and obey the physical shape and match the stub of his leg. Then his foot won't itch anymore because his foot is not there, even in the etheric form. And in a way that's sad. The error in your body was not always there, so all you have to do is change it back to the etheric mold and it will be correct, just as it's supposed to be. And a big question there is how good are you at believing?

You also change things with your mind. If you decide that you are going to be sick, I don't give a darn how well all your organs and everything else work, you will be sick. And it is one of these things that is very difficult to get across because people don't like to admit that they are sick. And you should never do it anyway. But if you've got a nagging headache, don't think to yourself, Well, I'll ignore it and it'll go away. No way! You've got to be more direct than that. Tell it to go away. You've heard the old story; someone steps on your toe so your toe is hurting. Then someone hits you on the side of the head. Now your toe doesn't hurt anymore, but pretty soon, you become conscious of this and both of them hurt.

But what did your mind do when it paid attention to your head and ignored your toe? That's what you've got to learn to do on command. The easiest way to do it, of course, is with something like a headache where you can simply let go of it. These are some of the things you can do by thought control. It is not easy. I told you that the one thing in these classes that would probably make you unhappy is it all sounded so easy and yet turned out to be so hard to do. And that's exactly what you're going to bump into and that is "B", thought control.

It is the total answer. If you learn nothing else in the first 50 years of your life except total thought control, it will have been well worth it. But how do you learn this?

We can control things with our thoughts. Okay, how far? With this etheric pattern, this master blueprint, there are so many interesting things you can do. Take for instance a seed, an ordinary seed. If I took out a piece of corn and put it there, and you could really get still and touch it with your psychic sight, you would see faintly and kind of shimmery a corn plant standing here because that seed carries with it the etheric mold, the etheric shell if you will, into which that seed will be allowed to grow.

I saw this demonstrated most beautifully in Rev. Bradley's class. She had three or four men who specialized in just that. We would line up 50 seeds, give the men pads of paper and say, "Sketch what each seed is going to be." Well, there were three or four of them that were good; but there was one young gentleman who was just phenomenal. I mean, sure, if I put a corn kernel out here you're all going to know that's going to be a corn plant and you could fake it and draw one. And if you've seen a radish seed, you could draw that too. But I, being the nasty person that I guess I basically am, brought several vials of orchid seeds from home. If you've ever looked at an orchid seed under a microscope, they look like tiny little specks of dust. They are very small, among the smallest seeds there are. And so on four little disks of black paper, I had four different kinds of orchid seeds. If I had gotten the vials mixed up, even using the microscope, I will tell you, honest-to-God, I could not have put the labels back on the bottles right because they are so similar, even at 600 power under a microscope.

But this one fellow really amazed me. Not only did he sketch roughly what the plant was going to be, but he knew the color of the flower. That really blew my mind because I planted those seeds and four and a half years later he was proved right. And he spotted every one of them. A number of the men, by looking at the etheric form above the seed, decided that one wasn't going to grow. It looked perfectly healthy, but it was dead. And so, of course, we put that one in a germinating cup to see if it would germinate and it did not.

So these are the things that you can do. Well, that's kind of fun and games. It's fun to do at parties and stuff. Put a couple of fairly good-size seeds in a little package, pass them around and ask everybody what it is. Okay, you're sitting here holding a package that has a lima bean in it. What is it? You'd be surprised how many accurate answers you will get. If you calm down and just go by first impression, that first impression is often right.

One of the ultimate forms of mind control is, of course, the control of pain. Those of you mothers who gave birth to children know about pain. Those of you men, who have not had children, thank God you have not. It is considered one of the most painful experiences that can occur. So at least, in that respect, all of us guys are lucky. But much of the problem here is your state of mind at the time.

Now Rev. Bradley was a stickler for following through with what she thought should be done. One time she had an impacted wisdom tooth and she went all over town to find a dental surgeon who would extract it without anesthetic. They looked at her, of course, as if she were an absolutely foolish black woman. She must have weighed 200-plus pounds, so when she came sliding into an office, it was something to behold. But then to make a request like that! I guess she was almost unceremoniously thrown out.

She finally found one who agreed. He said, "I will have the nurse standing by with sodium amytal and if things don't seem to be going right, may I put you under?"

"Of course."

So she arrived at the appointed time, went out in the lobby and picked out an article in a magazine she thought she would be interested in. Then she went back in, sat down in the chair, got up with her etheric, walked back into the waiting room, sat down and read the article for a little over an hour. The doctor by pre-arrangement was supposed to open and close the door to let her know the procedure was over. The doctor later told her that he never felt so silly in his life, and he kept all his other patients away so they wouldn't wonder what he was doing.

When she popped back into her body, the doctor was amazed. There was a minimum of bleeding; there was no pain, even after she got back into her body. And there was none for a very good reason. All this time the nerves had been sending to the brain: ouch, ouch, ouch, this evil man is hurting me. But she was in the other room so she didn't answer the command. And pretty soon the nerves stopped sending. After a while they get tired of sending messages that you're not paying any attention to. That's exactly what happened. I think this occurred on a Friday. She conducted message circle Sunday night and church. It didn't bother her at all.

Now, there is another way you can do this, the old beautiful East Indian way of taking a large sewing needle and pushing it through your hand and pulling it out the other side. If you are in control, you can do that and there won't be a drop of blood. I would not suggest that you go home tonight and try sewing your fingers together. Get a little more control first.

But this is a common thing in some parts of the world. People in the Western world are amazed at this. Yet I'll bet there are a hundred thousand people, certainly in India and Nepal that can do it at the drop of a hat, simply as an exercise. It is taught to small children at the lamasery as a way to prove they have control. Instead of your little junior coming to you with a sliver in his finger, screaming and bawling; if you've got a sliver in your finger there, the priest would come up and take another stick and push it the rest of the way through and pull it out. You're not supposed to flinch because you are in control. Notice I said, "Supposed to."

There are many, many things that we will get into as we go along and the name of all of them is this thing of thought control. As we talked about before, thoughts are things, thoughts are real. You will hear me spout that so much, you're going to get tired of it. But I want you to know it to be true because it's extremely important.

One of the things I didn't touch on I'll just mention in passing. This spiritual energy thing seems to be almost not akin to natural laws of physics. There's getting to be more and more evidence that thoughts travel faster than the speed of light. They had a good opportunity to check it out on the last series of missions to the moon but no one aboard the ship was a trained psychic. I wish one of them had been; we'd have gotten more information. But there are some very peculiar things about thought. Remember we talked about how plants can receive your thoughts and you can hook the right instrumentation to them and find out what they know. You can put them in what is called a Faraday Cage, a closed, six-sided cube of fine wire charged with thousands of volts of electricity through which waves of the electromagnetic spectrum have a great deal of difficulty passing and it doesn't bother thought transference at all. Baxter, I think, in one of his ultimate experiments, put a plant inside a Faraday Cage with 500,000 volts of DC current on the outside. On the inside he put the plant in a box of lead and grounded the lead. And the plant reacted beautifully. Every time he sent it a message, it reacted.

So there's something peculiar about thoughts. We don't know if they travel faster than light. It appears that they do. Two of the experiments that were done on the second moon mission show that it is as fast as light, if not a little bit faster, because it takes, of course, a distinct time for a radio signal to go from here to the moon and back. But thought impressions of ESP cards were getting there ahead of the radio signal. So as I say, if we had a really trained super-psychic aboard, then we would have a lot more information.

Man's concept of god. This is one that we've touched on a number of times because it's very, very important.

First of all, prehistoric man: notice here we've got listed nature spirits and gods in the form of man. Early primitive man made a god out of anything he did not understand, and most of the time he made gods out of things he was afraid of, which is normal. I mean, good grief, can you imagine what a big bolt of lightning did to an early caveman-type person? And we've only known what lightning is for a couple hundred years. They were out there, it was raining, and here comes a brilliant bolt down out of the sky, slams into a tree, splits it open, and sets it on fire. My God! If you want a god, there's a good one. If you want something to be afraid of, there's number one. They had a god for lightning, they had one for thunder, they had one for rain, just go right on down the list. Almost anything you can think of, they had a god to represent it.

But then an interesting thing occurred—gods in the form of man. And thank heavens we have a few really fine anthropologists who believe in studying primitive people and not trying to help them for their highest and best good. Any time man gets out there with his helpful attitude, he does nothing but destroy. The Australian Aborigine existed in a gorgeous, pure culture for countless thousands and thousands of years, and was essentially destroyed in twelve years by well-meaning people. That's a shame, but competent people talked to primitive people before they began to convert them to our good ways, and they have found out some very interesting things.

There was one beautiful story. Did any of you see the movie, "The Sky Above, the Mud Below"? I spoke to one of the Frenchmen on that expedition when he was speaking at the Adventurer's Club and it was the most interesting thing to hear him talk about the natives carving a totem. If you remember the picture, they cut down a tree and carved it to look like a native with war paint. When the explorers asked why the natives made the statue look a certain way, they got an answer that almost floored them.

"Because when you carve it like that, it looks just like him."

The scientist asked, "Who do you mean by 'him'?"

"The one standing right there," the native answered, pointing to a spirit.

The researcher couldn't see the spirit so he didn't know if the statue was a good likeness or not. Isn't that interesting? And at that point in time, we suddenly find primitive (I hate that word), we find primitive man making gods out of people that they honored, or people that they were afraid of. And it carries right on through time for quite a while.

Finally, Egypt is where we touch upon the highest form of the formalized worship until we get to modern times. And certainly it is one of the most beautiful. But here again, they had a god for almost everything. And they had beautiful combinations, mixtures of men and animals as gods. I mean, sphinxes are beautiful. I don't think anyone would think of a sphinx as a horrible creature. I'd like to have one in the backyard, a live one. Ra, the solar god, the head of a cow and the body of a man—

that's a gorgeous combination. One of the disasters was Ibis, the body of a man or woman and the head of a long-necked bird with a bill. This never quite fit. They had gods for all of them.

Incidentally, we might point out a little thing here that is often misunderstood. Akhenaton, Amenhotep IV, has been given an awful lot of credit for creating the concept of a single god. Unfortunately that's not what he did at all. He simply brought the whole philosophy of Egypt around to the worship of Aton, which means nothing but sun. Of course, now, he was justified because life cannot exist without the Sun. So from that standpoint he was right, but he was not the father of the single god concept, not at all. The single god concept came about probably in very early Hebrew days. And there they just simply made lesser gods angels, instead of gods, and kept just one.

This is why Tutankhamen was buried in such splendor. Akhenaton was his father-in-law and when he died (or murdered, they're not sure which) and Tutankhamen took the throne, all the priests came to him and said, "Hey, look what the old man did to our temples." Tutankhamen said, "Okay, we will rebuild them." And he reopened all of the temples to all the various gods. But even though he died very, very young, at eighteen or nineteen, he was buried in brilliant splendor because he had all the priests on his side. Politics, even back then.

Then we get into a modern concept, and this I think is most fascinating. I don't want to sound callous, but the early Christian and Hebrew concepts were no better than the primitive ones because they made a god that was vengeful, an eye for an eye and a tooth for a tooth. They put him on a throne with a big book, keeping marks after your name and all of that. But it turns out that's not the case at all because we've got to look at God in the total abstract. And the two statements that you see written down here are two of my favorite questions to every high entity I have ever met or any high entity I have spoken with when they were working through a medium. These are the answers I have gotten over the last twenty-five years: *God is in all things, through all time.*

And then I really pin them down. "What is God?"

And you get those two words, 'God Is.'

No elaboration, no fancy words.

So it goes—the universe has always been and will always be. And God, this overriding force, this master plan that you would call it, is in all things through all time. And remember, if you bump into this question on a test, 'What is God—GOD IS.' And really, if you look at it even in the religious connotation, that is the way it should be. On one hand they make a god all powerful, invincible, and totally supreme; then they start restricting him with things he can't do, or things other people can do to him.

No way. It simply doesn't work.

The Aura

Guideline: RIGHT THOUGHT IS THE WAY

I. The Aura
  A. Visibility
    1. Physical eyes
    2. Psychic eyes
  B. Which Aura?
    1. Physical aura (aura C)
    2. Spiritual or etheric aura (aura E)
  C. Indicators in the Fine Structure of the Aura
    1. Illness or disharmony
    2. Anger and excitement
  D. Colors
    1. The Spectrum
      a. Low to high frequency
    2. Meaning
      a. Generally high or low
      b. Smooth or toothed
  E. Reading the Aura
    1. Only with Spirit help, a guide or teacher

**********WORK FOR THE WEEK**********

Concentration: Abstract spot in the mind's eye Meditation: Ten minutes each morning and evening

I know there are several books written on auras. One is simply called *Auras* and tells about the etheric E, and unfortunately, much of it is repetitive. I'm sure you have all spotted this in those psychic books you have read. You will find someone saying exactly the same thing a dozen ways. This not only helps get a point across, but lets us talk a little bit about the aura itself.

First of all you will notice your guideline, 'Right Thought is the Way.' That, I believe, would go without comment.

The aura itself can be seen quite easily. In your outline, under 'Visibility,' you have both kinds of eyes being involved here, physical eyes and psychic eyes. The psychic eyes will generally see an aura, especially in the dark and, further along, when we start having a few dark circles, you will notice that you can perceive these auras whether you are looking at the person or not. You've heard me mention here several times that a medium will be talking to an entity and we will unconsciously turn and look at where that entity is standing. Not that it helps to see that entity any better, it is just a habit.

To see the aura with your physical eyes is quite easy. I generally have a very bright aura and many people see it. Tonight Tao Sing tells me my aura is green, so possibly you can see it around me. One of the things you want to watch for is eye fatigue.

Many people think they are seeing auras and are not. I would ask you to look up and see one of these lights for just a few seconds and then look away and start blinking your eyes. You will notice that you see an image of this light. This is because the image of that light was focused on the back of your eye and was very strong. The nerve in the back of the eye simply remembers what it looked like. If it takes some while for this to pass away, this in no way has anything to do with the aura. This is also easily seen when you drive home tonight and see oncoming cars with bright lights. You can blink your eyes after the car has gone past and you will see the headlights in motion. This is purely a physiological effect. It has nothing to do with seeing an aura. If I were standing up against something with a high contrast, and you were to stare right at my forehead, after a very few seconds you would begin to see a glow that is around me. Now if you shift your vision from my forehead to my left hand, you would notice that the outline image would shift also. This again is eye fatigue. This area you would see by using that kind of vision would only be from six to eight inches wide. Again, it is a physiological effect. It is not the aura.

There is a green aura around me about fourteen inches wide and rising above me. This will not move as you shift your eyes. I would ask you to practice doing this. Look at someone against a particular background and, if you see a halo around them, shift your eyes immediately. If the halo does not move, you are seeing the aura. We always hear it referred to as the aura, but you will notice I have 'Which Aura' in your outline. I've called them aura "C" and aura "E" for our identification. Other authors do not use this terminology. The physical aura we call aura "C" because it is colored. Generally it is highly colored. It can be any color you can imagine. A spiritual or etheric aura, I will call aura "E." The word etheric is our "E." This one is more difficult to see. It is more of a glow without a definite color and it will generally be very extensive. It can radiate from a few inches to several feet. You can find a beautiful display of the auras when there is a spilling over of aura "E" into aura "C" because it allows the color to extend a long way.

As I am standing here, my etheric aura is reaching to about the third row back and, because I am familiar with the feel of vibrations, I can feel her right at the surface of it. So as I am standing here, my etheric aura is sticking out there something like eleven or twelve feet. You will notice this as you become more and more aware. The surface of the etheric aura is smooth. In other words, it is a repeat of body structure. If I move my hand, my aura "E" moves with it and I can feel it changing as it moves across the wood and plaster of the wall. And you can learn to feel this. Imagine, if you would, that you had a long feather, a long peacock feather, and you were feeling things with this feather. If you stopped at something at which just the tip of the feather is touching, it would be very hard for the nerves and muscles of your hand to know that the feather was being touched. But, if you moved it a foot to where the feather is more substantial, you could find objects quite easily. This is the thing where, when you are working properly, this will bring you up short. You will walk into a dark room and find a door standing open. As you approach the door your etheric aura starts receiving the surface of it, the edge of it, trying desperately to warn you so you don't walk into it and smash your nose and get a black eye.

The aura "C," the colored one, is only a characteristic of your being alive. When you die and your body stops functioning as a unit, its aura "C" disseminates. It simply collapses. The aura "E" goes with you as it is part of the etheric body and therefore part of the spirit that makes up you as an entity. As I have mentioned in the outline under 'Indicators,' you can use aura "E" to detect things. In aura "C," you can see illness, disharmony, anger or excitement. They are difficult to tell apart in many cases. Let's just take the first one, illness and disharmony. The top of the aura "C" will be jagged; in other words it will have teeth in it, like radiating spokes. This shows that something has upset the person. The color aura is not remaining homogeneously attached to the rest of the form. Imagine me standing here with an outline of myself about two inches out, but a very accurate outline, another outline about two inches beyond that, and another outline about two inches beyond that. The color aura is generally restricted to about six to eight inches, unless it spills over into the etheric aura. Then there is a lack of smoothness, a lack of conforming to your contour. It is an excellent way to spot illness and disharmony.

To pinpoint an illness requires a study of the fine structure of aura "C." This is done extensively in the Eastern world. As I have told many people, and they usually have a funny smile on their face, the fine structure of aura "C" cannot be seen through hair. In other words, the surface of my arm here has enough hair to interfere with the fine structure of the aura. The fine structure of the aura is only about three millimeters tall, which is about a third of a pencil diameter. So it is very, very close to your skin. It fits you just like a perfect little glove. If I wanted to have someone examine the fine structure of the aura "C," they would have to look at this part of it where there is little hair, where the hair simply covers it up. Obviously, then, if you are going to examine a body for illness by studying the fine structure, we must remove all their clothes. In this day and age of medical practice this is not unusual. Can you imagine someone in the Victorian ge, where there was some concern about even using a stethoscope around nice young ladies, asking a patient to strip clean and lay over there on that flat table? It is looked upon with a little less excitement today, but it is absolutely necessary if you are going to study the entire body in its fine structure.

This is a remarkable little indicator. There are two major things to watch for. Imagine this little three-millimeter pile of energy, in a half dozen or so very fine parallel lines. Any place that the body has a problem, these lines will change direction. In other words, if you are looking at a spot, you will see all the little pieces of the aura bend up, they don't meet. They bend up as if they were trying to get away from the surface. This is a perfect example of an illness or an injury that is caused by excitation, like inflammation, something that has a higher body temperature, like a bruise, something of this nature.

If the fine structure dips in, then we have a condition below that area. The cells are not doing what they are supposed to be doing. The best example of this, of course, is cancer. We see it most often, of course, in scar tissue. Scar tissue, at the surface of the body or deep in the body, influences these little fine structure lines of this aura "C."

I have only used this skill, with beautiful results, one time. I was at the lamasery in Hawaii and we studied the aura. The Buddhist follows this concept of aura detection expression of the psychic sides of medicine.

We had a gentleman who was laid out on the table and we were supposed to see if we could find anything wrong with him. Well, I was busy looking and looking at his aura and the fine structure of his aura and his etheric aura. The thing that impressed me the most about him was he had the brightest yellow aura I think I have ever seen. It reminded me of petals of sunflowers. It was just brilliant, brilliant yellow. Anyway, everybody was down there, looking at the body and running around like you had to do. The only thing that I could find there was a small place on his leg in which the fine structure dipped in. It dipped in very sharply. The fine structure went straight into the leg, so I was really looking at it. The priest saw what I was looking at. He handed me his pen and said, "Where does it go?" Because I could see it, just like I was looking across at you, I started marking here and there and went down a ways and marked here; so forth and so forth, until finally I had a mark that went clear around his leg. I said, "Okay, that's all I see." He said.

"Excellent. That's exactly where the gentleman had a broken leg two years before." They whipped out the x-rays and I had drawn a line exactly along the scar tissue where the new bone tissue had grown together. So it can be done. I've seen it work, but, it takes a lot of patience.

'Anger' and 'excitement' foul up reading someone's aura because they change the color of the aura. Let us assume that you have a blue aura, and blue, incidentally, seems to be a very likeable color. Many people are blue people, but, as you get angrier, your aura starts shifting to the lower end of the spectrum. In other words, it would start shifting toward red and, if anger continues to build up, the aura will zip thru yellow into orange, into an orange-red and into a very deep blood red. When it gets to a very deep blood red, look out! The person is very, very angry and probably something is going to hit the wall, and it might be you.

I saw a beautiful example of this one night at a party. Everybody was having a good time; many had more to drink than they should have. There were two men just horsing around, you know, it will start with a slap on the back, then something else and something else. I was sitting there watching this when I noticed that one of the men's aura had started out kind of greenish and was now yellow. So I sat there very carefully watching. Then it turned to orange, to orange red and started turning deep red, so I told a friend that was with me, "We'd better break that up, that gentleman is not playing anymore."

We had some difficulty in breaking it up because he had decided to simply flatten the other man. But we did avoid the problem. So in taking care of yourself, if you are walking along the street and you see someone coming toward you with an aura that looks like a fire engine, cross the street or go in a store or get out of his way, because it is a sign of violent anger, reaching a point of breaking its bonds. The other end of the spectrum, of course, is the more tranquil or quiet blue, to the purples, to the violets, this kind of thing. Very, very seldom do we see the same person carrying the same aura all the time.

This is because of emotions. As you get excited, the aura starts pulling in. This is an excellent way for an instructor to see one of his psychic students who is doing something right, because we can watch the person's aura. A person will pick up an object and, let's assume that you are all at the point of getting clairaudient, you hear someone say, "Hello," and you look at your students and one's aura goes close to his body and then comes back out. Immediately you say to your student, "What did you just hear?" He says, "Nothing." But he did hear it and that's the trick, learning to hear when something is said. So this is what causes you to have that funny feeling, you know, that pins-and-needles thing, with your stomach all done up in knots, very akin to anxiety. The anger thing, of course, that I mentioned is the color itself. The aura expands with an excess of adrenalin to the body, so the two are linked closely that way.

You've got to know the person very, very well to know if this or that color is their color. So the main thing you can do with colors right now is to see. Is it a high spectrum or is it the low spectrum? Is it a high or low frequency? Red, of course, is the low frequency end of the spectrum and blue and violet the high. The white or gold that is often portrayed around the pictures of Christ, of course, is put there by the artist. Very, very high teachers and very high people on this plane tend to have a lot of white in their auras. I don't believe I have actually seen a metallic gold one more than once or twice and both times it was surrounding the same person who was a Master Buddhist priest.

I've heard a lot of people talk about a black aura and I've heard many, many people say that an aura turns black just before the person dies. Well, I have sat beside people at their transitions and patiently waited for their pretty blue auras to turn black. They didn't. As I was sitting one day, observing a person in a coma, I got tired of counting their breaths so I looked at their aura and thought, "When their aura turns black, I'll know that's it". I sat there in one particular case, and waited and waited and finally one of my guides reached over and said, "What are you looking at? He's not there anymore." His aura had simply faded. The aura got thinner and closer and closer to the body but it did not change color. I personally believe that I have never seen a black aura, in this case black representing a real color, not just an absence of an aura.

So there is a subtle difference here as you see, you will notice that. John, have you ever seen a black aura? I don't believe so. It's written up in nearly every book you pick up and yet I can't find anybody who has actually seen one. I guess it's a good end point if someone has turned black, they're dead. So maybe that's why it is there. I don't know if anybody has seen one or not.

By all means the easiest thing for you to spot, as far as meanings to the aura, are the two very broad statements I have made here, colors simply representing generally high or low. By far the most important is the degree of smoothness. If the aura is full of little holes, jagged at the edge there is tension, there is anxiety. There may be anger and again, anger associated with moving toward the red. That's about all you can really do consistently. Now, if several mediums took one of you people and literally live with you, I'd say it would have to be a period of several months, where they could compare your aura to all of your daily activities, the aura while you were sleeping, and so on and so forth, we could get a blueprint, or map let us say of the colors that your aura went through. Then we might be able to tell when something was wrong, just simply by looking at the aura.

But people change too much. When I'm working in trance and Tao Sing comes through to speak, I'm surrounded by his aura which is brilliant green, with a gorgeous, gorgeous violet.

When another entity, Sir, comes to me to speak through me, my aura will become almost white, with a silver shimmer to it. So you see these are things associated with individuals. I think while each one of you do have your individual aura, and your individual aura color, it would take some time to find out exactly what it is. Try this as you develop and learn to see auras.

Watch your friends. You can get, well today it might be blue, the next day blue again. So as long as t you keep going along, then suddenly you find out the aura is orange and you say "Good morning" and he says, "Oh, shut up", now in his case you've learned what the orange means. But as I say, it is an individual thing.

Husbands and wives, of course, have the best chance at this because even with the husband hiding behind a newspaper at the breakfast table you can generally see the top of his head and you can peek and see what's going on inside. Be careful when his or her aura contracts. It means a lot of mental activity, something is stirring. When an aura expands quickly, this is almost always associated with a tremendous feeling of uplift, a feeling of ease. I've noticed it a few times.

I'm generally not very nervous when speaking. I guess you can see why, I do a lot of it. But sometimes if I'm with a group that I feel I've got to be careful, that I've got to be on my toes, that someone out here is waiting for me to stub my toe, I always get that feeling that my aura is zipping back and forth, like you're testing, testing. Then finally, as I calm down and get into my little groove and say "Well, if he proves anything I'll ignore him anyway", then zoom, you can feel it spread out and it is a most beautiful feeling. This is the feeling you'll get in the morning because at night your aura has been kind of confined because of lack of activity. You'll get up in the morning and say, "Isn't this a beautiful day" and you just feel, swoosh, and this is the aura extending out, a beautiful thing.

In section E of the Outline is the subject "Reading of the Aura". I think you can see what I'm going to say by simply what I've written underneath it, "Only with Spirit help, a guide or teacher". Many people will give you readings of your aura, and I would be willing to bet you that they look at your blue aura and their guide or your guide says, "Well, that means so and so". And then they will look at the fine structure and they see a fine little yellow band, the guide says, "Well, in that case, that means so and so". Because they think they are reading your aura and it's only a crutch for the clairvoyant and/or clairaudient activity. Now there may be some hard and fast rules to aura color, to aura texture, aura width and extension. As you know, they can now photograph Aura "C" and on some of these highly enhanced electronic versions, possibly Aura "E". So maybe we will get some very definitive, scientific answers to it.

But by far the main thing for you to watch, as you start learning to see auras is changes in the aura; how smooth it is, how jagged it is. For those of you who are married and can pin your looks on your wives on their next round to the kitchen table, you might examine and see if you can find their fine structure and see what you can find out.

I have it on good authority that appendicitis scars are beautifully outlined by the aura. I've never seen one that close. I've been tempted, of course, on some of our beaches, but you might have an awful time convincing the young lady that you were looking at her aura. It is all in the interest of science but it is an excellent excuse for watching a skimpy bathing suit.

The Concept of Vibrations

Guide line: What my eye cannot see, my mind can know.

I. Concept of Vibrations
- A. All things
  1. Non-living
  2. Living
- B. Space
  1. Between particles
  2. Time
- C. Waves (light, radio-active. Not radioactivity.)
  1. Water like (sound)
  2. Tuned beam
- D. The Scale
  1. High and low
  2. A system that works
- E. Psychic waves or vibrations
  1. Thought control
  2. Psychokinesis "PK"
     - a. Focus of psychic energy
     - b. Practice makes perfect

**********WORK FOR THE WEEK**********

Concentration and Meditation:

Ten minutes each morning and evening. First three to four minutes be still. Ask aloud for your guides and friends to give you information you can check. Make sure you know what they send. Thank them for the help and close your silence after ten minutes. Check what they have given you, so that in your next silence you can acknowledge what you received. If you could not check what was received, ask for another test. This is testing your reception as well as the spirits' ability to send.

As you can see from your outline, the lecture itself is going to be relatively short for a couple of reasons. One, we don't know a great deal about what we are going to talk about. What we will do is go through these things and I will point out some things for you to watch as you go along. As time goes on, and we work more and more in this field with some of the scientific equipment that is being made by the Chapel, we might be able to answer some of these questions much more accurately than they have been answered here before.

Your guideline tonight is a direct quote from one of the Buddhist Sanskrit teachings, "What my eye cannot see, my mind can know." I think you will know what that means because that's what we have been talking about. To see something with your eyes is one thing. To see something with your eyes and your mind is to know it. That is what we are trying to teach you to do.

You will notice I have headed the whole thing "Concept of Vibrations." That is, of course, simply a term that's convenient to use.

You will hear people when they are giving messages or when they are doing healing or any of this kind of activity use terms like, "When I touch your vibration," or "When I come into your vibration," and so forth. I believe, in reality, it is something to say because, on a psychic level, we are not at all sure what these vibrations really are.

If you will recall, some time back we talked about the evolution of things. Everything from dust balls to stars to planets and all those kinds of things. I mentioned in passing that all things are vibrations. At first this might sound a little odd, and yet, even if you break matter down into its smallest divisible particle, it suddenly ceases to be what you think it is.

One of the most difficult lines to draw when you get into the study of very, very simple kinds of things is this number1 and number 2. We will simply state that all things are made of vibrations and that there are two kinds; either non-living or living. Now that sounds like a fairly easy distinction to make and certainly for higher animals it is. I know you can see me and say, "Gene's alive. He is breathing, he is moving, he is walking." Okay, that is fair enough. But when you get into some of the more simple forms of things that are alive, it gets very, very difficult to define exactly what you mean when you say something is alive.

For instance, you can say I am alive because I use oxygen. I breathe air and use the oxygen. If I dropped a strip of magnesium ribbon out here on the floor, it would absorb oxygen, yet it's not alive. It gets extremely touchy when you get into very simple forms of life. Remember when we were discussing evolution of a grand scale? We literally started off with molecules that could duplicate themselves and then moved on to viruses. Viruses fall into that group that are very nebulous as to "Are they alive and if so, when?" I think one of the most beautiful examples of that is the tobacco mosaic virus. I imagine some of you have seen pictures of it. It was written up in *Life Magazine* many years ago. It is a very simple molecule because it is a virus. It can duplicate itself, therefore it is alive. But when things are not quite right, if the temperature is wrong or the culture in which it is growing is wrong, it crystallizes and turns into a small pale brownish-gray kind of hexagonal crystal. I have seen vials of these things and you can pour them out and look at them with a magnifying glass and no way could you convince us that the thing is alive, because at that particular point it's in a total resting state exhibiting none of the characteristics that we could consider to be life. But if you take a few of these little crystals and drop them in a culture dish with the right kind of media, the right temperature, the little crystals break out and become viruses again. Then they start reproducing and making more of the same kind.

So there's the key. What is life? It is the ability to reproduce itself. It is the only one that holds hard and true. There seem to be exceptions to almost any other one you could name. Even that one, the example I just gave, the tobacco mosaic virus, is very difficult when it's in crystal form because in nature you can find crystals and you can collect crystals that have grown from a solution, and you can watch them grow. You can grow salt crystals in a concentrated solution of brine if you want to in a glass.

But the point is they are not duplicating themselves. They are simply adding to what they already have. Notice there's a subtle difference. They are not duplicating themselves; they are adding to what they already are. That's why a crystal (a salt crystal, a quartz crystal, an amethyst crystal, whatever) is not alive. It is not making more of its own kind; it is simply making more of itself. That is the subtle difference.

Okay, what do vibrations have to do with you? Well, since I have said that all things are made of vibrations, be they living or non-living, obviously then everything is made of vibrations. But what's the difference?

The major difference in the vibrations that you see around a living object is the aura. There is a very fine line to draw here. Only living things have an aura "E."

Now, a non-living thing can have a field of energy around it that looks kind of like a halo, but this is not to be confused with an aura. So as you go along and see auras and are able to define the difference between aura "E," aura "C," and a field of energy, you will then have at your disposal a foolproof way of deciding if it is alive or dead. If it's living, it will have those two auras, "E" and "C." If it's dead, it will not.

The field of energy is what many people see around things. First of all, if you see a bright field of energy around non-living things, have your eyes checked, just to be on the safe side. You might have a spherical aberration or something in the lens of your eye. But if you just simply see a small diffraction line around something that is not too bright, this is purely a property of the light being refracted along the surface of that object. Don't worry about it.

The other thing is you will notice that the field of energy around a non-living object does not change. It will always be the same, day in and day out. Your aura, either "C" or "E," will change with the emotional state you might be in either consciously or unconsciously, so a true aura will always change. Subtly, agreed. Sometimes very subtly, but it will change.

If you are looking at something around that candle, it does have a field of energy around it. Around that particular candle, it's kind of pale blue, but it will always be that color. And it will always be that same distance from the candle because it is simply a product of matter sitting there in space. That's all. Don't confuse the two things.

With matter, we are so used to saying that things like this podium are real. I can feel it; I can hang on to it. It's ponderable; it has mass, weight, and occupies space, therefore it is real. If you were to take one small atom out of this complex hydrocarbon (wood) and start tearing it apart, you would get down to some very, very small subatomic particles. And we call them particles simply for a lack of terminology. But they are not ponderable. If you were small enough and they were big enough, you couldn't hold them like this. They are not little balls of stuff. They are distortions of normal space. An electron is apparently like a depression in the surface of the water. Have you ever seen a water spider, this insect that runs around on top of the water? If you are looking at him when light is reflecting off the water, you will notice the water dips in where his feet are resting, because he has weight pushing down on the surface of the water. That's what an electron looks like, in a two-dimensional concept. In a three-dimensional concept, it's extremely difficult to imagine and absolutely impossible to analyze mathematically. So simply assign it a size, a diameter, and so on and so forth, and go on from there because it's something that works. But in reality, it is not that.

As I say, these things seem ponderable and solid and real, but there's far more empty space than being real. And not just because this is wood.

If we had something out there that's metallic, like the shield of this light, the shield would be visual, of course, because it is metal with little cells. They have cell structure. But the metal part of it is almost all empty space.

You will remember when we talked about the size of the universe and the distance factors involved, they were appalling. If we took a couple stars that were really quite close together, made them about the size of a small orange and set one here, the closest next star to that would be ten miles away. So look at the space involved here, this enormous gap. And if we took one small piece of this wood and enlarged it to about the size of the state of California and could look at the way the atoms were arranged, if they would stop running around, you would notice about three feet between them. So here again, we would see a little bundle of energy and three feet and another little bundle of energy and three feet and another little bundle of energy.

So all the things you see look solid simply because they reflect light.

And this is, of course, delusion.

This of course can be the key to why an entity can walk through that wall. If your vibrations are fine enough, there's an awful lot of space where you can walk through. You simply walk through it. What is the space between? What about this thing in between the particles? A long, long time ago, well not too long ago, but before a lot of you were here, most of the scientists thought that space was filled with ether.

Michelson did a lot of very beautiful experiments and it turned out not be to true. He was sure he was going to prove it was true, but being a good scientist, he admitted that he had proved it was not true. So what's between them? It's easy to comprehend space and yet how very difficult to really realize it. For instance, take the air in this room. It's very beautiful if you stop to think about it because we can see through it, we can feel it as it is moving, that kind of thing. But it looks pretty empty. It also has these little particles, but it's mostly space and it has a lot of weight. You are not aware of the weight of the air in this room, but if you took it all out and didn't collapse the building, it would make a tremendous change in the weight of this whole chapel.

So these are some of the things that look obvious but are difficult to imagine. Then, of course, the $64 question which says, "Between these particles is space and time." Okay, what's time? It gets very difficult to discuss time without getting into relativistic theories, so let's just use Einstein's simplest definition that time is nothing but the motion of matter through space. In other words, if there's no motion, there's no time.

For convenience, let us leave it there. This, of course, is the so-called fourth dimension that a lot of our science fiction writers like to write about and some of the programs on television have, in a very exciting way, presented. It's not like that, however. It is not nearly as dramatic as we would think. Traveling into the past? Yes. A little farther on we will teach you how to do it. Travel into the future, no. The future has not occurred yet so there is no place to go in that sense of the word. For now just remember that time is the motion of matter through space. Just a definition, that's all.

All of these kinds of vibrations seem to follow waves. This is section C from your outline. Here again is one of those things that is easy to think about and sometimes easy to picture in your mind, but very difficult to see as it really is. "Light." Incidentally, you will notice that I have put here 'radio-activity,' not 'radioactivity.' It constantly amazes me to pick up books on our particular philosophy or offshoots of this and see how very lax some of the writers are about the terms they use. They talk about communicating mind-to-mind and call it radioactivity. Well, no way. Radioactivity is a very precise, very detailed physical condition. It is the degree, of course, of certain elements with the giving up of energy. It gives off particles. It is dangerous to you because you are alive, and to an entity because it disrupts them. An entity cannot visit the core of the Sun for that very reason. They stay away from those areas. So remember to watch that word, radioactivity, because what it really means is radio-activity. In other words, the vibrations or waves are working like radio frequencies. Frequencies that you cannot see, that you cannot feel, that you cannot touch, but with the proper detecting equipment, namely a radio receiver, you can convert them to sound waves so you can hear them.

Into this group fall all the forms of life. That word "life," when we use it in the normal sense of the word, should be looked upon as the whole electromagnetic spectrum. Everything from the farthest red, pure heat waves, and even farther in that direction, going across the visible spectrum, which is a real small piece of the electromagnetic spectrum, on out past soft ultraviolet, hard ultraviolet, x-ray, heavy x-ray, and finally on up into the realm of cosmic particles. It is really quite amazing how different the world would look if we could see something through different eyes. Owls, for instance, see a far distance into the near infrared. This is how they can find mice in twilight or almost total darkness. They cannot see in total darkness but they can see quite well in light where our eyes are absolutely worthless. Most insects see strongly in the ultraviolet, so they look at things entirely different than we do.

They just recently found some beautiful research on that, like being able to tell the difference between butterflies when they are photographed by an ultraviolet camera. With the ordinary eye, with the ordinary camera, they look exactly alike. When you photograph them in ultraviolet, which is the way the butterfly is seeing the other butterfly, they look quite different. So we have this whole range of things. All are forms of life.

When you start working in dark circles you will start perceiving different things, either physically or psychically. At present, let us just stay on a physical level where you are using your physical eyes. Colors of those kinds of light will be very difficult to discern because, if there is a low light level in a room, your eyes are not nearly as accurate as to what the color is because it takes a certain amount of intensity of pure light so that you can see the color. Most of the time the things you will see in the dark, a dark circle let us say, have a smoky blue-gray cast, sometimes a little on the green side. Very seldom will you visually see anything much different than that as far as color goes. Psychically, in a dark circle you are going to see whatever color the entity wants you to see. If he wants you to see an orange football, you will see an orange football. But your physical eyes are somewhat handicapped, so you have to work within that framework.

Waves can act as sound waves act. You can hear me talking because my vocal chords are smashing little bumbles of air and they are radiating out in ever-widening circles. As they go past your ears, your ears hear a sound. If I threw a rock in the water, you would see these little ripples go out in the water. Sound is exactly the same thing, but in this case, it is three-dimensional. In the case of the pond of water, it is two-dimensional. As I am talking to you, my sound waves are not coming out in a single plane, but they are radiating in all directions, behind me as well as in front of me. Sound waves move at about 1000 feet per second. In the case of light waves, they move about 108,000 miles per second. So there are many different frequencies we can work with.

The tuned beam, of course, in physics is the laser. Some of you have seen a laser work. If you haven't had a chance to, I suggest you do so. They are fascinating to watch. They can do a lot of very interesting things. Some marvelous things they are doing in micro-surgery are utterly impossible without the laser. The tuned beam I am talking about is your mind. In other words, instead of having a radio that plays all the stations at once, we want you to learn to listen to one station at a time. That is what I am talking about here. With practice this can be carried to a very beautiful degree. There is nothing more fun than to sit with a group of mediums in a circle and have a closed beam between you and another medium. Tell that medium something and no one else in the room knows you have said it because you can literally build a small column between you and someone else along which you can send information and no one will know it is being sent unless they stick their mentality in the way and intercept the message. It takes good practice but it can be done. Usually, if I want to sit here and send an emotion or feeling to Nancy or one of the mediums in the back row, I can sit here and simply do it. You will all feel the wash of it because I don't tune it in. It would be a little hard; I can only see part of Nancy. The young lady here with the orange T-shirt would probably get clobbered because I can see her more than I can see Nancy. Here again, it's learning to use the tools you have available. Fine tuning is the way to do it. And the things you can do with it are just utterly incredible. The one I was talking about there, talking with one person, was a simple one.

Okay, section D about 'The Scale.' When we are talking about vibrations, you will always hear people talk about a higher vibration or a lower vibration. High or low can either be related to a vibration, to a frequency, to a color, to a speed, or to a velocity in the case of sub-light particles. But under no condition do I want you to think of it as high or low spirituality or high or low as far as a rate of development. It is very easy to get in the trap of 'this entity has a higher vibration.'

In other words, 'That vibration is quicker than this entity's, therefore; this entity is a better entity than that one.' No way! Don't do that. This entity just simply might like the more leisurely pace. To hell with this jumping up and down! This entity decided to just poke along. So don't get caught in the idea that, 'Oh, this entity has a very high vibration, therefore, he is God-like.' No way! Jesus, who was relatively God-like, does not have a vibration that will blow your mind unless he wants to do it.

He takes a very gentle, casual, easy feeling. So when you bump into your entities, you will notice this immediately. Some will come in like gangbusters; others will kind of drift in. Don't judge them by their rate of vibration because that is simply a system that works for me to distinguish that an entity around you has a high vibration so you will know which one I am talking about. Not that one is higher than another, not on any kind of scale because it depends on what they want to do. Around here we try to limit it when we talk about teachers and high teachers. Here again, you have to be very careful. What is a high teacher? How much higher than a teacher is a high teacher? We have masters and ascended masters. Well, how much higher is an ascended master than a master, and how much higher is a master than a high teacher? Here again, terminology. Don't get caught up in it. Know the entities around you. Know the people, and remember, they are individual people. Know the ones you are working with and accept them on that level and that level only. Try not to label them. Mankind is probably one of the best labeling creatures there is and that is one of the most dangerous things he does. So don't do that.

All the things we have been talking about here fall into ordinary laws of physics. They obey and fall within the categories of the electromagnetic spectrum; therefore, they should act like all the other things in physics. There's getting to be more and more evidence that thought does not obey the electromagnetic spectrum, though. We don't have firm proof yet, but it seems as though thought communication with our people that were in space in orbit around the moon got there faster than the radio signals. Now it wasn't a conclusive test because first of all, nobody in the satellite or space station was a competent receiver. The Russians have done some experiments the same way and their results are the same thing. It is right at the edge of saying, "Yes, thought is faster than the speed of light." My high teacher said it is and considerably faster, but, I couldn't prove that to you right now, but we will as we get more experiments going in this.

You have to remember the difference in speed here. When I say, "Hello," and Nancy hears it in the back of the room, if at the same time I had given a little spark of light, it would have gone around the Earth six times before Nancy heard my voice. So look at the difference in speed here. It is appalling. So you can see it would be very hard to measure.

The other experiment that looks very suspicious is a very good device called the Faraday Cage, which is a couple of screen boxes, a six-sided cube, with a receiver, namely a man, sitting in the middle. The screen, which is copper wire all soldered together, is charged with high voltage, either AC or DC, depending on the test they are doing. This blocks the electromagnetic spectrum. Radio waves will not go through it. So in the case we are discussing here, they encased the box inside and outside with lead.

The plant inside with 50,000 volts applied to the Faraday Cage received the thoughts as if there was nothing in between. Thoughts do not obey the laws of radio waves. They do not obey the laws of light. Whether or not they break all of the laws of those two magnificent factors of physics, we don't know. But some day we will. So as I say, for now so that we can at least talk about it, it is something that works. We will use that until scientific data defines otherwise. Then we will have to make up some new names for vibrations, thought waves, and things like this. Who knows? Maybe one of you will be able to pick that name.

Okay, one of the most interesting things you can do with psychic waves and/or vibrations is in section E. First, you are all learning thought control and you have all mastered thought control by now. You are all doing stillness. You can take one thought and just set it aside and look at it. You will really get better at it as time goes by. Keep at it. It is one of these things you have to keep working at. One of the most intriguing things you can do is psychokinesis or psychokinetic effect. Some time ago we had talked about this thing of moving things with your mind. I would like you to start actively practicing doing it. Nothing quite convinces you that you can really do something completely impossible as when you do it. That seems to wipe out the impossibility of a task about as fast as anything I can think of. We can sit here all night and tell you so and so could do this, so and so could do that. That doesn't really mean anything to you until you do it.

Okay, what I want you to do when you get home tonight is get a piece of aluminum foil and cut it into a big square. Fold it from corner to corner and crease it. Open it up and in the opposite direction fold it again, corner to corner. Now we are back to our little triangle which now has a crease down the middle of it. Here's where it gets tricky. Open it back up so that the creases are away from you and fold it so that the creases are on the outside and fold it in the other direction once more. Now I want you to take these things that are at 90° and pull them all under and re-crease all the corners. Anyway, the whole point is you will end up with a little metal pyramid. Aluminum foil works best because it is too easy for thoughts to go through paper. So make it out of aluminum foil and take a large pin and stick it in the end of an eraser of a pencil or a wad of clay or something so that it will pivot on the point and just barely set it down on the pin point. But the whole point is you can move that foil with your mind. That is what I want you to practice this week in addition to your other exercises.

There are two ways you are going to try to do it. Try to reach out and simply touch an edge your mind and push it. Mentally, just reach out and touch it. For some reason, it is easier for some people to pull than push. Don't ask me why. Try both ways.

Reach around it and pull toward you to see which works the best.

Do not set this under something that is glass right now. Set it someplace where there is not a draft or a breeze because then you will never know what is moving it. If you put it in a glass aquarium or fish bowl, it will be harder for you to move because you will have to learn to go through glass. Learn to turn it first. Once you can turn it, then you can place it in glass.

There is nothing that upsets a jeweler more than to stop the radiometer in the store windows. This can be done. If you don't stop them carefully, you break them. So when you get to the point of working through glass, stop them gently.

I have to tell a story I tell all the classes. A woman came to class and she could do this better than I think any woman I ever met in my life. She kept telling me how good she could do it. She said her pinwheel was on the mantle and she just drove her husband absolutely crazy. He would be sitting in the room paying attention to nothing. She walked through the door, glanced at the little triangle and it would spin. He watched this for the better part of a month and finally appeared on the scene one night wanting to know when these classes started again. He either had to learn to do it or get a divorce, he didn't know which. He learned to move it but he couldn't do it as well as her. She could spin it. She wore out so many it was ridiculous because she would get it spinning and the needle would go through it.

There are many other funny little things that can pop out and are difficult to define. One of our students can move it much easier if she exposes everything from her waist up. I am sure that's interesting for her husband and her guests, but . . . there does seem to be a correlation to skin areas and certain psychic effects. For instance, reading without your eyes is greatly enhanced by exposing your chest area. We don't know why. Maybe the cells can actually do something. We are not sure.

Anyway, give the pinwheel a try. Try it both ways. Try pushing it or pulling it because I haven't any idea how to tell the difference between pushers and pullers. There seem to be two classic kinds. Incidentally, if you noticed the films of the Russian lady who can roll things, it's very easy for her to push pointed things, like a compass needle. She will push it in the direction she wants it to go. Blunt objects she pulls toward her. Now, again, what this subtle little difference is, who knows?

Anyway, that is what we are talking about when we talk about psychokinesis, moving something without touching it. It can be done, believe me. A little later on we will be doing some experiments with other objects where you can all have a chance to test and show off your abilities. It is something to be proud of. You have heard me talk about that before. Be awfully damn proud of these things because we jokingly call them spiritual gifts, but they are not given to you. You earn every darn one of them. So be very, very proud of them.

Meditation: Stilling the Mind

Guideline: RIGHT MEDITATION ILLUMINES MY WAY

I. Meditation
   A. Eastern Concept
      1. Control of mind and body
      2. Seeking Nirvana
   B. Western Concept
      1. One with God
      2. A passing fad—why?
   C. Spiritual Concept
      1. Stilling the mind
      2. Receptivity
         a. Universal pool
         b. Friends and loved ones
   D. The Master Way
      1. Turning off self
      2. Your better life
   E. Delusion
      1. Reading between the lines
      2. Your downfall

**********WORK FOR THE WEEK**********

Concentration and Meditation:

Ten minutes each morning and evening. First five minutes get still, produce your small spot. Change this spot into a flower. Last five minutes, change your flower back into a spot and hold it there. You will see only your small spot and the background glow.

You'll notice the guideline, 'Right Meditation Illumines My Way,' is a direct quotation from Buddha, as you can probably guess.

Meditation itself is the only major topic for this evening. Before we look at the major categories, let me say a few words about hypnosis. We are constantly asked if hypnosis will help or hinder you in becoming clairvoyant, clairaudient sensitives, or whatever terms you want to use. In all cases where it has actually been done and scientifically evaluated, hypnosis does not help. However, there is a fly in the ointment, as is always the case in psychic work. If you think something is going to help you, it will. In other words, if I could convince all of you that if you went home tonight and stood in the middle of the room, balancing a glass of hot water on your head, it would make you more clairvoyant, you would believe it and it would work. This is the problem when you try to evaluate a test involving people opening psychically through the use of hypnosis. As I say, scientifically, no. And the reason is quite obvious—hypnosis is almost directly opposite of meditation. Hypnosis is an act of suppression. It is getting rid of that part of the mind that acts as a check and balance, that part of the mind, you might say, that acts as a governor.

Hypnosis is spectacular and can do many things, but because it is a suppressant to the mind, it also cannot do a lot of the things claimed for it. Many of the early works in hypnosis ran into certain obstacles. A classic example is to use hypnosis to get rid of a habit. Let's say I was going to use hypnosis to stop smoking. If a hypnotist got me into a deep hypnotic trance and told me that cigarettes were going to taste horrible, and that I would get sick to my stomach every time I smoked one, he or she could convince my unconscious mind that it would really occur. Minutes later, if I tried to smoke, this would occur because my mind would tell me it was going to happen. And as you know, whatever your mind tells you is going to happen, will. But there are no safeguards to keep me from replacing my smoking habit with something else, because you haven't stopped and faced the basic psychological problem that caused me to smoke in the first place. One most often sees a person take up the habit of eating in place of smoking. I have both habits, for whatever that's worth. But it is true that most smoking is a nervous condition of wanting to do something with our hands. The double problem of compulsive eating is now you are exercising many of the basic reflexes of the body. You are moving your hands, your jaws, you are tasting things. Unfortunately you also get fat. But if you want to use hypnosis for the ordinary kinds of development that we are talking about in psychic awareness, I would say don't use it. Now there are some fantastic things you can do with hypnosis, for instance improving memory and sleep teaching, these kinds of things. All of this falls outside the psychic realm and is purely, let us say, a sub rosa conversation between you and your subconscious.

Unfortunately, you don't talk to your subconscious very well and once something has been implanted, you have an awfully hard time talking your subconscious out of the idea. Hypnosis is one way this can be done, but only by someone who really knows what he or she is doing, who has a thorough academic background, certainly in psychology, and I would hope farther into a Ph.D. field having to do with neuro-psychiatric problems.

Okay, I've said that hypnosis is the opposite of meditation. Let us look at some types of meditation.

A, the 'Eastern Concept,' is most beautifully exemplified by those followers and practitioners of yoga, attaining absolute control of mind and body. The main thing they are after is number 2, the seeking of Nirvana; a seeking of perfection, a seeking of heaven, for Nirvana is the equivalent of heaven in our Western concept. This can be carried out to a tremendous degree. I am sure some of you have seen, certainly on television, maybe in person, certain yogis who, under deep, controlled meditative trance, can almost stop breathing. They can stop their heart action. They can hold a hand out and run a hat pin through it and pull it out the other side. The intriguing thing that still puzzles physiologists is they see the person do this, but the hole does not bleed. All you have to do to cause a great argument is to ask why it did not bleed, because certainly the hat pin pierced some cells and undoubtedly erupted little capillaries, but for some reason no harm was done. In fact, a few minutes after the act was done, there is absolutely no indication that anything abnormal happened to the hand at all.

This is exactly the same thing we see with the famous firewalkers. Here you want to be a little careful. We have firewalkers and then we have firewalkers, and they are quite different. We have some that are done with trickery, and we have fire walking that is carried out under yogastic control to prove their control of their bodies. This has been beautifully studied in northern India and I think one of the most thorough studies was done by Younger in 1972, in which they taped to the soles of the feet of the yogis that were going to perform this act, small recording thermometers. They're just very small things but have little markers in them to show where the temperature went up or down and it stays there. Without exception, after these gentlemen walked across hot embers left from burning wood (or hot rocks, like they sometimes use in Hawaii), the little thermometers on the bottoms of their feet consistently showed four degrees cooler than they did before the people stepped out upon the coals. A yoga teacher would scold his students, "You were overdoing it, and you overshot the mark by four degrees." Would that we could all do that!

A beautiful example of how the mind can control things was done at the same series of experiments. When Younger's wife asked if she could walk across the bed of coals, the priest said, "Yes, if you will hold my hand." She was wearing a long dress typical of the British at that time, and as she walked up to the edge of the pit, she reached behind her to gather up the end of her dress so that it would not drag over the coals. The priest said, "Why are you doing that?" and she said, "I don't want my dress to catch fire." He said, "It won't." So she let go of the dress, took his hand, and walked slowly across twenty feet of coals with no sign of scorching or burning to any degree.

So here was the mind of this yogastic priest in complete control of the vibrations of energy at the level of that fire. No heat went beyond his mental barrier. If you get a chance to see Younger's experiment, it was photographed, though of course the film was rather poor because of the time it was done. I've seen it a couple of times on television, I think it was on "You Asked for It." If you get a chance to see it, it's worth staying up for. You'll probably have to see it on the late thing. But if you notice it in your TV guide, watch it; it is beautifully documented by the British Institute of Psychical Research. But what does it gain for the person? Certainly it would be startling to everyone in this room if we could fill the aisle here with red hot coals and run back and forth from the door back up to here, and it would show great mental control. And the immediate question comes up, "So what? You've shown you have the ability to control temperature." Is this going to change your life? Is it going to allow you to have one day happier than the day before? Probably not.

So let's go on a little further, to Western concepts of meditation. And here is where I, as a medium, clash with most of the spiritual organizations. All of you now know what I mean when I use the word God. So if I were to say that the Western concept of meditation was to be one with God, you would remember back to the talk we had in those two lessons in which we discussed God, and you would notice that we are now in communication with the Ultimate All, the Universal All, the I AM, to use several of the other organizations' phrases. But most people, when they think they are at one with God, or in tune with God, they still visualize him as an elderly gentleman on a white throne, and that they have now opened their mind to the point where they are saying, "Hey, Sir, do you have anything to tell me?" It's a lovely concept, but it is not true.

And the next comment is, 'It's a passing fad.' Why? We have a number of people in the room who have studied various kinds of meditation for some time and I'm sure they could tell you about class work they started, trying to meditate this way or that way, following it very strenuously for a while, and then the newness wears off and they stop. And I think a great deal of it has to be attributed to our news media. We have many so-called wise men teaching meditation and it is literally a fad because it is not carried to the next step.

Here it is again, if you can sit in a corner in total silence for two hours, great. But what does it accomplish? Does it help you? Unfortunately, the answer is no.

There is a very specialized kind of meditation called transcendental meditation that I am sure all of you are aware of, at least you've heard of it. This is one of the most unusual forms of meditation in that it is a technique for the body to rebuild vital energy. Now this sounds strange, but let us look upon this exactly in the same light as perfect sleep. Your nervous system requires a certain amount of rest to rebuild and prepare itself for the next period of activity. Transcendental meditation can do this in a matter of minutes, where it might take four to eight hours to do it by very restful sleep. For those of you who would be interested in this kind of study, it is available, certainly in our area, I believe now almost nationwide. You can explore it. There are some books written on the subject, but not a great deal. The problem is that you cannot put into words an experience. The Zen Buddhist masters are constantly screaming at people who write books on Zen, *If you are talking about it, you are standing outside the gate.* So this is the problem—how can you describe something that cannot be verbalized?

However, these different forms of meditation all fall short of what we are trying to do. And then the next meditation item, 'Spiritual Concept,' for lack of a better term. 'Stilling the mind.' Opening your receptivity to what? To a universal pool of knowledge or to friends and loved ones who have supposedly disappeared. I have to put the universal pool in here because all of you know of the gentleman Edgar Cayce. As you know, he did not consider himself a spiritualist, in that he did not talk to spirits. Hugh Lynn Cayce, who is now handling the publications, has changed some of that, but if you read the two original books that Cayce approved of before his passing, you will see that some of the later books are not quite along his line of thinking. But he believed he was dipping into a universal pool of knowledge, one in which was found absolutely everything that was ever possible, past, present and future. This is the same universal pool that Dr. Jung talks about in some of the Jungian philosophies. An interesting gentleman. A spiritualist, incidentally, but he didn't admit it until after he was 65 years old because he decided he would wait until he was old enough so that nobody could do anything about it. A brilliant man, nevertheless.

'Friends and loved ones,' you are all aware of this, you know our concepts of reincarnation, our concepts of being on the spirit side. The only thing that is keeping you from being aware of them is your mind and that little part of your mind we are working on. We are trying to teach you to still your mind.

'The Master Way,' D. This is what makes the difference. If you learn to still your mind and sit there and look at pictures all day, great. This is a wonderful light show, but it doesn't help you, just as being at one with God didn't help you. Just as being in absolute control of your mind and body didn't help you.

But you must turn off yourself, that little nagging you that's upstairs, stirring things up so frantically, so that you can have a better life. And you will simply have it as a consequence of knowing what is right and wrong, of being guided by those loved ones, teachers, or guides who will be around you. Here, for the first time, you can use your mind to live your own life, to help you be happier, to help you live a more full or content life. It is an incredible thing, and as you set about doing this, the first few times it will come as a surprise. You will be bothered by some problem, let's say, and so you relax and get quiet and suddenly you have the answer to that problem. And you will undoubtedly spend the next ten minutes trying to think of some other reason why that funny solution came up in your mind. But after everything else is thrown out, you will decide, 'Okay, someone told me.' And that someone is important for you to get to know. The better you know them, the better, the fuller, and the happier your life will be right now. Because we don't have to look toward tomorrow, I don't have to plan for some great day in the future when we are going to achieve Nirvana or reach heaven. We can experience a tremendous difference right here, right now.

E, 'Delusion.' This is something I have harped on now several times but I MUST get this across to you and it cannot be gotten across to you too strongly. 'Reading between the lines' and 'Your downfall.' As you open yourself to the psychic realm, you must learn not to try to anticipate what an entity is going to present to you. The other evening, a gentleman here mentioned that when he was working in his silence, a cross or crucifix appeared in front of him and I told him to thank them and negate it, to push it away. The reason I was being what might seem harsh is because I want him to reach the point that when an object comes in, I want him to be able to tell the difference—did he project it there, or did someone else put it there? I know that sounds simple but it is so very, VERY important.

One of the tests you can do in your meditations—you will remember now that you've got your little dot, you've turned it into a flower, and you take it back to a dot. Next time you go into your meditation, not here as we are going to do in a little while, but at home this evening and in the morning, let's take another big step. After you change your flower back into a spot, don't jump from a flower to blankness, change it back into a spot. I know this might sound hum-drum and routine, but it is a sure pathway. So in your five minutes you will get still, make your little spot, turn the spot into a flower, change the flower back into a spot, and then make the spot go out. Make the spot get smaller and smaller and smaller until it is gone, or make it simply recede from you, or simply turn it off like you would a light bulb. And then immediately, when the dot is gone, and don't kid yourself, when the spot is gone, ask aloud for an entity to show you something and leave it up to them. The moment you perceive something, be it the face of a loved one, an object, or a light, say aloud, "Thank you," and stop your communication right there.

That's going to be the hardest thing you've ever done in this course. The first time I was told to do that, I looked at Rev. Bradley as if she had gone right straight out of her skull. I thought, 'Are you kidding? Once I've got something from the other side you want me to throw it away?' However, the old girl was right. You must not be caught in the game of watching pictures go by, because suddenly your mind will start putting pictures in there, along with other information. And at this stage you might not be able to tell the difference. And that is delusion. And that's a problem. It is like the old philosophy, 'If you tell a lie long enough and loud enough, everybody will believe it.' Your mind is much easier to convince than that. If you sit here watching pictures go by and the part of you that is open psychically says, "Hey, Gene, that dog that went by came out of your mind," and Gene says, "Oh, shut up, I like to look at the dog," very quickly you will have lost the ability to tell the difference between Gene putting the dog in there and Tau Sing putting the dog in there. And once you have reached that point of delusion, it is extremely difficult to backtrack. It is like learning a bad habit. So any of you who might have taken piano, you know there is a right way to finger the keys and you are taught the right way, and a little ways down the line there are some chords and chord changes coming up that you cannot play if you have not learned the right way to finger those keys. And that's exactly what we are talking about.

If you start now with bad habits, you're in trouble. If you have any doubt as to whether or not the object you see was given to you by Spirit, make a note of it in your book and forget about it. As you go along you'll find out which is which. Some people will learn this very quickly. Believe me, there is a difference. I cannot describe to you the subtle difference of your mind saying "Hello, there, Eugene" and an entity saying "Hello, there, Eugene." There's a difference, a subtle difference, but it's a very REAL one. And once you identify it, then you're home free, but please take it slow and easy, because the fast way leads to a solid brick wall that you will not be able to climb over. So remember this for your little meditation period because this is the biggest pitfall in opening your psychic ability. For instance, we have talked about the use of the mind to move things. We were talking about the little pinwheel that you rotate by the power of the mind, so on and so forth. You will practice with this if you like, and play with it, and suddenly one day you will notice when it does what you command it to do; you've felt yourself touching it mentally. It is a subtle thing, but you will know the difference. And that's what we are after, knowing that subtle difference.

Spirit Evolution

Guideline: I AM STILL AND KNOW!

I. Spirit Evolution
   A. On the Spirit Side
   B. Breakthrough
   C. Communication
      1. Mental
         a. Clairvoyance
         b. Clairaudience
      2 Physical
         a. Knocks and raps
         b. Trumpet, etc.
         c. Etherealization
         d. Materialization
   D. What They May Like
      1. Mental
         a. Intellectual equals
         b. Their way of thinking
      2. Physical
         a. Incense
         b. Music
         c. Flowers
         d. Water

**********WORK FOR THE WEEK**********

Concentration and Meditation:

Ten minutes each morning and evening. First three to four minutes be still. Produce your spot. Hold it about one minute, then reduce it to nothing. Ask aloud for your guide to show you something for your highest and best good. Study the object, describing it aloud in detail. At the end of your ten minutes, thank Spirit for their help and close.

'Spirit Evolution' is rough in some ways but possibly helpful in many other ways. The middle section will be rather easy going and the last part of it full of all kinds of interesting questions. So let's dive into it and see what happens.

'Spirit Evolution.' We've discussed evolution on a broad scale before, physical evolution of animals and spiritual evolution of developing spirit. Now we are going to talk about spiritual evolution or spirit evolution on the spirit side. In other words, not while you are here.

As you know, one of the most important things you do here on the Earth plane is develop your awareness. This is one of the most important things you do on the other plane as well. I love the comment that Mark Twain made about it when he was discussing heaven and hell. He said, "I understand that when you go to heaven you will study and progress, study and progress, and study and progress, and if that isn't hell, I don't know what would be." Well, there's a little difference, because the kind of progression that you can do on the spirit level must be beyond carnate understanding. In other words, it must be even beyond the wildest concept that you and the people here and now can imagine.

We often wonder if it is not like some great school where we go from grade to grade to grade. Not quite like that. We have tried to decide what is your goal, who tells you which direction to go, and we have simply been told that your direction will be shown to you. How you get there, how fast you get there is up to you, but you will know where you are going. One of the biggest things that pops up, for instance, is if you are giving readings to people and they ask, "What happens to a child who goes into Spirit?" Is that child always going to be a small child? Well, I'm sure from the material we have already covered you know certainly that is not true. A small child is not always going to be a child. It is going to grow up. What do we mean when we say that the child is going to grow up? Here we are very, very strongly trapped by our own physical world. In other words, we can see a small baby getting bigger and bigger as it literally grows.

But that is of absolutely no consequence. Maturing of the mind is growing up. This is the main line of spirit evolution.

This is why we see many, many times people with grown-up physical bodies that are children. As you look at a baby as it grows up and gets physically bigger, what do you use as marks for its rate of maturing? You can see it learn to stand up and walk after many spills. Finally it begins to learn to make sounds and finally it begins to talk and with the act of talking comes a rapid maturing of the mind. Why is this?

For instance, if you take a baby chimpanzee home, take it away from its mother so it does not know its chimp mother, and start raising it up at home by giving it all the loving care you would give to your non-furry baby, it will be ahead of the human baby in development. At some point the human baby begins to talk and then suddenly, if you compare the two, the little chimpanzee is left standing alone while the human baby goes racing ahead and becomes man. Why? What is so significant about the ability to talk? Well, we'll find that this is not significant at all because a spiritual entity cannot talk in the sense that I am now talking. They can do it with various devices, with trumpets and things of this nature. So if it isn't actually the process of talking, what is it?

It's the converting of thought images into formal form that can be translated from one person to another. Now that's a big mouthful. It simply means that I develop the ability to convey to you something that I see, sense or detect in some way. The technique we use here is horribly inadequate when you compare it with the activities on the spirit side. I know this may sound strange to you now but when you first have an entity step into your vibration and give you an emotion, let us say happiness or elation, it is finer, more beautiful, more perfect, more pure than you have ever experienced up to that time because they are not relying upon image pictures, they can actually touch you emotionally. This is something you will spot many, many times. I'm sure many of you in this room have spotted this same thing. You will pick up an object for psychometry, or you will pick up a billet for a reading and suddenly you are overwhelmed, you are happy, and your eyes fill with tears. They are communicating on a pure level and in this communication is the key to what they are learning to do. We will get into details of what they are learning to do in just a moment.

Remember now, when we talked about a spirit child growing up, we are talking about its maturing mind, not its physical body. It no longer has a physical body, just as you and I will not have one when we go into Spirit, but this does not stop us. We go on and sometimes at much faster rates because we are not hampered by a physical body. Imagine, here I am now, I've stood up here and talked to you for some eight to ten minutes and I could have given this to you emotionally and by direct mental contact without ever uttering a word in probably a thousandth of that time. Yet we are slaves to the spoken language because we are Homo sapiens and because we have not all developed thought transference, which, of course, many, many primitive men and many of our animal friends of today have. But man has gone him one better. He has learned to speak. How sad.

Then man invented a thousand different languages to speak in. So when we bump into, let us say, psychometry, and you receive an image of a baby walking around and you say, "I have here a baby," and the person says, "Oh, yes, this was so and so, but my, he died thirty years ago. Is he still only that big?" Well, you can see the concern about the person for whom you are reading, but stop and think for a minute. If the individual had come in looking like he did after thirty years of growth, would mother have recognized him? Of course not, but mother recognized him as a baby still walking around. This brings about one of the biggest problems that we are discussing here tonight. When an entity appears to you, two things are involved. One, how good he is at doing it and two, how good you are at receiving it.

Now the reason I say, "How good he is at doing it," is twofold: can the entity marshal the proper set of thought and energy to impress me the way he wants me to see him, or is he going to do it by some other clever means? Probably the most difficult form that he can use is, of course, direct materialization. We will get into that in a few moments. So don't expect your first spirit entities to do this. He would probably scare you anyway, because we are not used to having people suddenly pop in and be there. You will get used to it, believe me, you will. That is one of the things he has learned to do.

Sometimes entities have not learned how to communicate on an abstract level. These are the ones that are easier for them to do: 'knock knock' or 'rap rap,' or you hear their footsteps or some other little thing that they can do.

Now, every highly-developed entity can knock and make the sound of footsteps. So do not classify them as underdeveloped entities because they like to knock on things, but it is easier for an entity to do this. To get to the point where they can project so that you can see them requires a fair amount of practice and diligent work on their part. To get to the point where they can speak to you clairaudiently requires a little more. You suddenly get to the point that you can see the funny kind of balance system. You only go about a quarter of the way to their vibration and they come down about three quarters of the way to you, so honor them with their efforts to communicate. You are looking through a keyhole into the other world; they are patiently coming downstairs to you. So honor them, please.

How long does an entity stay on the entity side before he reincarnates? Unfortunately the answer is, "As long as he wants." We, with our regimented form of living, would like to think, 'Well, you're allowed four score and ten here, four score and ten there,' and so on down the line. Keep it all neat and orderly, but that's not the way it is. If you are doing something on the spirit side that you feel is of help to you, you will do it until you consider it finished.

Spirits can have a lot of fun. Rev. Bradley, about whom you have heard me mention many times, was my teacher before she passed over and is certainly the same loud, boisterous, overemotional person I knew on the Earth plane. She has found a number of off-colored jokes that I have not heard before and loves to bring these in when she is speaking in trance through me, or if I am in trance allowing her to speak. This can be embarrassing. She is just the same as she was the last time I knew her and loved her dearly. She's been gone now about two years, but lately she's been making little hints that it's getting time for her to go on and do something else. So one of these times she's going to pop into our circle and say, "Okay, Gene, I've got to go and be about my own business," and she's going to be gone, to do what she knows is right for her.

Tau Sing, the one you've heard me talk about so many times, and I have kind of a thing going. When I am on this side, he is on that side. When he is on this side, I am on that side. We have been doing this for thousands of years. I don't know if this makes progress any faster, it makes you feel much closer to your teacher because I've known him and he's known me for some time. The actual steps of what they learn, the actual lessons they are learning, cannot really be understood by us because they do not fit into any category that we conveniently think in.

One time I asked one of the teachers, Rod, "What do you do to have fun?" He said, "What do you mean by fun?" and I said, "Well, other than going hiking." Good heavens, they can project just about any place, they can see any kind of a view they would want to see. "But what else do you do?" I asked. "Well, we play hide and seek." I thought, well, that's about the most mundane thing I've ever heard in my life. He caught that thought and said, "Not if you can hide anyplace in the solar system." That put a little bit of dimension to it. So here we have a game of hide and seek going on, where one time I will hide on Titan, the large moon of Saturn, and if they find me there I'll suddenly slip around and hide on the dark side of Mercury, slipping across billions of miles of space as fast as my mind can think of moving. I'd like to learn to play that kind of hide and seek.

Okay,"B." 'Breakthrough.' Hideous word . . . I don't like it, but everything now is a "breakthrough."

This breakthrough I'm talking about could easily be equated to, 'When did Spiritualism become a going thing?' When did people know they were communicating with spirits? Well, of course, Spiritualism in America started in the east, since the little girls heard the raps and knocks and the entity answered them and gave them factual material, but I'm certain that it goes much further back than that. No one could tell me that when Christ was talking to any of his guides, teachers, any of this type of person, that he was not doing exactly what we are talking about now.

But why are teachers or guides helping you? Probably for one of the rarest of reasons on the face of the Earth. They are helping you because they want to. That's a rare commodity these days. I've heard many, many lectures having to do with the little gold stars or the additional check after their work that they get for helping you on the Earth plane. Yet when I have pinned any of them down and asked, "What good is this to you, to talk to me?" They will answer with two quick things. One, their ability to communicate with me helps their awareness. Two, they love to help. Isn't that appalling? They are not getting paid ten dollars an hour. They are doing it because they love to do it, which, if nothing else, gives you a wonderful feeling about these unseen people that are around us. The things that you do here and now will speed up your rate of spirit evolution on this Earth side. If you learn the significance of some of your emotions and learn to control them, you won't have to master them somewhere else. If you develop so that your mind is in complete control, you've gained a number of steps. So how long is it going to take you to reach perfection? I had to check that answer out. Okay, just as quickly as you want to, and he pops back with a beautiful quotation, "There are none so blind as those who would not see."

Okay, 'Communication.' Most things in a spiritual realm or psychic realm break down into two major categories, mental and physical. Remember we are talking about from the spirit side, not you talking to Spirit.

'Clairvoyance,' 'clairaudience,' I am sure you are all very much aware of. 'Clairvoyance'—in this case we are talking simply of psychic seeing, clear seeing, not necessarily seeing a future event. They may show you a present event as well, but it is sensed with the psychic eye. 'Clairaudience' is them learning to impress upon you, as if you were hearing. So this is psychic hearing. I can probably show you here by using an analogy, something that I would like you to think about. I will pick up this microphone. Let's assume this is your left ear and this box here is your brain. Someone out there makes a sound, let us say someone drops a rock. The waves of compressed air hit this, then through a series of nerves turn it into electrical energy and it goes to your brain and in here you say you heard a rock drop. Now how can a spirit do that without dropping a rock? He can simply reach in here and give you the electrical signal and your brain thinks you heard a rock fall.

If someone says hello out there, the waves hit here and the nerves turn them into electrical energy and it goes to the brain and the brain says, "Wow. Somebody said 'Hello.'" Our entity reaches in here and releases the same little series of charges and the brain says, "Hey, somebody said 'Hello...'" That's what it's all about. Now don't you see how that takes some training on their part? Because if they touch that nerve wrong it might say, "Get out of here," or "Shoo." So not only do they have to be able to do it, but they have to know what impulses mean what to your brain and that takes a little training. This is why, to help them, I have been telling you to talk out loud to them, because conversely, if you were thinking abstract forms, they must look at all those little electrical signals and decide what you are thinking about. If you are not thinking clearly, they might see a beautiful pattern, something like the 4th of July with all the firecrackers going off, but they won't know what you are thinking. So for now when you are working with them, please say it out loud, verbalize it, so you force your brain to work.

The physical things, again, are those that you are very familiar with except the last two items. Knocks and raps I think all of you have heard by now. Trumpets we will be getting into in dark circles. A trumpet is nothing more than a conical piece of aluminum, shaped like a long trumpet that an entity can build a sound box inside, a voice box if you would, and by shaking the voice box can make his voice be heard outside the trumpet, just like the old-fashioned phonograph.

Remember the old-fashioned phonograph with the big horn on it? If you shook the needle, static came out the other end. Well, they shake the needle with a little better control. As I say, this is just one of the devices that are used; there are a lot of others.

Okay. 'Etherealization' and 'Materialization,' here are two things that get mixed up so often and yet they are quite simple.

Just look at the first parts of those two words, 'ether' and 'matter.' As all of you who have studied physics know, there is no ether in space. So that's what "c," etherealization means, something that is not there and yet visible. So here is an image made and projected by an entity, made of light and energy that you can see with your physical eye, but you cannot touch it. You could pass your hand through it and it would have no substance. Materialization is obviously the next step. It is solid, it is matter, and it is real. In this we find aports and a number of other things. Those last two items are two of the most difficult things for an entity to do, and generally, these two items require an established circle working in harmony so that you have a good field of energy in which the spirit can work. We do not know all of the geometry and all of the detailed physical relationships between the energy we have in our own self and the energy they can use, but a very high entity can do it.

D, 'What they may like.' This one is the most difficult, because it steps on a lot of people's toes. If we step on your toes in the next few little words here, I'm sorry. If you are setting up for communication, an entity is watching your little light go on, and the first thing you are going to notice is that they will seek out intellectual equals. Now that sounds awful, but it is true. If you are going to sit in your meditation or in a small circle and giggle and cut up and have a good time all the way through, you're going to attract no one but that same type.

If, however, you get serious and open your mind and seek understanding, then you will attract those who will work with you at that level of thinking.

For instance, as I'm sure all of you are quite aware, I was a Buddhist. So, naturally, if I sit around the house, especially if I have a stick of incense going, I am surrounded by Buddhist entities, dozens and dozens. Just mentioning it, I am surrounded now, because I would think the way they want to think. Just because they are in Spirit doesn't mean that they have suddenly reached ultimate knowing. They still have their own likes and dislikes, just as they had here, just as you and I have here. So they will welcome their own way of thinking. So in meditation, for instance, in the front room where I have a Buddha, and if I have incense going, I would be surrounded with Buddhist priests and yellow-robed monk figures.

I would be very surprised to have a Southern Baptist entity walk in and say "Hello," and I think the reason is obvious. I can tell you about one which shocked the dickens out of me. Don and I were having a circle at the house. We had been speaking to several Buddhist priests and one of them wanted the circle to be closed with the prayer "Om Mani Padme Hum" repeated three times. We did so and just before we broke up the circle, Sir, a very Christian gentleman, appeared beside me in full regalia of the high church and he said, "What are you heathens doing?" Well, I almost fainted right there on the floor because I think a great deal of Sir. Then he laughed like mad and unbuttoned the top of his white and gold cloak and held it open and he was wearing a saffron-yellow robe of the Buddhist priest underneath. So watch this. Sometimes in some circles you will get deeply religious people and no one else.

Sometimes in circles you will get people who are just having a lot of fun and I use that both in the intoxicated sense as well as any other way. Because they are people, I want you to remember that. Even though it is easy for us to put them up on pedestals, remember they are people.

The physical things they like; if, in your meditation, an entity who would be your guide comes in and asks you to do something for him, as long as it isn't outlandish, please do it. If he tells you to take all your clothes off and walk out in the middle of the street, find a higher teacher and ask him why, simply because at this point in time, it would be against the law. However, he might ask you to light a candle, ask you for incense, or he might impress upon your mind a certain kind of music, or request that there be flowers in the room. One thing that is often requested is a small bowl of water in the center of the circle. Now all these things, of course, are simple crutches. There is nothing magical about them. All the decorations in this building here, all those candles, and all flower arrangements are sort of predetermined because they are going to have a wedding here, and that's exactly the case with spiritual entities.

A spiritual entity will like a certain thing. For instance, as I say, at home when we have a circle and we want to have a lot of Buddhist priests around, we light a stick of incense. The fastest way to bring in the Catholic set, let me call it, of the high teachers, is to play the Gregorian chants before the circle. This attracts them like mad. I happen to like Gregorian chants so that's great. If you don't like Gregorian chants I feel sorry for you, but if the entity requests it and you can fulfill it, do so. The incense is a very strange thing. It comes, of course, in all scents, and even though they don't have physical noses, they sure know the difference. Because I have one little priest who likes one brand of incense that smells like lotus flowers. For a long time I couldn't get that brand and I got bawled out every darn time I asked for his presence. Now I have found a place to get it and he is locked into that.

That might be a crutch and it might be an awful problem for him, but it is his problem, and if you want him to be around you, then use that particular kind of incense. Music in your meditation is too distracting. As you go along and start having individual circles, try different kinds of music and see what feeling this brings to the group, what entities it brings into the circle. This can run the gamut. At many circles they will sing many very religious songs from the old-fashioned hymnbooks. During one of the most beautiful circles we had up at Denver, with about fourteen people in the circle, a gentleman came in and asked for a song. You can imagine fourteen people, none of them singers, trying to sing a song and nobody knew the words. So we were sitting there trying to figure out what to do when someone suggested singing "Silent Night." We all knew that one and we sang it and the whole set of us were all of the same vibration. That was one of the most beautiful circles we ever had. The ceiling went away, the walls went away. We had materializations, trumpets that were just fabulous. So if they ask it, do it.

The water thing is a fun thing. Water, as you know, picks up odors, like if you have a bowl of water sitting in the ice box and you open an onion and set it in the ice box, the next morning that water is going to smell like that onion. Well, I had an impulse to set out a bowl of water because they can impress things into it. I have an entity that likes to put his cologne in the water, and it's beautiful. So watch for these. Know that you are treating them just as you would your friends. If you were going to have your friends over tonight for dinner, and they hated sauerkraut, you would not serve sauerkraut. If you are planning to have your spiritual friends come in, do what they like and you will be greatly rewarded.

Healing

Guideline: PERFECT HARMONY IS LOVE

I. Healing
   A. Mental Healing
      1. Visualization
      2. Absent
      3. Prayer
   B. Physical Healing
      1. Vibratory concept
      2. Passes with the hands
      3. Field transfer
   C. Limitation
      1. Mental attitude
      2. Preset
         a. From the spirit side
         b. NO KARMIC DEBT
   D. Protection of the Healer
      1. Mental clearing
      2. Physical clearing
         a. Washing hands
         b. Snapping fingers

**********WORK FOR THE WEEK**********

Concentration and Meditation:

Ten minutes each morning and evening. First three to four minutes be still. Produce your spot. Hold it about one minute, then reduce it to nothing. Ask aloud for your guide to show you something for your highest and best good. Observe the object until you are sure of it in detail. Try to change it in some way. IF YOU CAN CHANGE IT, IT IS YOUR OWN MIND AT WORK. Spirit will not allow its projection to be changed. At the end of your ten minutes, thank Spirit for their help and close.

'Healing.' Let's dive into a rather interesting subject and one we've been discussing for nine weeks, even though you might not realize it at this point. Healing is one of the most important phases of psychic or spiritual development. This is because it is needed more on the face of the Earth right now for individual people than probably any of the other psychic gifts because, just as you've all noticed in your meditations, if you are not feeling well, you cannot meditate easily. So it must follow that we must take care of what is bothering you first. We've been talking about this directly and indirectly for the last eight lectures because we've been talking about harmony, we've been talking about perfection, we've been talking about evolution and how you live, and all those things that go together to make the complete, perfect picture.

Our guideline for this week is perfectly obvious: 'Perfect Harmony is Love.' Love is one of those magnificent little four-letter words and probably one of the most misunderstood in the English language. We have to look at love on a broader scale. It is much easier to talk in terms of harmony than it is to talk in terms of love, because if I say love, some of you think one thing, some of you think another. If I talk in terms of harmony then you are all thinking the same thing. So let's go through healing and see what we've got here.

Healing breaks down into about twenty categories, as far as types of healing are concerned, but we don't want to make it that complex. For those of you who will go on into advanced studies and specialize in healing, there is a lot of detailed information from teachers that will be made available to you. There are many different techniques and we are, in this case, simply breaking them down into the two forms of mental healing and physical healing simply for convenience. There are many excellent healing books on the market so please do not think because I'm handling only two here that I'm throwing out all the other forms. I am not at all. Many authors break it down into too fine a series of divisions because it is so easy to make something complex, but it does not have to be that way.

How do you heal? By my previous lectures you should all know that you heal by bringing about harmony. How do you do that? First of all, by getting yourself in harmony with yourself and the universe. I'm sure those of you who have had any musical training know that if you pluck one string of a violin, the string immediately adjacent to it will also sing. It is singing by vibrations being transmitted both through the instrument and through the air to that string. The intriguing thing about it is that the string now singing is of a different tone than the string you touched first.

So it is with you and healing. Each one of you consists of a whole bundle of vibrations. Visualize yourself as just one vibration. If I were to stretch out a rope in front of me and snap the rope, you would see a sine wave going back and forth from one end of the rope to the other. For the present, just consider yourself one of those, a little wiggly line that repeats itself, each wave never deviating from the pattern. If you reach out and grab the rope and hang onto it tightly, the smallest portion of it will stop vibrating and the other portion will continue to vibrate. So if someone is ill, we say their vibration is not in harmony with their etheric self.

As you will recall, back when we were talking about the etheric self, we stressed that *thoughts are things*. Thoughts change the etheric mold and this can be devastating to health. If we had the time and you wanted to try an experiment, you could take your thumbnail, start looking at the center of it, tell yourself how sore it is, how bad it hurts, that it feels just like it got smashed in a door, and if you go along with that for a little while, you'll have one sore thumb. The only thing is, you must learn to turn it off, because you're telling your thumb that it's sore, and the nerves from your thumb tell your brain, "Yes, I am sore," then your brain says, "Good heavens, yes, you are sore," and on and on until soon you're running around with a black and blue thumbnail. And trying desperately to blame it on someone other than yourself.

This is the biggest problem of healing. This is why Christ said, "Physician, heal thyself." So isn't it odd, the one thing we have the greatest difficulty doing is changing our own habits. How easy it is for us to suggest that someone else change their habits, but we leave ours intact. So what can we do about it?

Much of the healing activity that goes on today that you generally read about is very, very poor. It deals with symptoms, not causes. Many so-called healers are charlatans of the first order. We have a few true healers among us, thank heavens. We don't today have a Jesus Christ walking among us, at least that we know of, from the standpoint of healing, but I'm sure that all of you have seen some of the beautiful representations of psychic works, Kathryn Kuhlman and some of the others, each with their own particular dogmatic concept of how it works or why it works, but it's all the same thing. Oral Roberts directs his prayer to Jesus Christ. Kathryn Kuhlman sends hers directly to God. I would direct mine to a spirit doctor or simply to Infinite Spirit. They are all names for the same thing. We're talking here about a power, a force that is so great that it can correct anything. Notice I said "can" correct anything, not "will." It *can*.

Okay, we've decided that we are going to be a healer. Well, first of all, let's look at the criteria you can use to decide whether or not you're going to be a healer. I won't get into all of it; there are some very peculiar aspects. One, you probably love animals. Two, you probably get easily upset with other people's emotional problems. When you visit a person in a hospital, you feel almost as sick as they are; these are characteristics that we see in healers. And the problem is, like with most activities, people will not take the time to be what they say they want to be. Now, as I've said before, and you've heard me harp on it, "Thoughts are things," "So you think, so you are, so you think you will be, so you will be." If you think you are never going to be a healer, I suggest you try something else, because you will not if you carry that thought.

Let's assume now that you *are* going to be a healer. What can you do to start? Unfortunately, that first step is the one thing that most people will not do: *master your meditation to the point of visualization of what you are doing.* This is the most difficult thing to do. For instance, right now you've all got close friends, husbands or wives, or someone you know who is not here right now. Close your eyes for about ten or fifteen seconds and visualize their face right in front of you as if you were looking at a colored picture of them.

Okay. Did you get it complete? Could you get exactly what they looked like? This is important. For instance, if you come upon someone who is in need of healing, let us say they have a gash on their arm; they are lying there conscious or unconscious, their blood running out. The first thing your mind does is go to the negative and say, "Oh, look, how horrible!" The first thing you've got to do as a healer is to forget what you saw. You've got to *see the person as whole*, as if there's nothing wrong at all. Now that's why I say that healing is contrary to what many other spiritualists and psychic teachers will tell you, because many call healing the easiest art. I put it almost on top of the list as the most difficult to really control. How difficult it is to look at an injury and not see it! The moment you see it you are imaging the injury, the very thing you do not want to do. The very thing you cannot do, if you are going to heal.

So visualization is something you've got to practice every single time the thought even crosses your mind. In your daily activities, practice it. Close your eyes for a second. A lot of times I'll close my eyes and visualize my friend Don standing there, and later in the day we'll be talking and he'll say, "Were you thinking about me about 2:30?" Yes. Visualization is the way to lock all these things together.

Now you've got to go more abstract. Here sits someone beside you who needs a healing. Right now, do not be concerned with what is wrong. After you have developed a very fine degree of healing, you can then correct a particular problem, but that is of the highest order of healing. Right now, work for the person's highest and best good. Wrap them in a white light of harmony. Keep yourself in a perfect attitude so your vibrations can strengthen theirs. It is just like matching cog wheels. If you bring them together quickly they might not match, but if you do it slowly, you can make last-minute corrections so they will fit together. This is the same thing you will do with healing. You will feel your way along.

Don, most of you know, is a healer and has been for a long time. One of the things he was told to practice was to sit in silence with his hands about twelve inches apart and see the force flow between them; this force will flow counter-clockwise.

Many times in dark circles I have seen Don sitting there like this and it would look like he was holding a pale bluish-gray cube between his hands. He said that as he works with this, he is able to push and feel the energy, as if there is something there.

These are some of the things that you can do to build up your confidence. This is what is so delicate about this kind of thing. *You must KNOW it will work!* You can't hope it's going to work. You can't assume that everybody is going to help you do it. You must do it yourself.

An easy way to get around this, of course, is absent healing or healing by prayer. Thank heavens for these other two forms. If everything had to be visualized, we could probably count the healers of the last many centuries on one hand, because that method is difficult. For example, if you want to replace the human heart, you have to visualize it cell by cell, little vein by little vein, capillary by capillary, and put it together the right way. You can't do this. Few people know that much about the human body, but you can do it by sending into the etheric double a vibration that will replace any vibration that is not in harmony. And you do this in absent work or a prayer by simply willing your vibration to the other person. It is just as simple as that, but there is no way to really describe it.

We're going to practice healing by visualizing the person seated in the chair and the healer standing above them both wrapped in a cone of white light. Just wrap them up in the most beautiful cone of white light that you can project. White light is used, incidentally, because it is a product of all colors and is, therefore, in total harmony.

Absent healing by prayer is an extremely powerful force. Much can be done by setting up prayer circles. I'm sure all of you have read the work on prayer circles, how one group prayed over and cursed one row of bean plants and prayed over and loved another row of bean plants, and the leaves on the little row of beans that were cursed withered up and died, while those that were loved flourished. The same thing happens to you and me, as people. We are susceptible to all these things.

Physical healing is one of the most spectacular methods to watch, but you rarely see it. The vibratory concept is simply that if I am feeling good, any of you can look at me and say, "Hey, Gene's feeling good tonight." How do you know? You can feel the edges of my etheric system sending out vibrations that are in harmony with me. How many times have some of you who are going to be healers walked into a hospital room and saw someone lying on a bed, maybe with their eyes closed, and before you even got close to them, they smiled because they sensed the presence of a harmonious vibration? It's a beautiful thing and when you see it in action, you will never forget it.

If there is anything in the practice of healing that looks very mysterious and peculiar, it is passes with the hands. And yet it is extremely important. To see a healer come up to someone and hold his or her hands out and pass them over the body without touching the person, the audience will say, "Oh, ho!" But it's not fake, believe me, the healer is doing something. He is literally using the edges of his aura, the etheric one, to smooth out and comb the disharmony in the patient's auric system. And now that he's got this energy all gathered up, what's he going to do with it? Well, he can let it soak in and take on the problem himself, if he wants to (if he's stupid) or he can get rid of it.

There are many ways to get rid of it—healers will often simply shake their hands or snap their fingers. It's just like scraping moisture off your windshield early in the morning to make it clear. Exactly the same thing. If something in the etheric shell is not clear, I wipe the droplets away and get rid of them.

Passes of the hands is one of the most powerful methods because it is easily felt. When the healer is working, I think almost everybody will notice heat from their hands or a tingling sensation. These sensations occur because of flowing fields of energy, and hence, this last subject, 'field transfer.' You must be careful because this one can be done unconsciously, so you do not want to set yourself up to take on the illness of someone else simply by being around them. It is easy to do. "Those who live among the lame will also learn to limp." This is very true. How often have you been around someone who is sick or at least is complaining all the time, and pretty soon you are feeling the same low way? Don't any of you get caught in that trap. By now you know enough about meditation, or know enough about turning things off and on, not to put up with it. This is one of these transfer effects like if the string is plucked, the other string will sing and you're simply in harmony with it.

All of the books you read on psychic or spiritual healing will deal heavily with the psychic centers, or *chakras,* located in the etheric body. These are sources, or focal points, where energy can flow in and out of the system. It is wrong to visualize them as spots in the nervous system itself, even though the names are used to describe where they would be, because they exist in another form of space, not in the three-dimensional now. They exist in the etheric shell, or the etheric mold, and you will learn the seven major centers as you go along and develop more of your healing.

The limitations of healing are only two and the second one is catastrophic. The first one is 'mental attitude.' Here again, we are getting back to 'thoughts are things.' If you can give yourself and your vibrations wholeheartedly to a healer, knowing that their influence is going to bring about harmony within, it will do so. If you sit in the presence of the healer thinking, "Well, I'll bet this is not going to do any good," you can bet your life it is *not* going to do any good. If you look at it this way, "You are responsible for your actions," then an illness or something bothering you must be something you brought upon yourself. Isn't it one of the prime laws that we are not allowed to interfere with anybody else? Then would it not follow that maybe I should not heal you because I'm interfering with something that you brought about, because of your own fault, or something you needed to learn? Put it all into mental attitude; if you think it can be done, it can. If you think it cannot, it cannot.

I get a kick out of people Don has helped with healing. Many people who go to a psychic healer expect something exciting, at least one or two skyrockets. They expect something spectacular, maybe a hot, shrouded, steaming room or someone running around in a toga. All of this might help, but it's not necessary for healing. Healing is simply a matching of vibrations, a dampening out of unwanted vibrations, and an amplifying of those you want left there. One of the teachers told us you should take two units of time preparing yourself, one unit of time for the actual healing, and three units of time for cleansing yourself. And these can be broken down into minutes, not hours. So when you are thinking in terms of healing, it's not that you're going to set aside the next twenty-four hours and heal the pimple on the end of your big toe, you are going to do it in a matter of moments.

The second limitation of healing is the preset condition. This is one that you have no way of knowing. This would cover, of course, those people born blind, where we have some of the great healers working with them and they do not see, they do not respond, and this is probably the reason why. For this go-round, this lifetime, they decided to include the additional challenge of living blind. And if this is a preset condition, there is absolutely nothing you can do about it, even though you would love to.

So you can look at things two ways. As those of you who are going to be healers start healing, you will have some beautiful successes. You will also have some healings where nothing seems to happen and you must not let this bother you. You are doing the best you can and you are using the highest form of energy in the universe. Whether or not that person accepts it, whether or not the patient responds in harmony with it, is beyond your control. But you have opened the gates and through those gates will flow enough power to do anything that needs to be done. And I have put here, in big capital letters so you will remember; there is NO KARMIC DEBT in the classic sense of the word. You may remember my tirade about that some time ago. It's funny how hard that concept is to kill. I guess I'm going to be stomping on it the rest of my life. Just two days ago, while talking with an elderly lady who accepted my concept of karmic debt eighteen month ago, she complained about her condition (which is similar to cataracts), and she said, "Well, I must have seen something awfully ugly last time around because it's making me go blind." I spent the next half hour verbally thrashing her, trying to convince her that something out there is not making her go blind because she saw something she shouldn't. If she accepts that, maybe we can get things on the right track again. Karmic debt simply doesn't exist. Don't blame anybody else for your problem—you probably did it yourself.

'Protection of the healer.' We've covered it in a number of ways, mental clearing and physical clearing. We mentioned washing of the hands, you've seen many of the healers shaking their hands or snapping their fingers; mentally, it is simply getting yourself back in order, dismissing from yourself all vibrations that give you a feeling that you have taken on the problem of the patient.

Here is one place in the psychic realm where you can know when something is happening. When you observe a healing, place your hands in the air with your palms forward, facing the healer. While the healer is working with a recipient, see if you can feel a flow going through you. It's interesting how subtle something like that can be. You are sitting there and sitting there and suddenly "Oh," you can actually feel it running around your hands in a little tight circle. But, as I say, right now try to limit yourself, unless you've had other healing training, of course, to absent healing and prayer.

And don't forget this thing of protecting yourself. When you step into someone else's vibrations, you will take on that vibration and you must get rid of it. You must get rid of it just as deliberately as you take off your coat when you come inside. And it must be done deliberately. Remember, "Thoughts are things." They're just exactly that. Washing of hands goes back, way back to the old Biblical treatises and to early Jewish mythology and it is simply handed on down to us.

Let's review our exercises for the week. Driving here this evening, I was talking to one of my little guides and he was running around eavesdropping among you folks and I said, "Gee, now they've had eight classes and they're meditating twice a day, they must have half their notebooks filled up by now," and my guide said, "Don't kid yourself."

So as you now work, the most critical test at this point is opening your psychic centers. Ask aloud for your guides to show you something for your highest and best good. Observe the object until you are sure of it in detail, and I mean detail like color, shape, temperature, an odor if it has one, everything you can think of. Then try to change it in some way. And you will notice that this is in big, bold print—IF YOU CAN CHANGE IT, IT IS YOUR OWN MIND AT WORK. Spirit will not allow you to change its projection, and this is one of the ways you can tell if you've been kidding yourself or not.

The first time I did this, I had an awful lot of fun because the image I was seeing would not change, so my mind put in another image to see if I could change that one. This was before I could talk to my Padre. Rev. Bradley saw what I was doing and said, "I didn't tell you to play with two images, stay with the real one." So I had to get rid of the one I could play with. This is powerful medicine. Do not deceive yourself, do not be deluded. If the picture you are given, let's say, is a young man, clean shaven, and you put a beard on him, go back to about lesson four or five and start again, one at a time for a week at a time because *you've GOT to be able to tell the difference between delusion and the real thing.* If you can't tell the difference between them you are in real trouble, and I am in real trouble as your teacher.

So, as I say, this is very harsh medicine. But try it. You will be surprised how easy it is and what a tremendous inner-knowing it will give you. I think we've discussed before, when given a horse, try to change it into a zebra, and if it won't turn into a zebra, be awfully proud of yourself, you've got the real thing in the palm of your hand.

Mediumship and Psychic Communication

Guideline: THERE ARE NONE SO BLIND AS THOSE WHO WILL NOT SEE

I. Mediumship
   A. Mental
      1. Mind as a receptor
      2. Clairvoyance and clairaudience
      3. Impression
   B. Physical
      1. Outside the mind
      2. Knocks, raps, materialization
      3. Independent voice
   C. Why
      1. Help in your daily life
      2. Helping others
      3. A step toward ordination
   D. Responsibility
      1. Top secret
      2. Your action—your reward
II. Psychic Communication
   A. E.S.P.
      1. Thought forms
      2. Mind to mind
      3. A stagnant box

**********WORK FOR THE WEEK**********

Concentration and Meditation:

Ten minutes each morning and evening. First three to four minutes, be still. Produce your spot. Hold it about one minute, and then reduce it to nothing. Ask aloud for your guides and friends to make themselves known. Keep order. Know each one of them. Close your silence after ten minutes.

You will notice in your outline tonight that the talk is considerably shorter than some you have had to wade through. The topic is, as you see, broken down into 'mediumship' and 'psychic communication.' We will discuss those in detail as we go along.

Many, many times the two titles are used totally at random and it is not quite true, there is a very small difference and we will get into that as we go along.

Your guideline for the night: 'There are none so blind as those who will not see.' This is probably the most fatal kind of blindness there is. It is one of the kinds of blindness that we are trying to fight all the time. We tell you to stop, stand still, and look and see. If you really choose to stop and look and see, then there is absolutely nothing that you can doubt. So keep in mind that not seeing is a very sad form of blindness because it is one that you control yourself. Try never to be guilty of it. You are never quite so wise that you cannot learn, so avail yourself at all times to the experiences of life.

Okay, 'mediumship.' The main difference between mediumship and psychic, or psychism, is essentially the religious connotation. We will get into that, as I say, in detail.

The main thing that a medium will do is communicate with a spiritual entity, someone who is dead, and someone who's on the other side. They will communicate with them and acknowledge them as an individual. A psychic will not. A psychic does not believe that this capacity exists. That is the main difference between them.

You will notice that under mediumship I have broken it down into four categories, so let's pay close attention to A and B. These are the two major categories that your sensitivities fall into. These are the two major categories into which all phenomenon occur. So let's go through them carefully.

'Mental mediumship.' This, of course, is one of the things we are teaching you. Your mind is a receptacle. Look upon it, if you will, as a radio. The only reason your radio works is because you're able to tune into a particular frequency, to tune into a particular show. Can you imagine what your radio would sound like if you did not have that capacity, if you got all the stations at once? We're trying to teach you to tune them down so you can pay attention to one particular station. That, of course, has its own fantastic rewards. A reward that, when you start to use it more and more, you will be appalled that you've lived as long as you have and not used it.

Using your mind as a receptor, use clairvoyance and clairaudience. In this particular case, you're going to take them for exactly what they mean. Clairvoyance, in olden days, was considered divining the future. Here, I want you to consider clairvoyance simply by direct means: clear seeing. Clear seeing in the here and now, clear seeing in tomorrow, either one. We don't care. The past, present, or future, clear seeing.

The other is clairaudience. Take it exactly the same way: clear hearing. Of course, these are on a psychic level, not a physical level. These are not using your physical eyes or your physical ears.

Remember when we talked about the nervous system? How if an entity wanted to impress you with something, they would simply reach in and touch a nerve and give that nerve the right impulses and then your brain would see or hear or feel or taste what the entity wanted you to experience? They can also, in a very grand way, give you impressions on a grand scale. Hence number 3, 'impression.' You will be staring at a scene and suddenly you are aware that if you get very still and don't turn your physical body, because that doesn't help, but turn your clairvoyance ability around, you will notice you seem to look behind you as well. Suddenly you are in the middle of a scene that only exists on a psychic level. It is an incredible experience. It is something that as you go along, and especially start working in dark circles, you will be amazed at the sensations that you will receive. As I say, here again, it is the entity literally reaching in and touching a set of nerves that, through experience or his own training, he has learned that if he touches them with that "frequency," you will see thus and so. Or your mind will make you think you saw thus and so.

So this is the way to work and this should give you the key to this vague division between mental and physical mediumship. Mental mediumship occurs always within the mind, never exterior to it. It is always you, this thing upstairs that is doing it. Clairaudience, of course, sounds like someone is talking to you. In fact, if you have what is laughingly called "three-dimensional clairaudience," you can tell where the sound is coming from. Just as if you all closed your eyes, you would know where I'm seated simply because your ears could zero in on me and you'd know where I am. The same thing happens but it is all in your head. If someone discusses this with you and you are commenting about clairvoyance and they said, "You must be crazy, that's all in your head," you can say, "Yeah, it sure is." Because that's exactly where it is.

Back again to the little radio set. You are going to hear us harping on this time and time again. Learning to fine tune. Learning to sense a vibration. Learning to zero in on a particular part of the image within your mind. By doing so you will see more clearly, see in more detail as the entity wants you to see it.

Now, of course, I've been talking here in terms of an entity that knows what they are doing. I've been talking in terms of an entity that has been around enough. Enough incarnations, enough lifetimes, enough time on the spirit side to know how to do these things. You will find the whole gamut; you will find some who don't know that well how to impress you with something, but as they work with you, you also work with them. Remember when we first started that I asked you to talk out loud to these entities for a very simple reason. When you are thinking, the thoughts that go across your nerve system are nothing but energy; they are thought forms. If the entity is not extremely adroit, he will not know what that thought form image is or which one he should listen to. But if you frame it aloud, if you say, "Yes, I see the green car," then your thought form image is that green car and nothing else. If you sit there and mentally think, "I see the green car, but I'd rather have a blue one," now the poor entity is wondering what happened? I've shown him a green car and now he's thinking of a blue car. Did I impress him wrong?

So here's a case where you can help them learn and, of course, help yourself learn at a fantastic rate of speed. These impressions will run, as I say, the gamut to anything you can imagine. There are some very critical ones that are difficult to analyze. For instance, let us assume that you are seated in dark circle. One of your teachers, guides, or protectors is standing nearby and you suddenly feel a weight on your shoulders. Then the medium in the circle says, "Did you feel so and so touch you?" "Yes, I did."Then comes the big question, "What happened?" Did he physically touch you, like I could physically touch any of you here, or did he reach into your mind and press that set of buttons that made your mind say, "Someone touched my shoulder"? This gets to be an extremely difficult thing to decide, and that's why we have physical mediums.

Remember, again, by sheer definition, physical mediumship occurs outside the mind and the ones I have listed here are the ones you are already aware of: knocks, raps. Materialization we've touched on a little bit. We will touch on independent voice in a moment. That's a real fun one.

If you and your husband, or you and your friend, or whoever you are staying with, is sitting at home some evening and suddenly you hear, KNOCK, and boy you sit up and say, "Honey, did you hear that?" "Hear what?" What happened?

Was he just asleep at the switch or reading a book or watching the news on TV and didn't hear it, or did only you hear it? If only you heard it, then it is mental; you heard it in your mind. Now, the same thing, KNOCK. Both of you hear it at once. Bang, physical mediumship. Here is something that happened outside the mind.

I've often been questioned, could they not have both been simply thinking and sensing on a psychic level and therefore using mental mediumship? It could be the case, but odds are a million to one against it, because no one in the world has exactly the same vibratory rate. So for an entity to affect people who are different in the same way, it would take a very high entity.

Yes, certainly Tau Sing could step in here and snap his fingers on a clairaudient level and you would all hear it, because he can match your vibrations that easily. But as I say, it is extremely rare.

So the only way you can really tell the difference in knocks and raps is if you have an unbiased observer, and that is usually the most fun. Of course, you can scare the devil out of your neighbors, but watch for these kinds of things. Check them out because many times if you don't check them out you don't know which occurs. Remember, a physical manifestation as far as sound is concerned is going to be heard with your physical ears, and therefore anyone else in the room can hear it. If the entity literally KNOCKS, he is creating sound waves that your ears hear. If he reaches in to your brain and touches that little nerve and your brain says, "knock," then nobody else is going to hear it.

This thing of materialization we are going to get into in a couple more lectures. I simply put it here to remind you that it is one of the faculties of physical mediums.

Let's see, you've been seated in class now for some ten weeks, that's seventy days, one meditation in the morning and one meditation at night, that's one hundred forty sessions. You've all got at least two notebooks now filled with exquisite detail. Haven't you?

Never neglect that teeny little factor. Just recently I was visiting some friends, husband and wife, who have studied the psychic world for quite some time. The only trouble is the wife is jealous of the husband because the husband is developing faster than she is. So I asked her, "Have you been doing your two periods of silent meditation each day?" She said, "No. I do it as often as I can, but the kids are yelling, the faucets are leaking, and the clock is ticking." She gave me many reasons why she couldn't possibly do it. I turned to her husband and said, "How about you?" He answered, "Yes, sir, every single morning and every single night." Guess why the wife is jealous of the husband? Unfortunately, her jealousy is not going to help her a darn bit. All she has to do is get back in the swing of things and do what she's supposed to do and then, maybe, she'll catch up with him. Just between you and me, I doubt it.

Rev. Bradley used to scold us because of our meditations. I'm so thankful you poor children don't have her, but she always told us if you miss one silent period a day, you have lost a week. I won't quite go that far. I don't miss them anyway. Please remember that this is the only way you are going to get control of this thing. That's the reason I'm going to pick on you, because certain forms of physical mediumship require fantastic training. If I were to tell you that in order to become a really fine physical medium, you would have to study for the next ten years before you produce any phenomenon, I wonder how many in this group would do it? If I told you that you had to do it for five years, some might. If I told you two years, maybe a few more would. If I told you one year, twice a day, every single day, more of you would try.

Some of the really complex forms of physical mediumship are only achieved after years of absolute control and study. I would like to say it was easier than that. So help me God, it is not. All you have to do is look around you. We have very beautiful, fine physical mediums in the world today. It used to be a mark of pride because people were aware of what they were. The really fine physical mediums of today I think can probably be counted certainly on two hands, maybe on one hand that live here within the United States. Because most of you are not willing to put out that much time in order to achieve anything, let alone something as abstract as physical mediumship.

Number 3 on your list, 'independent voice,' I put under physical mediumship. In all honesty, it probably does not belong there because independent voice can occur whether you are a medium or not, whether they are using any energy from you or not. It is almost totally dependent on the entity that wants to say something. For instance, I can recall one time that was real fun. First of all, how many times have you been puttering around the house or driving a car and suddenly from behind you hear someone call your name? This happens countless number of times. The first thing you have to do is to find out, was there an observer? Did the other person also hear your name called? If they did, then that is physical mediumship. If they did not, the entity may simply have touched you mentally, and it would fall in that first category.

One of the cutest ones I have ever bumped into was when Don and I had taken a whole group out to the desert. We were south of Death Valley, trying to keep warm, so we had zipped the sleeping bags together, but that doesn't help a whole lot. We had our little dog Annie with us, so she was sleeping between Don and me. We crawled in there hoping to get warm, and Don in a rather low voice said, "God, it's cold." Then a voice between us said, "Uh huh." I very seldom use that term, and so he thought, "What?" So he turned over and said, "What did you say?" And I said, "Not a thing." So both of us had heard it. It turned out later, of course, that we found out who it was; it was our little Indian guide. These people are always with you and they take every opportunity to answer you. He was simply answering a question; yes it was cold, 27 degrees.

There are many, many times when independent voice will come into play and it is spectacular to observe. It will simply be a voice speaking out of the air. Everybody will look, and his or her eyes, at least, will focus on where the entity is. I can only remember one time in which independent voice was occurring when the entity could be seen either psychically or physically. Independent voice requires a very special kind of control on the part of the entity, and they are not going to waste energy making themselves look like people and also use independent voice.

Over at Harmony Grove last year was one of the most beautiful experiences. Danny was one of the mediums over at the Grove, and one of his guides was a little girl, just a little squirt who ran around him all the time. He was paying no attention to her at all while he was standing at the lectern with about five mediums sitting behind him. No one was paying attention to the little guide and so she came pouting around him and with a voice about three feet from him said, "Why won't he pay any attention?" Well, all the mediums heard. He turned around and apologized and said, "I'm sorry honey. I'll pay attention," and then he chatted with her.

It occurs when you least expect it. So if you hear your name called and somebody else is there, see if they are chalk white because they don't know what's going on, and that will tell you what has occurred.

We have only had one case of independent voice here at the Chapel. It was the case of an entity around me we call Sir. He delivered a prayer one evening, surprised the devil out of everybody. So it does occur, but it's one of these things that you cannot predict. You cannot make them do it. They will do it if and when they want to do it.

I notice 'D' here on my rough notes about how much time will you spend on developing a gift. A young man decided he wanted proof that there was something beyond ordinary senses, so he went to a lamasery in Nepal and told the lama what he wanted.

The young man spent the next thirteen or fourteen years studying and never left the lamasery. When he did leave, he could see without his eyes.

The most spectacular demonstration I have ever seen of this in my life was up in Los Angeles. They had about a 100-gallon aquarium full of goldfish: red ones, white ones, yellow ones, black ones, whatever kind you want. He had a net about that big around on the end of a handle. They had sealed his head up to the point that I'm surprised he could breathe, he certainly could not see. Then they had people in the audience come up and stand beside the aquarium and tell him which goldfish they wanted. With that net he would chase that goldfish all over the aquarium until he caught that goldfish, and put it in a little bowl.

That was without a doubt the most spectacular demonstration of seeing without your eyes I can imagine. I have seen him play table tennis, but immediately when you see this you think, "Uh huh, he just has darn good ears." But if you've ever tried to catch a goldfish with both eyes wide open, you will know why I was so impressed about that particular one. A few weeks later he was in New York and got arrested for riding through Central

Park blindfolded. They felt it was unfair to the pedestrians and everybody else. But he was able to do it, and he sacrificed, like I said, something like thirteen or fourteen years to learn how to do it.

A little later on, when we get into what we call billet reading, I will show you how you can see without your eyes in a limited way, not like him. To be able to pick something up and simply lay your hand on it, and then to read it is much easier than you think. There is a very simple series of routines in which you can teach yourself to do this. It's especially fun when you're playing cards.

'Why.' Why? That's always a question the little ones ask, and it is a question I hope all of you have asked all through your adult life and will continue to ask. The most important one, of course, it is helping you in your daily life, in your here and now. Remember what Jesus said, "Heaven is here and now." You can both acknowledge it and make it heaven, or you can turn it into the goriest hell you can also imagine. It is up to you.

Learning to control your mind is the first step, controlling it to the point that you can bring about those things you want. Then of course helping others. You don't have to put this first. I'd put this second, not first.

We have a great many Christians and pseudo-Christians who feel they must help other people and to hell with themselves. Well, unfortunately they haven't read the Bible very closely. They haven't really looked at their own activities. Remember the little warning that Jesus gave in the Bible, "Why are you concerned about the mote in thy brother's eye, when you cannot behold the glean in your own?" So this gets back again to if you cannot help yourself, then don't kid yourself, you're not going to help anybody else. So make all of these things work with you, first and foremost.

Number 3 is for most of you who want to go on toward ordination here at the Chapel and become a reverend. In this particular point, here at the Chapel you don't just simply go through a series of courses and answer a bunch of questions, because I feel if you are an ordained minister at this philosophy, you must demonstrate clairvoyance and clairaudience on command. It would be dumb if we sat here and talked about clairvoyance if I couldn't see anything. That's ridiculous. Like I've always told all the students, I will never ask any of you to do anything I cannot do or demonstrate. That's the main point here at the Chapel. You will be ordained here when you can prove to us that you are ready for ordination, and not before. So keep an eye out and we will get into that later on for those of you who do want to go farther on.

When you do become a medium, some of you are that already, but I want you to think seriously about D, the responsibility of it. We've talked very lightly about a lot of these things but the responsibility is fantastic. What I've got here is top secret. I guess I'm hung up on WWII semantics, but anyway it's got to be that because if you are giving a consultation to someone or giving a reading or answering questions for them, you will know more about that person than they know about themselves because it is just that way with anyone who has that kind of ability. I feel it is much more a sacred trust between a person and a minister, a spiritualist minister, a medium, than between a doctor, a psychiatrist, and an attorney or anything else. Because you can lie to your doctor. You can lie to your psychiatrist. You can lie to your attorney. You cannot lie to a fine, competent medium because they will know, and more subtly, they will know what the individual has forgotten. That's where the great responsibility comes in. Never under any condition, even when you're working here at the Chapel when you have psychometry circles, go chattering to someone else in the class, "Oh, I found out tonight that Helen did so and so and so and so." First of all, it's none of your business. It's nobody else's business but Helen's. So watch these things.

You must honor them because of this second thing I've got down here, 'Your actions and your rewards.' You will be known by your work. You've heard that from me many times, and I'm sure you've probably heard it most of your life. If your work turns out to be a slipshod mess, pretty soon you'll find you're not working anymore. If you use it wrongly, there are many things you have to pay for.

There are some very clever ways, incidentally, that you can use several forms of mediumship if you want to use it wrongly. Like picking the right teller at a bank, someone whose vibration you can match exactly. Hand her a blank piece of paper and she will cash a $100 check. However, then you leave, and at the end of the day she's got an awful problem. But that's her problem. Or if you're in a place that has a lot of diamonds in a vault, you can simply walk in the thing and say, "Who knows the combination of that safe?" Then if anybody in the room knows it, their mind will give it, automatically. If we hook you up to an EEG and someone stepped up to you and said, "What's your girlfriend's name?" 'Helen Smith' comes up because your mind will simply and automatically answer a command. So, what you do is you tune in and you walk outside and you write down the number, come back later and end up in San Quentin, but that's beside the point. So your actions can be used in all ways. Remember that. It's up to you.

If you use them in a negative way, you're going to have all kinds of problems, I can assure you. If you use them in good ways, I think the results are quite obvious.

Now, what about this thing of a psychic? I've got to be real careful about how I say some of this. To me, the major connotations, as far as difference goes, is this thing of religious concept. A psychic believes when they are communicating with someone that they are either talking to your mind through a 'mind-to-mind' contact or to an infinite pool of knowledge, the Jungian concept.

Unfortunately, that system only works to a point. I doubt very, very much if Tau Sing would be tolerant of being called an infinite pool of knowledge. He's an individual, just as you and I are individuals. He has every right to be acknowledged as an individual.

This infinite pool of knowledge is open to many people, if they do a little studying and go into that area. It is open to the so-called field of ESP, extra-sensory perception. I have glowing fights with some of the parapsychologists over this, but one day they will know the difference. Some of them would just faint dead away if you were giving them absolutely perfect valid information and they found out it was coming from their dead grandmother. They would simply drop on the spot. However, that's where it's coming from. If they won't admit it, that's their problem.

Pure ESP is generally limited, like I mentioned here, to thought forms, to mind-to-mind contact, with the exception of dipping into the infinite pool of knowledge, which is a system incidentally that Edgar Cayce used, for those of you who've read Cayce's books. Please, and I'm going to get stones thrown at me, please don't read anything but the two books he wrote, because some of the other stuff is not what he believed or taught at all. If you want to read them, they are, *There is a River* and *Green Mansions*. I would recommend those two. He was probably one of the finest psychics that ever lived. He was not a spiritualist; he did not believe in spirit communication, he did not believe in reincarnation, he did not believe in communication with the so-called dead. He was purely an ESP phenomenon and a fantastically fine one. Because of his limited way of looking at and using the ability to see, he dealt with the same crap that almost all pure ESP psychics do. They miss an awful lot of important information. That's why I've written down here, it's a limited way, 'a stagnant box.'

If we get a hold of a really fine psychic and work on them long enough, we can turn them into mediums, whether they like it or not. We do this by simply pointing out that a lot of the information they are getting is coming from mind-to-mind contact, but the other mind is on the other side, not here in someone's physical body. So as time goes on I think we're going to see the two merging. Probably psychic will win out because it is simply more popular. "Medium" carries with it the old English connotation, which is awfully close to Salem for comfort. We may end up someday all calling ourselves psychic, but at least right now there is a sharp difference between the two. We make that big difference in performance.

Mind of Man and Its Power

Guideline: RIGHT ACTION MEANS ATTAINMENT

I. Mind of Man
   A. Brain (Seat of the Mind)
   B. Nerve Complex
      1. Drugs
      2. Hallucinogens
   C. Electrical Activity
      1. Control
      2. Testing

II. Power of the Mind
   A. Almost Unlimited
      1. Master your concentration
      2. Master your imagery
   B. Voodoo and Black Magic
      1. Spirit law
      2. Familiars
      3. Your decision and your reward

III. Dreams
   A. Psychic
      1. Lesson
      2. Prophetic
   B. Physical
      1. Emotional
      2. Physical organic upsets

**********WORK FOR THE WEEK**********

Concentration and Meditation:

Ten minutes each morning and evening. First five minutes get still—produce your small spot. Change this spot into a flower. Last five minutes change your flower back into a spot and hold it there. You will see only your small spot and the background glow.

A simple lesson for tonight and yet it is one that can cause much upset. You will notice your guideline at the top, 'Right action means attainment." This is taken directly from the Sanskrit of Buddha. It was one of his commandments and would be on a par with the commandments of the Christian religion. I think it is quite obvious that it doesn't take a lot of mental gymnastics to see that it is true. Since you are responsible for your actions, if you want to achieve something or attain something, it requires right action on your part. So let that be your thought for the week.

I am constantly amazed when I hear a long, excited discussion over what is the difference between mind and brain. I have heard some of the most circular discussions you have ever heard in your life on that subject. You will remember, if you go back through a lesson we had a few weeks ago when we were talking about this body thing, that the brain is nothing more than a very elaborate, organic computer in which your entity is living in. The mind, or that intelligence thing that makes you the individual you are, is found throughout every cell of your body, but its seat is the brain. In other words, this ball of gray stuff that you've got sitting up on top of the end of your spine is the brain. It took man a long, long time to find out if that was true. For many, many centuries they were sure that the most important part of man was in his heart and this is why you will see that all through older literature and even repeated in our modern day, the Christian concept, "Let your heart...etc., etc., etc.," all the time referring to the mind.

They thought the seat that made you "You" was in the heart. It was carried to extremes by some of the cannibalistic tribes when they would murder someone. They would cut out the heart and eat it so they would be as strong as he was. I've never quite understood their logic. If they could kill him, he must not have been as strong as they were. But they mustn't leave any stone unturned, so they did this religiously.

It was carried to the extreme in the New World of the Toltec empire of what is now Mexico where the living, beating heart was extracted from the sacrifice and offered to the sun god which, if nothing else, must have been one of the goriest forms of sacrifice, certainly in the New World. Somewhere along the way they found out that if you hit a man on the head hard enough, he becomes unconscious, yet his heart keeps beating and still he doesn't function.

So this was their first hint that the brain had something to do with it. And then finally, through some accidental work in the Egyptian empire of Tritoni, they cut a hole in a man's head to let out a headache. Surprisingly, a great number of them survived.

We find their skulls with the bone tissue partially growing back over the hole. Many times the hole had literally been knocked in there by the point of a rock. At this point about all you can say is thank heaven; surgery has come a long, long way. This began to give them some hint of what was going on because they damaged certain parts of the brain through these operations and found that a person could no longer walk, that his left or right side was paralyzed.

So then came the dawning of the nerve complex, your next little step down, which simply is a string of organic wires that connect the brain to all the various muscles and organs in your body to keep it working.

If there were any doubts at all that the nerves were nothing more than conducting pathways for electrical energy, the Russians last year erased all doubts by giving a man back total use of his left arm which had been severely damaged by an internal nerve injury, by simply rethreading it with fine platinum wire across those sections of the nerves that were broken. His arm had begun to wither, to atrophy due to lack of exercise. Within eight months his arm was back to normal, using his right arm as a comparison. And, as far as we know, he is doing as well today as he was when the wires were put in. So we can literally be rewired like a house. You can go too far however. The spine is a bundle of nerves, much like a big cable that the telephone company would use, with millions of little connections, but none of them are labeled or color coded. So when something goes wrong in the major nerve trunk, right now we can do almost nothing about it, except for spiritual healing.

The nerve complex throughout the body is simply that, a channel of messages that your brain sends to have something done. If you are ever in doubt about the complexity of the brain, stop and think what happens when you walk. It's hard for us to remember when we were little children and had trouble standing up, but now you can walk and jump without really thinking about it. Your brain can go tearing along, giving you the right messages to several thousand sets of muscles, to make your legs bend, to make your body lean forward. This is most beautifully seen in pigeons. Have you ever seen a pigeon walking along? He walks with his head bobbing. Do you know why he is doing that? It is because he can't walk any other way. Just like, if I want to walk, I have to lean forward and put my foot out in front of me because I am a biped and upright. When I put my leg out, my center of gravity starts forward, but if I should just put my leg out and not touch the ground, I would fall flat. Well, the pigeon puts his head out and its body would fall flat on his chest so he puts his foot out to stop it from falling. He does it again and then puts his other foot out. Next time you watch a pigeon walking, watch this. There will be a head movement for every one of his foot movements. Disney of course took advantage of this. I don't know how many of you have seen their little thing on birds where the sand pipers and the dippers are all running around in time with the music and having a great time. Some people, I'm afraid, think those birds were taught to do that in time with the music, but they weren't. They can't move without doing it.

Now, what about this network you have that tells you all these interesting things? It tells you you're standing upright, tells you you're dizzy or you're not dizzy. Well, you can do all kinds of things to that network. Other than outright injury, the use of drugs causes the most damage, because they are literally nerve blocks or hallucinogens. Many drugs are a must and we should all be thankful for them because they do a great deal of good. The hallucinogens fall into another category, however: marijuana, LSD, etc.

I have tried hallucinogens and find that they hamper spiritual development. They do it for a very obvious reason—they take away your control. Anything that takes away your own personal mental control, I don't give a darn how beautiful a trip it sends you on, it is not advantageous because you cannot control it.

As we develop along here and start having circles, you will see some spiritual trips; let's call them that will make anything any drug user has even seen fade into insignificance. The idea, I think one of the most beautiful ones, is when we are in a dark circle, and a very strong entity comes in, removes the walls, the ceiling, and suddenly you can see the stars and then slowly you become aware it. It is almost as if you are not in the room but you are standing someplace looking around at a beautiful landscape. It's impossible to give you that feeling because one part of your mind is saying, "Hey, look, you're sitting in the chair" and the other part of your mind is saying, "Oh, no I'm not," and neither part of your mind is dulled by the drugs. There was a question asked a couple of times ago as to whether or not LSD can permanently damage the psychic centers. I sent this story off to one of those gentlemen in UCLA who is doing work on LSD and he said, to his knowledge, it does not, unless it has reached the point that it has done major nerve damage simply as a chemical and not as something else. Of course they are only working on ESP now. So for any of those in the audience who have had one or two trips on acid, the only thing I can say to you is don't do it anymore. You don't need it. It does not give you what you are sitting here tonight trying to achieve. Stick with us a few more weeks and we can show you how to get exactly what you are hunting for.

Okay, the nerve complex, as I say, works by electrical activity. Just lately there has come to the forefront, with much writing and ballyhoo, much about watching your alpha wave response and controlling it. Here again is another proof that the brain and the nerve network is simply a fantastically-sophisticated set of electronics and a magnificent creation, but nevertheless, no more than that. The control that you can exhibit, since you are watching your alpha wave response, is that you will be able to control that particular portion of your electrical energy that your brain is doing. In other words, increasing or decreasing or staying in that particular sine wave or configuration. As far as I know there has been very little work done on this in connection with psychic development. I suspect that somewhere down the line we're going to see a lot of that work done, but it has not been done yet. There will be various kinds of testing such as the lie detector test and all of these kinds of things. I have one at home. It's an awful lot of fun testing various victims that happen to come for a visit. It is amazing that the biggest response you get from a person is the very first inclination that you are going to ask them something they are afraid you might ask. Boy does the lie detector respond. It really goes off the scale. These are some of the things that we are coming to experience in parapsychology. Some of it will be very interesting; some of it will have no application at all to our kind of work.

We've been talking about the mind. Okay, what about the power of the mind? I think we have drilled enough. It is almost unlimited. You can do absolutely anything with your mind that you want to and I mean in three-dimensional reality. This cannot be stressed too strongly. Remember, Christ fed the multitudes. He didn't do this with the help of some little black box. He did it by using his mind. Ananda, one of Buddha's prize students, planted what we would now call a bean, a row of them, made them grow, flower, fruit and be ready for a harvest in about six hours, just by sitting and staring at them. He did it with his mind. You've heard me talk about little tricks of the mind to move something, like making something rotate. Or put a grain of sugar out here and concentrate on moving the grain of sugar. It's an excellent exercise. It is frustrating until you learn the little knack, because it is simply that. You can all do it. You can all do it and will be surprised how quickly. 'Power of the Mind.' 'Master your concentration' and 'master your imagery.' What you cannot visualize you cannot have. What you can visualize is yours. Unfortunately, that law is just that simple. If you can visualize it being in your possession, hence the power of positive thinking or positive prayer, it is yours.

Because the power of the mind is unlimited, almost unlimited, we have to talk for a minute about voodoo and black magic. Voodoo is a combination of psychic and spiritual activity, coupled with hypnosis. Much of what you have read about voodoo is real. It may be fancied up slightly in some of the Hollywood movies, but believe me, with enough control you can kill by thought. You can kill by thought as surely as you can by using a gun.

Black magic falls into voodoo simply because it is different from white magic. I'm often accused that all of the things I believe and manifest are works of the devil, and therefore, obviously, I'm a worker in the black arts. The only comeback to that is no. I am a worker in the white arts. I will not deny that black arts exist. Both use the same power, black or white. The only thing that keeps me, and I would assume all of you, from playing in the realm of voodoo and black magic is spiritual law. Whatever you send out is reflected back. Burn that into your mind. If you send out hateful thoughts to someone, it will be reflected back. If you send out dishonest ideas and concepts to someone, it will be reflected back. So then it simply stands to reason that you all have to come over to my side of the boat and play with white magic. It is your decision and your reward.

After you have finished these classes, and after you have had enough circle work that you can project something, you can bring about something. If you want to go off on a tangent using spiritual power to live someone else's life or change someone else's idea to your way of thinking, that is your problem. I would warn you here and now NOT to. Almost all of them end in suicide or some other very unhappy set of circumstances. It is your decision and the results of that decision will be your reward. Whether you play the game of white magic or black magic is up to you.

A 'familiar' is a formless mass of energy that can be created by a powerful individual and it will bend to that individual's will. It has no conscience of its own. It is not a spiritual entity. It has never been alive. It is a little device, or thing, that is responsible for almost all of the fancy legends we have coming out of Europe like vampires and werewolves and ghosts who tear things apart, a ghost who kills, this kind of activity. They almost all fall into that category. There are many, many spiritual entities that spend their lifetimes on the spirit side doing nothing but breaking familiars apart. The reason is that if I were to make a familiar, let's say with big eyes, big teeth and lots of hair, something very creepy standing over here, and I told him I did not like green and he was supposed to destroy anything green, well anybody wearing green in here would immediately be in trouble. And when he got outside he would raise Cain with the lawn and bushes. So let's assume that I created him and gave him this command and then I died. Now he is only going to take commands from me. Let's assume that I had not developed enough spiritually and on the other side I realized I had left a monster behind and I had no way to contact this mindless bundle of energy who is carrying out my orders to destroy anything green. Here is where many of the spiritual entities step in and will literally dissolve the familiar and let him go back into energy. There are some classic cases on record in which these things did exist. There are some even quite modern ones.

I can tell you one that happened in 1946, at the Balboa Naval Hospital in San Diego. A young man in the Navy had a back injury and was paralyzed from about the middle of the back down. He was very fascinated in ESP, witchcraft, black magic and everything else, and so he decided to create for himself something that would be just his. And he made a great big white polar bear. He had seen polar bears before so he could image them very, very well. And over some six or eight-month period he visually imaged in his mind and projected a polar bear with great big feet and white hair. Everything a polar bear was supposed to have, including a polar bear's temper. Well, you can imagine what happened. His illusion got out of hand and anyone that he did not like, the bear was against. And he suddenly found out that he was having a whale of a time keeping his pet bear from hurting anyone. His nurse or doctor would come in to give him a shot or to take a blood specimen. This registered pain and fear to him. BANG, here was the bear and it took a great deal of mental effort on his part to keep the bear from becoming three-dimensionally real and carrying out the unconscious commands that "this person is hurting me, protect me." Well, as the story goes, and as I say this story has been documented in the psychiatric works, one of the doctors whom I knew, who was also interested in ESP, spotted what was going on and got to this young man and discussed it point blank and said, "Look, I know you have created a force and you are about to lose control of it." Very quickly, then, through some psychiatric work, purely on a non-spiritual level, they gradually undid the bear and released him. But if it had gotten out or hand, we would have had one of the best horror stories imaginable, in Balboa Park. So when you go back and read some of the old fairy tales, remember that much of the time it involved a little thing like that. As I say, it is your decision and it is your reward. Don't go that way. We have a lot more fun in a different way.

Now we come to 'dreams,' one of the most difficult parts of psychic study. Dreams are difficult because there are two major divisions, psychic and physical. Every time you dream does not necessarily mean that you've had a psychic experience. You have to be able to tell the difference. Now I had a lady in my class one time who had a magnificent technique. If she was just dreaming, it was in black and white. If it was a psychic dream, it was in living color and three dimensional. I have always dreamed in color and three dimensions, so I have to rely on something else. Generally, when you receive lessons in the dream state in which you go somewhere besides the present time, you might not know what you studied. This technique is used all the time—we receive information we will be using a few steps down the road. If you don't need the information right now, they'll just file it away in that enormous set of memory banks in your brain so it is there at the time you need it.

Some of your dreams will be prophetic. In other words, they are going to be telling of events to come. Here I would ask you to remember you are all keeping journals. Some of you who have had dreams that may be prophetic, I would ask you to keep them to yourself, to watch them and analyze them to see how they come out. See if you can get to where you can tell the difference between psychic activity and physical activity. Physical dreaming is brought about by two main stimulants, emotional and physical organic upsets. The emotional, of course, is for you who have active imaginations, who go home and remember one of those furry little monsters that I created here and wake up screaming tonight.

There was one who kept me awake for a big section of my youth when I saw "The Mummy" and "The Return of the Mummy," and things of this nature. If I see those on the late, late shows, they still send chills up my back. Nevertheless, many other emotional upsets will cause dreams such as a sense of failure, a sense of accomplishment, this kind of thing. Generally dreams will only be understood on a purely psychological basis. Those brought about by organic upsets, like if you go home tonight and have Champagne and lobster before going to bed, are the most classic. It's guaranteed to do something. So, don't do that. However, there is another one I've noticed. Very, very beautifully, just these last few weeks, we've had these quick, quick changes in temperature. I'm one of these cowards who sleeps under an electric blanket and I don't have to be fully awake. I just reach over and poke the button when I get cold. But most of all, when I turn on the blanket, if it starts getting warm, I have the most fantastic dreams imaginable, simply because I am hot. So it's little things that can upset you, like an uncomfortable bed. How many of you have tried to sleep at a friend's home or on a vacation or on a trip? You did nothing but doze off and wake up again, all night long. So you can learn quickly which kinds of foods you as an individual should not eat before going to bed.

The emotional level is something more or less at the whim of our emotions. Until we can get to the point where we can control them absolutely, emotional activity is something that is simply there. There is no easy way to tell the difference between a psychic dream and a physical dream. By checking your notes, you can see which dreams were prophetic. Which ones came true and which ones you later found out benefitted you. The reason

I say you must write these down is because there will be little clues along the way for you to be able to say when you wake up in the morning, "Hmmm, that was a psychic warning of something that is going to happen," and you take immediate action. I can give you no hard and fast rules because every one of them is different for every one of you. I'm sure you have all seen the huge volumes on dreams. My mother has one of those, bless her heart. She's quite psychic. Sometimes she will have one of those beautiful psychic dreams and look in her dream book and decide, "Oh good heavens, the world is coming to an end." So she will get calm and then she can tell the difference. We all can. It's just learning how. It will become quite easy. So don't consult your dream book to see if that blue car that smashed into the side of your car and broke all the glass had some mystical meaning. Get familiar with your guides and guards and say, "Hey, was that really my car?" If it was, pay careful attention to where the car was and the time of day.

I had a woman who was the most accident prone lady I think I have ever seen or known in my life when I worked in Denver. She would buy a new car and within six months it would be replaced part by part because she would smash it and she had the most beautiful prophetic dreams on every single accident. She would do nothing about them. Finally she told me at a Thursday night class that she had had a dream last night. She was going down a road and this kid on a bicycle came across and she swerved right into a post, the post broke off and fell over and smashed her car. It didn't hurt her, thank heavens. And I said, "Well, what time was it?" and she said it was about ten minutes to two. I said, "How did you get ten minutes to two out of your dream?" She said, "Oh, because I had on my gray dress and I always wear it when I go over to play cards and I leave about ten minutes to two." So I said, "Okay, don't go that way, go a different way." About three days later she called me and said she couldn't come to class unless her friend could pick her up because her car was in the shop. I said, "What have you done?" and she said, "I was in such a hurry, I was running late, and I knew it would be okay to take the old way and I ran right into a big post." So please learn to tell the difference. You'll save yourselves from aches and pains and you'll probably save me some late night calls. Be on your guard. You have to know you're going to have both kinds of dreams. Many of our sex fantasies and dreams are purely psychological. Very few of them will be psychic. They can be but very few of them will. So watch them. Fill them out in your book and then check and see if that happened the way you dreamed it would.

One day you will suddenly notice that many of your dreams are real, psychic dreams, not dreams at all because you didn't go to sleep before it occurred or you were awakened just before it occurred. You've heard me and seen me do this a hundred times. When you go to bed tonight and start to go to sleep, you go down a little slide and bang, it's morning. If you can learn to start down a little slide and then stop there, you'll be surprised at what you can do. Note the dream that occurred immediately upon drifting off to sleep, it may be of great significance. You have to analyze them because each of yours is a little bit different.

Materializations and Manifestations

Guideline: ALL THINGS ARE MINE, IN TIME AND ON TIME

I. Physical Materializations (Objects)
   A. Aports
      1. Long-lasting physical
      2. Short-lived physical
   B. Teleports
      1. From where
      2. Be observant
   C. Fakes ("I was told to bring this to you")
      1. Do not alter the concept
      2. Should be exposed

II. Physical Manifestations (Spirits)
   A. Etherealization
      1. Controlled (dark circle)
      2. Uncontrolled (at night)
   B. Ectoplasm
      1. From the medium
      2. From the circle

III. Physical Manifestations (Objects)
   A. Made visible in dark circle
      1. Flowers, crosses, etc.
   B. Knocks and raps
      1. Active
      2. Passive

**********WORK FOR THE WEEK**********

Concentration and Meditation:

Ten minutes each morning and evening. First three to four minutes, be still.

Ask aloud for your spirit guides and friends to give you information that you can check. Make sure you know what they send. Thank them for the help and close your silence after ten minutes. Check what they have given you, so that in your next silence you can acknowledge what you received. If you could not check what was received, ask for another test. This is testing your reception, as well as the spirit's ability to send.

Your guideline, which will definitely frustrate you, is 'All things are mine, in time and on time.' I personally hate that statement, and yet it is so true. Until you are ready to handle a particular gift or until you have learned to handle a particular gift, you will simply not be able to use it. It's as simple as that.

This is why we have been hammering away at controlling your mind. The key to all these things is to absolutely control your mind. While this may frustrate you too, you will hear me, other teachers here at Chapel, as well as spirit teachers, all using variations on that theme all the time. While you might not like it, just as I don't like it, it is nevertheless true.

Tonight we are going to discuss materializations. This covers a whole gamut of things.

A figure most of you are familiar with, who displayed this control, of course, would be Jesus. Jesus displayed this kind of control over material and physical objects as readily as you and I breathe. He is not the only one. There are a great many Buddhists and Buddhist priests who did everything he did.

We have to look upon this as another reason why Jesus told everybody, "These things ye shall do and even more." Knowing that there was more to do than he did, it is up to you to first learn what he did, and then go beyond. If you want a challenge, I think that's an adequate one.

As far as using mental energy to do things, as we discussed, there is turning the little aluminum pinwheel; moving things by the power of the mind. When you start working in some of the psychometry circles, you will have to do things like that to give you actual practice. There is another thing you are going to get tired of hearing, PRACTICE MAKES PERFECT and it does, pure and simple.

I have broken this down into several categories and so we will simply run through them. There is a particular phase of spiritualism, or psychic activity, that is without a doubt the most difficult to believe until it happens to you.

I can sit here all night and show you aports and teleports and talk about these kinds of things, and there will always be a doubt in your mind until it happens to you. Then, it is a revelation that will just absolutely blow your mind.

You will notice how I have broken it down:

Physical Materializations of Objects
Physical Manifestations of Spirit
Physical Manifestations of Objects

It is rather important that you keep those major headings in your mind because as you start working in dark circles, there are some do's and don'ts that are predicated by what is going on in the circle. Soon we will have a discussion of dark circles where we will get into all the exacting details, but let us just look at these for now.

'Physical Materialization of Objects.' You will notice I have broken it into two things: aports and teleports. The big difference between the two, and these I want you to remember, an aport never existed before. It is made from energy and given to you by a highly-evolved spiritual being. It is given to you as a gift or as a compliment or a reminder for what you are doing.

A teleport exists in the three-dimensional here and now. It is simply a material that has been de-materialized, brought to the circle, and re-materialized. I love that word, "simply" dematerialized.

If you can do the things, for instance, that Jesus could do—feed the multitudes, stop the storm, or hear thought—then moving physical things around or changing them to energy would be no problem whatsoever.

Aports come in two kinds: long-lasting physical and short-lived physical. On the short-lived physical, we don't know an awful lot about the reason why they leave. I will give you an example in a minute where we do have a reason in this particular case, but I can give you a couple others where there is no reason at all.

However, a long-lasting aport, physical object, can be anything you could imagine: a feather, rock, twig, leaf, anything.

One of the most exciting things, of course, is to receive an aport. I had a cross sent to me, given to me by Sir and Tao Sing to wear at my ordination. I didn't bring it tonight, but I will when we start circles so you can see it. And it's a fantastic thing to obtain because, as I say, when it happens to you, then it really means something.

Probably one of the most interesting ones occurred back east. I think it was in New Jersey. Rev. Packard had a series of circles going on where they were practicing materializations, and all kinds of these things. He had an American Indian guide who simply loved to bring him anything he could think of. They would have their circle and when they turned on the lights, there would be little piles of sand on the table, twigs, rocks, bird feathers. The Indian guide brought anything he thought he might like or he thought might please him. He would simply bring it to the circle and materialize it.

Rev. Packard decided, however, that he had enough of these trinkets, and one night at circle he asked the Indian guide, "Please bring something that no one in the circle would have access to in any way." The poor little Indian, of course, couldn't figure out what the devil he meant. So he asked the reverend what did he mean, and what would he consider that kind of thing?

The first thing that popped into the reverend's mind was a six carat, blue-white American cut brilliant diamond. So he told the little Indian, "You can bring me a rock. You might as well bring a "rock" rock.

Two weeks later, at one of the circles, nothing exciting happened as far as the activity in the circle. They lit the candles after the circle was over. There was a pile of beautiful sand in the middle of the table, and sitting on top of the sand was a six-carat flawless blue-white American brilliant diamond.

And needless to say, the reverend was a little excited. He kept it for quite a while. He finally took it to Tiffany's to have it appraised. I don't remember now what the appraisal was, but the gemologist at Tiffany's said it was the most flawless diamond he had ever seen in his life for a diamond that size. He immediately asked where it came from, and the reverend, of course, beat a hasty retreat.

Several years before his death, he gave the diamond to the Carnegie Museum and it is in their permanent gem collection. They really pinned him down as to where it came from because they wanted their notes for the collection to be complete and proper. He thought long and hard about telling them and decided he would not. He told them that a very close and dear friend had given it to him. This information came from his diary. It was published after his death and I'm very curious to see if the museum changed the label on that stone, but probably not. Those are the aports that last a long time because they are simply made to last.

Now, a short-lived physical aport is a whole other ball game. First of all, they are quite rare, and thank heavens they are, because if they were not rare, it would be awfully frustrating.

Probably one of the best documented was written up in just about every psychic journal there is about ten years ago.

There was a little old lady in San Francisco who was attending message circles and séances every place she could possibly go. At this particular one, her grandmother walked up to her, talked to her, and she identified her, and all this kind of thing.

As grandmother was getting ready to leave, the little woman with tears said, "Won't you give me something to remember you?" Well, the grandmother was wearing a shawl draped around her neck and she reached up and pulled a piece of lace off the shawl and handed it to the little woman. Needless to say, the little woman was very excited. She kept it and showed it to anybody who would look. She was so excited about it that she showed it around for about two years or so. Some of the physicists at Berkeley, who had heard of it, decided they should look into it.

They approached her to ask if they could examine the piece of lace. She was happy they would pay attention to her keepsake from her grandmother; so of course, she let them look at it.

They put the lace through all kinds of tests. The first thing they found surprised the devil out of them. They found it was not made of thread, it was not made of string; they could not unravel it.

They worked on it with a very high-powered x-ray microscope and finally ran some critical analyses. The closest thing they could come to is that the material was, of course, not string at all, but was a white, gelatinous protein of some kind. It was opaque and white and from a few inches away under normal light, it looked exactly like lace.

I have seen enlarged photographs of it. It must have been utterly fantastic, but they really exhausted themselves trying to find out what it was. They came up with absolutely nothing.

Shortly thereafter, the little woman died and started one of the greatest mysteries in the world of psychic investigation because the lace began to get thinner. It got thinner and thinner and thinner. They finally sealed it in a glass cube so that it was totally isolated. It continued to get thinner and thinner and thinner. And after a period of about seven months, the glass container was empty.

Okay, what happened? It is quite obvious that this particular aport was given to the little lady to help her feel more comfortable and after she had crossed over, that comfort was no longer necessary, for now she was walking with her grandmother. She didn't need the lace as a reminder of her and the lace simply dissolved back into energy.

We have no idea how aports are put together, but in that particular case, we can say we know the reason. That one was short lived simply because it was for the little old woman and no one else. The rest of us were just all very lucky that research was carried out on it while it was here.

I have seen three short-lived aports. I will only mention two of them. They occurred in three of Rev. Bradley's circles where we were working on materializations. The first one really floored me.

Without an awful lot of fanfare, one of the young ladies' American Indian guides brought her an arrowhead. It was about an inch and a half long and it was made of a dark gray-brown material.

As you know, I am a geologist and I recognized what it was and I can assure you it was a rock, but it was an amazing thing. A few days later, two days later I think it was, she came back to Rev. Bradley's and the arrowhead was about a half inch long. It was shrinking. It was exactly the same shape and she had not switched arrowheads because I remembered a very peculiar flake that had been chipped off the bottom of the arrowhead, a very unusual pattern. That flake was there but it was now about one third of its original size.

It got smaller and smaller and smaller and finally simply vanished. So here was an aport that lasted three or four days. Why? Good question. Was it not put together properly? Was it maybe not meant to last? When I got my crucifix, I tell you, I ran around like I was daring it to disappear. I hoped it wouldn't but worried about it for quite a while.

There is no explanation for some of these things. When you ask a high teacher like Tao Sing, he says it was intended that way, period.

In the case of the arrowhead, I didn't know Tao Sing at that time, but I knew Sir, so I asked him why it didn't stay. He said, "It served its purpose." I asked "How?" His response was, "That is not for us to know, it is none of your business." It involved the person who received the aport.

At another circle, there was a young lady who was scared to death every time we got in a dark circle and anything actually happened. That woman would absolutely crawl the walls. One time Rev. Bradley's teachers came in, materialized to the point where they were transparent, walked over, touched the woman on the head, and said, "I bless you my daughter." The woman almost died! I tell you, she kept insisting she was not afraid of the dark, but when the lights went out you could hear her chair shake.

She turned out to be a very, very beautiful student and went on and accomplished some very gorgeous things. Her deceased father brought her a small pink square stone. I did not get an extremely good look at it. I did not have my glasses with me, but I would assume it to be something like a spinel or a pink topaz. Of course, it was small so she didn't want to lose it. So she dropped it in a new tissue, folded the ends up, then twisted it at the bottom so it wouldn't get away and put it in her purse.

She got home, of course, and was telling the family about what had happened. She opened her purse, dug out the tissue, opened it up, and there was nothing there. There were impressions of the square stone in the tissue, and no holes in the tissue, it was simply gone. Why? I don't know. And those people who do know won't tell us.

I suspect it is none of our business. Aports are done for a particular purpose and probably only the person receiving it knows why, and maybe they don't even know consciously. But anyway, time goes on and we will be having some aports show up here. I have a number of entities around me, as do five or six of you, who can bring in things like this from time to time. And, as I say, it will not be extremely meaningful until it happens to you.

'Teleports.' An object moved any distance and brought to you by a teacher.

Again, these come as all kinds of things. I am wearing one, a small green disc, given to three people here at the chapel who are associated with Doc Tao Lu. They were made in Doc Tao Lu, de-materialized, brought to the circle, and simply deposited on the table with a clunk (dropped from mid-air). Teleports are very difficult to detect. You never know when it's going to happen.

In this case, Tao Sing asked me to set up a special circle, but I didn't know why. Another very important teleport was brought to Don Schwartz, who is one of the healers here at the Chapel. He has a high teacher named Amentorate, who is Egyptian, and Don wanted an amulet scarab. Amentorate tried to bring him a very nice one of amber, but it got cracked when he took it out of the ground.

So he brought Don a small limestone white scarab about so tall. It's kind of white-buff colored, a very, very beautiful thing. It has an absolutely atrocious odor about it because the limestone is so porous (Amentorate brought it from the tomb of a high priest that has not been located), but it absorbed the vapors, or what would you, from the preservatives used in the bread and beer that was buried with the priest. Don keeps it screwed up in a little film canister so it will hold that fragrance, if you can call it a fragrance, as long as it can. Every once in a while he will go unscrew it and sniff it to make sure the scent is still there.

The important thing about that particular scarab is that on the back it has a very simple series of hieroglyphs, vertically running from an eagle's head on down to the undersurface of the scarab, which says "Life is truly eternal," which, coming from Amentorate, is one of the things he harps about a great deal in circle, either talking through me or through Don.

So, those are the teleports we bumped into.

Now, notice item C, 'fakes.' Both of these utterly magnificent things that Spirit can do for you can, of course, be faked by man. I have had real bad times with some materialization mediums. They know I'm sensitive, but they forget that I can also see in the dark. So when they are running around taking things out of their pockets and dropping them here and there, I am wondering, "Uh huh!"

But I think the most pitiful kind of fakery that you bump into is the one I have quoted here where the medium involved has reached a point of such a delusion of himself or herself that they actually think that they were told by Spirit to go to the store, buy you a trinket, and bring it to you in a circle. This is delusion on a grand scale. If it is an out-and-out fakery, of course, this is the thing that should be exposed, and all organized groups do that constantly. But the one thing I want you to keep steadfast in your mind is that, even though there are people who fake materializations, it does not alter the concept of what Spirit can do.

And oh, there are some lulus.

There are only two physical mediums I know of in the United States that I would trust in this kind of work. It takes a great deal of dedication on the part of the medium. But when you go to a gathering . . . let's say you go to a séance and you have someone who is acting as a channel and teleports are appearing in a room of fifteen people. If you get more than three teleports, be very suspicious because this takes a great deal of energy. Spirit is not going to waste it on trinkets.

One of the most embarrassing questions I have ever answered is having someone walk into my office with a handful of things, dump out on my desk a dozen or so little stones or pieces of rock, and say, "Rev. Larr, which ones are real?" Well, after you get a little way down the line, you can tell they are real either simply by looking at them or touching them using psychometry.

Those I have trouble with, of course, Tao Sing and Padre fill me in. But it is awfully difficult to answer that question to someone who really wants you to say, "Yes, they are all real." Incidentally, as I have warned all of you in the past, if you ask me a question like that, I will answer it. You might not like the answer, but I will tell you the truth.

It is an amazing thing. I think some mediums may fake materializations because of the pressure to perform and satisfy people who may be paying to sit in the circle.

First of all, if anyone asks you for more than about $5, tell them to go to hell because it is simply not right. I know some, believe me I do, and several of them I have blown their minds when they showed me a gorgeous little trinket that their great grandmother gave to them and come to find out that great grandmother had nothing to do with it. So be careful of those kinds of things. They will do nothing but make you sick inside.

I follow a system just like Rev. Bradley, and I make a lot of enemies, just like she did. When someone wants to work, especially in a circle, they will have to satisfy me first, and if they don't, you are not going to be exposed to them, period.

This was a very embarrassing thing that I watched Rev. Bradley do because, oh, she was a stickler. I remember there was an old gentleman who is on the spirit side now, a fine materializationist, his name was Bill. He came to town and stopped by her place to talk to her late one evening. I was there going over some notes, and he introduced himself and talked for a few minutes. She simply reached over, snapped off the lamp, and said, "Okay, Buster, show me what you can do!"

Well, I can tell you, when you get a 250-plus pound black woman leaning on her chair saying, "Okay, Buster, show me!" that has to catch you off guard. However, he did very well. Some very beautiful little aports and teleports and some very beautiful manifestations we are going to be talking about here in a minute showed up. He then served at St. Michael's Spiritual Church, which was her church, and he was an absolute saint, it worked very, very well.

And I am going to follow the same lead. I have worked in probably a dozen spiritual churches and met an awful lot of people. But I would not ask you to walk across the street to sit in a circle with them. I am sorry, but that is the way it is.

Okay, as far as disclosure, if you are in an event that you know is fake, please don't start up and scream or shout and make all kinds of noises. Simply go to the head of the organization after the thing is over, report to them that you have seen thus and so, and simply chalk up the $2 you have spent as the same amount of money you would spend to see a side show. Leave it at that. I would, of course, ask you to do the other thing, too. When you sit with someone who is good, who is really genuine, let them know it. It really is important because a lot of times some of these people work awfully hard and work for a great many years and a kind word of congratulations, this kind of thing, means an awful lot more to them than the money they might make from a circle. Okay, let us run on.

'Physical manifestations of spirits.' The thing I want you to remember with etherealization is you can see them but not touch them. This is a phenomenon that is a pure energy field (you can see in the first part of the name that here is our ether again). If you take an etheric aura and toss enough energy into it, it will become visible in a darkened room or even in a room of subdued light if enough energy is used. However, if you were to reach over and put your hand against the entity, your hand would simply go through it because it does not have enough energy or enough molecular structure to be solid. Of course, you would never do that. I am going to remind you now but we will talk more about it next time. In a dark circle, never touch anything without permission from either the head of the circle or the materialized entity because you will upset things if you do.

Okay, there are two kinds of materializations—a controlled one in a dark circle and an uncontrolled one at night.

The controlled one in a dark circle is done simply to please you by a very high teacher or high entity. They will make themselves visible enough to appear to you with your physical eyes. Now, when I use the word "see" here, I mean with the physical eyes, not the psychic eyes. It will generally be less dramatic, color wise. It seems to be, oh, something like a bluish-gray, green, something like that. However, when you get an entity that is higher, he can be extremely spectacular. At a circle in Denver, at the chapel of the First Spiritualist Church, we had a materialization medium and Sir decided to pop in and did so with all his robes on. And that was the most gorgeous Christmas tree you have ever seen in your life. Glittering, glittering, glittering. White gloves, rings on his fingers, the whole bit. And it was something to behold. But I could not touch him for he was simply an energy field. He was not a real object.

The uncontrolled one generally appears at night. You suddenly wake up and see someone standing at the foot of your bed. Of course, our first impulse is to scream and hide under the covers, but after you get over the shock, if you haven't scared them away, say hello. It might be important. These will happen at unpredictable times, generally in subdued light because the bombardment of photons seems to dissipate the energy they use to make it. So it might happen in your bedroom, maybe with no light on, maybe some light coming through a window, or something like that. In the controlled conditions of a dark circle, of course, then it happens in total darkness.

One of the things that an entity can use to make the etherealization is called ectoplasm, item B. Ectoplasm is energy associated with your etheric body. It can be drawn from you with your permission and used by an entity to create something, to either create themselves or to create an object for you to look at. Most of the time the ectoplasm will be coming from the medium who is head of the circle. Or if there is more than one medium, up to maybe two or three mediums in a circle, it will be corning from them as well. Only occasionally, I think I have only seen it a couple of times, will you see it come from everybody in the circle. And it is so much fun when that occurs because everybody is sitting around in the dark, of course, and when something starts happening everybody starts straining their neck to see what's going on.

Suddenly you will notice that there is light corning up across your face.

You look down and there is a cloud, a fuzzy cloud, and it goes over here and it goes over there. Then you start really looking carefully and you will notice a beautiful pale blue-gray donut sitting in everybody's lap all the way around the circle. This is where ectoplasm is taken from everybody in the circle. It is a weird material. We know nothing about it.

I would love to get a chunk of it under a mass spectrometer, but Tao Sing assured me that it couldn't be done. So we will have to try some other way. I have taken far ultraviolet spectrographs of some of it, but it is very difficult to pick up. Anyway, when it is taken from you, you will notice two things. There will be a pronounced change in temperature. Generally, when they are using ectoplasm from me, I get cooler. However, I know almost as many people who will get warm.

So we can't say which it is, but there will be a pronounced change in temperature.

The odor of ectoplasm runs the gamut of smells, believe me. To me, I think most of the time it smells like an old musty house. Have you ever been in a really old house? Even though the house was as clean and neat as a pin, it has a funny odor about it that simply says "old." I have smelled some that was absolutely revolting. But, nevertheless, don't be too critical of the tools they like to use. If someone's ectoplasm is not Chanel #5, we will bless them and go ahead and use it anyway.

It will never hurt you. It is part of the energy field of the etheric body. It might shock you or surprise you if you find a medium sitting, especially in a trance, and ectoplasm is coming from their body, like out of their mouth or their nose. NEVER

TOUCH THEM! If you do, you literally might scare them to death. So just leave them alone and sit there and watch what's going on. When you sit in a circle and the energy is coming from the whole circle, don't touch your neighbor simply out of courtesy. It will not shock them because it is not being taken in that great a quantity from you as an individual, but you wouldn't touch them anyway.

I get a big kick out of some of the students. In one of the Wednesday Night circles, we had a spirit of a young man who loved to materialize things and show people things. He was a physical medium on the Earth plane and so were both his parents before they went into Spirit. He works with us occasionally. One night he came in behind Larry. He had been making little lights all over the room, just blink, blink, blink. And we were going, "Ooh, ah, ah." Finally, everybody says, "Ohhhh! Look up there!" So everybody's looking. Meanwhile, Larry's looking and looking and looking. Up here behind his head was a complete hand and it was just hanging there in mid air. Larry hadn't seen it yet, of course, and the entity knew he hadn't seen it, so he brought his hand down, snapped his fingers and put his hand back so Larry would look up. Well, Larry looked up, and when he made several comments, the whole circle just broke up because I don't care how many times you bump into that kind of thing, it is extremely exciting and a lot of fun.

So these are the kinds of things that will happen to you.

When ectoplasm is brought from the circle, it's generally focused into the middle of the room, and there you will see it pile up either into a conical shape or ovoid ellipsoid and then they will make something out of it.

'A physical manifestation of objects.' Okay, what are they going to make for you to look at? Here again is the same kind of thing. It is visible with the physical eyes. It is also, of course, visible with the psychic eyes. So when you are sitting in a circle and something appears there, the first thing you would do is blink, close your eyes and see which way you are seeing it. Is it physical or is it being impressed on you psychically? The first time you see something, close your eyes to see what is going on.

Okay, the items are simply made visible in the dark by the techniques we have talked about above, either by dumping energy into a particular shape so it simply glows because of its own vibration, or they use ectoplasm to make the shape.

What can it be? It can be flowers, crosses, anything you can think of.

One of the most beautiful manifestations I have ever seen was at Rev. Bradley's one night. She loved old-fashioned roses. I don't think I have seen any for a long time. The old fashioned cabbage rose. Remember the big, round pink ones like a big head of cabbage? They have a fragrance that just can't be equaled. Her mother loved these and apparently had a yard full of them. Every place in the yard there was two square inches, she planted another rose bush.

Rev. Bradley's mother, almost without fanfare, walked into the room and made three of them on the table in the center of the circle, and they were gorgeous! Beautiful pink. You could count individual petals, stems. I think they had three or four leaves on the stems. They were real, they were 3-D. They were everything you wanted. Their fragrance filled the room. Rev. Bradley asked if she could pick one up. At that time, I was clairaudient and heard the answer, "I don't think you can match their vibration." Rev. Bradley said she wanted to try anyway, so she reached over where the stem would be, closed her fingers, and the rose stayed there. Her hand went through it. Then she took both hands and reached over and got a hold of one of the roses, put her hands down around it and just closed her hands; you could see the rose sticking out both sides of her hands. She hadn't touched them at all.

So anybody seeing that begins to be very suspicious, "There's something unusual going on." But we enjoyed that for, I don't know, what seemed like an hour. I am sure it was probably a very few minutes and then they simply went out, like "snap" and they were gone. But spirits will do this and these are the kinds of things that happen in dark circles. I have had many, many circles in which those kinds of things occurred, and they are real fine and they are very, very beautiful.

Okay, the other kind of physical manifestation. Most of you are probably familiar with the first thing: knocks and raps. I hope you are by now. If not, when you get into circle, you certainly will be. There is an active and passive form. We will talk about the active one first.

The difference between the two is done by a surge of energy for you. The passive one is simply done whether there is an observer or not, and it is done by a very special kind of situation and I will get there in a second.

One of the most obvious ones, the knocks and raps bit, you will hear a lot in a circle. I think it most often comes from our American Indians. Tenetchcook, of course, my little Indian. We also have a little Indian squaw, Navajo, I think. She loves to sit under the table and pound on it from the bottom. And they love to get anything that will make noise, like a trumpet, so they can rap on it.

One of the loudest, most chaotic circles in my life—there were about twelve of us—and I think every single one of us had an Indian guide, and among them were several chiefs. One of the gentlemen was hard of hearing, so his Indian chief would bang on the table. And, of course, Constance didn't hear it and he would say, "louder." He said "louder" about two or three times and I wasn't really sure the table was going to survive, but then everybody else got in the act. Tenetchcook had a stick and he was banging on the trumpet. Constance's Indian was pounding on the table. The squaw was underneath knocking on the bottom. I forget who was where now. We had five or six places on the wall.

The runner on the drapes was also a very good sound for them. That tape is without a doubt the most total chaos I have ever heard in my life. Once in a while, they would all get together. They were trying to do this: "KNOCK knock knock knock knock knock knock," that kind of thing. But they were all out of rhythm. It was total chaos, but it built to such a point that everybody just broke down. We couldn't even hold any composure.

I think half of us were lying on the floor laughing. We couldn't even breathe.

But I was really quite surprised that the whole group survived. So if an entity comes into one of our circles and does something, please don't ask him to do it louder more than once because he will take you literally and then it can get out of hand.

Okay, the passive form, as I say, is the one where there is not necessarily an observer. This is generally restricted to a particular kind of thing we would call poltergeist. This is a very difficult thing to understand because it falls into both categories: purely ESP and probably spiritual as well. In every single case of poltergeist activity that has really been explored analytically and very thoroughly, they find a teenager with problems involved, emotional problems of some kind. And here is a raging battle going on as to who is doing the activity. Is it the unconscious state of the emotionally-upset youngster or is an entity doing what the youngster wants the entity to do?

I am sure you can see it would be very difficult to tell the difference between those two, like when you are turning your little pinwheel and I am turning my little pinwheel. I can turn it or I can say, "Tenetchcook, you turn it." If you are an observer, how can you tell which occurred? Unless you are a very fine medium, you could not. If you are a fine medium, you could simply see Tenetchcook reach over there and turn it. That solves your problem.

Poltergeist activity, though, we don't know. I have only explored one, personally, that was a real good one. And that was down here in San Diego.

Again, a young boy who was fourteen, a lot of emotional problems with his family, this kind of thing. And things would go flying around the house like mad. I don't think anything was ever broken—a great deal of care was taken there.

But one night I went down with a couple other people from the Chapel, and there a spiritual entity was involved as well as the pure ESP of the youngster. And we got to know the spirit entity fairly well and pretty well stopped the poltergeist activity. But during the evening, I was getting rather insistent that the entity come there, stay there, stand still, and talk to me. He did not like that so he was throwing pennies at me. And I was sitting on the floor, a candle in front of me throwing light on the room, and these pennies would appear and smash, boom, smash. He never hit me with one. He came close, but he wasn't going to hurt anybody.

So, as I say, that is a very special one and, of course, one that gets written up in all the fancy magazines. But don't worry about that one because I don't think we have very many teenagers here tonight. At least all the teenagers are swearing they are twenty-one and all of us are swearing we are teenagers.

So of the three we have covered tonight, the main thing is that center portion because this is one you are going to be exposed to in dark circles. Etherealizations using ectoplasm or physical manifestations of objects. Those will simply occur and I want you to be aware of what they are when they do. The top two, aports and teleports, will also occur, but I cannot tell you when or under what conditions. It is one of those things that when they decide to do it, they do it. There is simply no way to predict it.

Dark Circles & Your Next Step

Guideline: I AM NEVER ALONE! THERE IS NO WAY BUT UP!

I. Dark Circle
   A. Why a Circle
      1. Harmony
      2. Control
         a. About one hour
         b. Know the medium in charge of the circle
   B. Why Darkness
      1. Etheric formations
      2. Ectoplasm
         a. Medium
         b. Circle
   C. Red Light
      1. A lack of confidence
      2. Security
   D. Time
   E. Who

II. YOUR NEXT STEP
   A. Progress upward
      1. Watch for delusion
      2. Keep control
   B. More studies
      1. Keep your goals
      2. Don't go astray
   C. Conversion of others
      1. They must ask
      2. Do not force a change
      3. Your responsibility

**********WORK FOR A LIFETIME**********

You know what to do. The more you use Spirit the better you will become.

Dark Circle.' Most of the material we are going to cover tonight we have talked about before. We simply talked about it in different places along the way so it should not be new to you. Your guidelines, certainly by now you are very aware of, "I am never alone." This particular one is a Psalm from the Old Testament which is referring to being someplace where there is the absence of God, which, of course, cannot be done. Also by now, you are fully aware that you have many guides, teachers, and loved ones on the spirit side who are around you all the time. So for you to be absolutely alone, if you consider the spirit side as a form of companionship, is literally impossible. Even though we can sometimes emotionally or physically be alone, there are certainly a great number of entities interested in you as individuals who are standing there to keep you from danger.

A 'dark circle.' First of all, what is it? It is a room that is blacked out, a room in which there is no light. We have two of them in the building right now and we will shortly have two others. We will break this whole group down into small circles and you will be having circles of different kinds: candle circles, dark circles, psychometric circles, and so forth. We will start using and practicing what we have been talking about. Practice your mind control in these classes.

The dark circle, of course, is simply there. Okay, why a circle? Here again is one of these things. There seems to be something mystical about people sitting around in a circle. There is a certain harmony, a certain flow of energy that can be sent moving around a circle of people and it will be felt by all of you, especially as your sensitivity increases. You will not only feel the energy itself, but you will know where it is coming from. You will spot those people who are not necessarily the same vibration as you in the circle. It is just one of those things.

One of the things I want you to remember when you have dark circles is to try to always seat yourself in the same place. In other words, if we were to assign you chairs from the leader of the circle all the way around the circle, try to stay in about the same geographical position in relation to the head of the circle. It is just a convenient way of keeping track of where you are and also it builds harmony within the circle. The first night you have a dark circle, the head of the circle may shift you around. So if you are sitting next to your husband, wife, lover, boyfriend, and you are asked to move, please don't take it as an affront. It is simply what the medium often calls balancing the circle. Many mediums refuse to hold circles unless they are alternately man, woman, man, woman. I have only noticed this once. I think the one that I spot the fastest is where we will have very, very competent people. We will have four or five mediums seated on one side of the circle and students on the other side. That will really make the whole room feel out of balance. So if you are asked to move around, know that it is not some hocus pocus or mumbo jumbo, there is a valid reason for it.

Valid reason number one is harmony. If you are going to work together, you are going to work together to enjoy what Spirit can give you in a dark circle. It must be done with that in mind and with that as the first stepping stone. This kind of harmony can only be brought about by you.

First of all, get yourself calmed down and feeling at ease with those seated beside you and finally, with those in the entire circle. It is one of these things we can talk about but you really won't sense it until you do it. Then, after the first few times, you will kind of get the feeling of it. As you get in a circle, you will sit down, relax, and feel it. Go around the circle and everything will get peaceful, beautiful.

Another reason why you use a circle is for control. It is very awkward to talk about this because this is where we always get into the discussion of bad spirits or evil spirits. Of course, there is no incarnate devil; there is no incarnate evil. It is only a product of your own mind. We do have entities on the other side that are no farther along than we are here. I mean, just because they have crossed over and are standing on the spirit side does not make them a saint; it does not make them a super kind of person unless they have an awful lot of training behind them.

The kind of control I am talking about here is the kind that will generally be exercised by the head of the circle. He or she, with the aid of their high teachers or protectors, simply put a wall around that circle on the outside of it. You can feel this wall. One of the intriguing things you will sense in a dark circle when you first sit down is you will be aware of the four walls; you will be aware of where they are. Then somewhere along in the circle you will suddenly be aware that you don't know where the walls are. Pretty soon, you will swear the wall is standing right behind you. This is the kind of circle protection that they will put up. They do this for control so that undesirable, not evil, but undesirable entities will not enter the circle; there are an awful lot of them.

Okay, what do I mean by undesirable entities? I have just said there are no evil ones. Well, I think probably the most obvious one is an entity who wants to, literally, hog the whole show. An entity has suddenly come into your vibration and realizes you can hear him or see him. They will chatter like magpies until you shut them up. You will spot them sometimes at Sunday service when someone is giving messages from the pulpit. I catch myself, of course, doing some of the techniques that Rev. Bradley taught us; namely, snapping fingers to dismiss an entity. If you come into someone's vibration and here comes Uncle Harry, and he has had about thirty drinks and he is so happy that you can hear him talk. Well, the moment you acknowledge that you can hear, here he is crawling all over your shoulder chattering like mad. Generally, not with a great deal to say other than he loves you; but he won't let go. I mean here is someone who can hear him so, oh man, away he goes. You literally have to break the connection. As I say, one of the techniques is snapping your fingers and simply telling him to leave you alone. He, of course, will have to obey you if you say it and mean it. Notice I said, "mean it." I think we touched on that once before. Maybe I should remind you again. All spiritual entities will obey your positive command if it is a POSITIVE command. If an entity is doing something around you that is a little tense and a little upsetting, and you say, "Oh, I wish you would go away," but your mind is saying, "I bet he won't," guess what's going to be obeyed? When you dismiss an entity, dismiss him positively. Snap your fingers. "Leave me alone! Step back!" They will have to obey. It is as simple as that.

The other kind of control you can get here is one of a sense of presence. The closer a circle can work together, the better. Of course, it is just an extension of harmony. But you will suddenly find little, bitty differences in vibrations, in sensitivity, that you might not have noticed before and that is the time to bring them out.

By all means, be sure you communicate! Don't sit in on a dark circle like a bump on a log and watch things happen or feel things. Give out what you are feeling. The head of the circle will tell you if they can see the same thing and if they agree or disagree. After all, that is the way you are going to learn. Are you seeing this psychically or is your mind playing tricks? Okay, here is something you have simply got to learn. You can only do it by contributing.

The other reason to communicate out loud is that when you give out what you have received, the entity that gave you the information knows that it has succeeded. This is extremely important. It sounds redundant, I know. You would think that a teacher of any caliber would know when you receive what they wanted to give you. This is not true because of our faulty thought processes.

A good example happened way over two years ago. One of our ladies in class has Chief Pontiac as one of her major teachers. One night in a circle, he brought her a small brown rabbit and set it right in her lap. I saw him do it. She didn't say anything. So I thought, "I hope she remembers what I have told her." She waited until someone had finished talking and she said, "Rev. Larr, I have a rabbit in my lap and I think Chief Pontiac gave it to me." I said, "Yes, he did." This did two important things. It justified to her mind what she perceived and it let Pontiac know that he had succeeded. That is extremely important because then he took the rabbit away and gave her a bird; we spent the better part of the circle looking at all kinds of animals that Pontiac brought her. They do this on all levels. If someone comes to you in a circle, walks up to me and says, "Gene, tell Nancy so and so. Gene, tell Larry so and so. Tell Greg so and so," I will do it. Try not to interrupt someone else speaking, but remember what it is and give it out so they know they have a channel open. Otherwise, not only will you not know, they might not know. They work awfully, awfully hard so give them that courtesy.

The other kind of control relates directly to what we will talk about next. First of all, let's get rid of 'Why Darkness." I would assume no one here is afraid of darkness. We have had some fun with a couple of people who are petrified of the dark. The first time, there was a gentleman who was quite upset with the dark. He had just gotten over his phobia and was seated in circle without bursting with perspiration from head to foot. His teacher, twenty seconds after I blew out the candle, walked over to him, put his hand on his shoulder, and said, "Thank you!" and scared the hell out of him. I was so proud of him because he didn't immediately jump up and scream. Well, it took us another several weeks to get him back into circle. So don't be upset by these things. The poor teacher, of course, did not mean to upset, and there was nothing to be afraid of in the dark, anyway.

'Why darkness?' Well, the most important thing is the etheric form and the use of ectoplasm. Etheric forms that can be seen with the physical eyes can only be manifested in the dark. Now, many times you will see etheric manifestations in semi-dark, or even in daylight, but in almost all cases those will be objects you perceive with your psychic sight, not with your physical eyes. To see something with your physical eyes is why we use darkness. Now, yes, there are some high teachers, individual entities called archangels that can and have in the historic past appeared in broad daylight, in full sight, where everybody can see them, psychic or not, to carry out some of the miracles; but those are extremely small. Number wise, they would be almost vanishingly small. That is why I said, "essentially never." There are such events but they are extremely rare.

Why the darkness itself? Well, the main thing is to remember when we talked about energy levels. Light is a stream of particles moving in a wave vibration and they will tear. Ectoplasm especially, or an image made of ectoplasm, will be torn apart by light just as wind will tear a cloud apart. I am sure you have all seen little radiometers in jewelry store windows. It sits in the Sun and the little wheel will turn around as long as light is falling on it. This is because light has a pressure. Another beautiful place you see it is in the tail of a comet. Some of you, maybe, have seen big comets. They are a beautiful thing to see. Let us assume for the moment that this is the sun. Light, of course, is coming away from it in all directions. Here is a comet out here somewhere. It is coming toward the sun and its tail is going away from it. The comet is going to go around the sun and out the other side. But its tail, which looks so beautiful and so magnificent, happens because the light is pushing it away from the comet, not because the comet is moving. It is the light pushing the tail away and tearing it up into dust so that as the comet comes down around the sun, its tail is away from the sun. Finally, as it starts leaving, it will be chasing its tail into space because the light is pushing its tail away faster than it is moving. That same light pressure will tear apart the kinds of things we want our entities to build. I would remind you that ectoplasm is generally always taken from the medium in charge of the circle, and in at least the majority of cases, that medium will be in deep trance. It can, however, be taken from the circle at large and that is an awful lot of fun. I think I described this thing by looking down and seeing a little blue-gray cloud sitting in your lap and then you notice it goes clear around the circle because they are using this energy from all of us.

You will normally never feel this flow of energy. When a medium is in deep trance and a lot of ectoplasm is being used, it is dangerous to touch that medium because you will snap them out of trance. So don't do that. Regardless of what happens in a dark circle, never turn on a light because this will simply undo what the entities are trying to do. If you have a medium who happens to be in deep trance, it can be a real physical shock to them; so don't do that. Remember what we talked about. Don't touch these forms unless the entity that is making them asks you to.

The ectoplasm itself will not hurt you at all. It will not tire you or wear you out. To me, I think it is almost always kind of a soft blue-gray color, just like a little patch of fog. Then Spirit can embellish it. They can change its color, they can make it sparkle, they can make parts of it black, whatever they want to do with it. Look upon ectoplasm as kind of an etheric modeling clay. They can make it into any shape they want simply by the will of the mind. This allows them to do very many spectacular things.

These are things we aim for in dark circles. I will tell you right now, this will not happen in your first, second, or probably even third dark circle because we have got to get those other things there first: the harmony, the feeling of ease, this kind of thing. But after that, the sky's the limit.

Let's talk about red light. First of all, I think it's one of those things that I would ask all of you to be careful of. If you are invited to a séance where a red light is used, be first of all skeptical because it generally is used to bolster your confidence in what is going on. To me, it displays a lack of confidence in the medium that is the head of the circle. Any medium who is working in a dark circle can see in the dark as well as I can now. So certainly the red light is indicative. And the other point is the red light that is used is a very deep red light, far into the spectrum, and your eyes do not work well at that wavelength. So even though you can see across the circle and see the shape of the person seated there, you think that is going to make it all above board, but not true. The eye does not discriminate that well so there can be all kinds of things going on that your eye might not see.

I know of two fine mediums, magnificent workers who work with red light all the time because this is simply the way they were taught. They are the only two genuine mediums I have ever met who worked in red light. So watch that. It is supposed to give you a sense of security that you can tell what is going on, you can feel what is going on, but your eyes just don't work well in it.

It is absolutely contrary to what we were just talking about, the effects of light tearing something apart. A photon that is moving the tail of a comet does not give a darn if it is red or blue; it is still light. All of my teachers insist that those who work in red light force their guides and teachers to work an awful lot harder to overcome the pressure of that red light. You will never see a red light circle held here at the Chapel because of that reason. If we acknowledge that our high teachers and guides are working with us to the best of their abilities, it is up to us to take every step possible to make that work as easy as possible.

Okay, Dark Circle: 'Time' and 'Who.' First of all, the time is about one hour. There is a reason why we limit time. When you are in a dark circle and something is going on, even if it is just simply good vibes and good messages being given back and forth, assuming no materializations or anything like that occur, the time will go by so quickly that the first few times, you will be certain you haven't been in there thirty minutes. And if something really exciting is going on, like one night Nancy was heading the circle and the entities wanted us to dump energy into the middle of the circle. So here we are sitting there concentrating and getting still and dumping energy into the middle of the table. Suddenly, I etherically knew the table was moving but didn't know what it was doing, making real funny sounds. It rose high. Nancy reached out and touched the table (and the table is no light thing), but they had the silly thing rocking around and up. And then they started rotating it, and I think my tape recorder was on the floor and someone else's was on the floor and it just pushed them aside as if, you know, you reached over with your foot and kicked it. The table made about four rotations, I guess, and then sat back down on the ground.

So here is one of these times where they were simply using the energy that we were dumping to get us used to some things that are going to be coming up. But it seemed like a matter of seconds and our fifteen or twenty minutes were gone. It is incredible how time will vanish when something exciting is going on. The reverse is also true. If you have a dark circle with a bunch of people who sit around like bumps on a log and stare at each other like toads and frogs, the hour is going to seem like six. So don't do that. You get around this by it communicating back and forth. Anyway, as I say, we generally set our circles at about one hour.

Teachers sometimes go over time because you get so involved in what's going on. One of the longest dark circles I have ever attended was just a little under four hours. The only reason we had any way of knowing that much time had gone by is because we were recording on a tape of 1500 foot Mylar, which is three hours and forty-five minutes, and we heard the end of the tape slapping. I knew an hour had gone by; I was sure of that. I had been working in trance with a number of other people and I felt that an hour had gone by. But after I came back from my last little sojourn in trance, I started hearing a click and I thought, "What the devil is that?" Bob said it was the tape recorder and it has been doing that for about fifteen minutes. We turned on the lights and sure enough, we had been there four hours and we had absolutely no idea how much time had gone by. So watch that.

There are many different mediums lecturing and talking, but I want you to approach circles with caution. I would rather you get a few little building blocks on the ground first because there are some things that do go on which aren't genuine, but if you aren't aware of what's going on, it can really throw you off on a tangent.

I think a beautiful example of this is Rosita. She has a number of high teachers that work through her in trance, some very beautiful ones, and most of them are very soft spoken. So when she goes into trance, everybody's ears kind of automatically come up this way to hear what she is going to say. Well, one night everyone's ears came up this way, and one of her Indian chiefs came through laughing and yelling and said "Hello" and darned near knocked everybody off their chairs. Here we are straining to hear. Her first words are usually, "Good evening," or something like that and Bang! The walls shook!

If you didn't know Rosita and didn't know what was going on, you would think she had flipped her wig. Certainly something happened. She had another entity there we were not familiar with talking that way. He turned out to be a delightful individual and has spoken through her now a number of times. And he is just perfectly beautiful.

Don't be so fast to sit in every circle you find because some of them are beautiful, of course; some of them will be magnificent. But many of them will not. So I would want you to be a little careful as you go along.

Walk slowly. Be sure to take one step at a time. And after we have had a few circles, please don't start having circles at home until you know what you are doing because you can also get into trouble. The trouble is the one you have heard me talk about for thirteen weeks: self-delusion. There is nothing sadder than self-delusion. So don't have dark circles until you know what is going on and you know your guides and teachers and how to handle them. Then go ahead. If you want to get together and do psychometry with each other or something of this nature, please restrict it to the class. Don't go out of your way. Certainly don't drag someone in off the street and say, "Hey, I'll tell you your fortune," because your fortune is liable to be the county jail. Until you have that little piece of paper that says reverend, ordained minister, or something like that on it, you can get into a lot of trouble real fast. So don't pull them in off the street.

'Your Next Steps.' You will notice on your guideline, "There is no way but up." Of course, you have heard me talk about it a long, long, time. I would suggest that before you really dive into the circles, you go back over your outlines, go back over your notes, and make yourself familiar with what we have gone through. I think you will be really quite stunned at how much material we have covered. For instance, take healing. You will spend a lot of time on this because you will have separate classes for healing.

Healing is one of these particular so-called gifts that you have got to do. You have to actively, actively work at it in order to pin down some of the beautiful things that are available. Go back over your outline. Go back over your notes, the things I have been chattering about. Certainly look at the various times you have had work for the week. These are key. By now, of course, you all absolutely have control of your stillness and know exactly how to meditate and so on and so forth.

Well, one of the things we will be doing in circle is that we are going to make you sit there for five or ten minutes and be absolutely still. You will be seated in circle with a competent teacher. Most of them will be ordained ministers here at the Chapel. They will know if you are not still. When I was at the lamasery in Hawaii, our little priest would bonk us on the head with a stick if he found us thinking instead of being still. I think I have still got some bumps; but, nevertheless, I have harped about this now for fourteen weeks. You have got to do it in order to make it work.

You are going to progress upward. You are going to get better and progress regardless of what you do. I think that some of the things we talked about here you will be able to do a little faster in the future. And maybe you will enjoy it a little more. You have chosen this path or you wouldn't be here either in incarnate form or sitting here in this hall.

The most important thing you can do as you advance and start exercising your psychic ability is to watch for delusion. This is without a doubt the biggest difficulty of any of this kind of study. Be absolutely certain you know what you are receiving. Make absolutely sure by verification with one of the teachers here at the Chapel that you are on the right track until you have established communication with your high teachers beyond all question of doubt. It is one of these funny things. Delusion can creep in so very, very easy. You might be working around the house and hear something go, "knock, knock," and you think that might have been Uncle Henry. Ten or fifteen minutes later,"

"You know, I'll bet that was Uncle Henry." Then your husband or wife will come home. "Uncle Henry knocked on the wall!" In reality, it was a woodpecker outside.

Make sure you know. If it takes you ten times as long as anybody else in this room to develop your psychic gifts by being extra careful of delusion, the time will be worthwhile. I can tell you many examples; you know I have taught hundreds of people. I can show you many that went off on funny little tangents. But I think there are two major ones that upset me the most.

A high teacher will come in to someone who is just opening up and they will unfortunately choose a set of words like, "Behold and understand." Okay, that is a perfectly valid statement. Tao Sing has used it with me. Sir has used it with me. Virtually all of your high teachers will use it. But to someone who is just breaking away from Christianity or one of those other religions, the words mean, "God Himself is talking to me and me alone. That is delusion. Unfortunately, it can get out of hand because pretty soon you find these kinds of people standing on a soap box on the corner teaching the world because they are a direct channel to God. Well, they are not. It is delusion, as you know. Each one of them is God. There is no "A" God. So watch for these kinds of things. They are so, so very easy to get trapped in.

Probably one of the healthiest attitudes that you can use as you are exploring these kinds of techniques is question, doubt, question, doubt. Every night that we have classes, we will have the first 40 minutes or so as question and answer. So please jot down your questions so that we can get them out of the way and get them answered. If they sound dumb, I don't care. Please ask them.

If they sound so dumb you are afraid to ask them, ask them anyway. Someone else probably has the same dumb question and they are afraid to ask it, too. So someone gets enough guts and ask it. And believe me, those things that occur in your ordinary, everyday life are exactly what I am talking about. Don't ask me what the diameter of Omega Centauri is. I can tell you, but that is all. But if you are bothered by something in your own everyday life: "Will my teacher help me find a job? I have three opportunities. Which one should I do?" Okay, that is a good question. If you ask your teacher, you are going to find out something very rude and very shocking. He will not tell you; He will point out all the variations that could be there in those three jobs. Then he will say, "You choose." They are very good at that.

I fight with Tao Sing all the time. With as many people as we have in the classes, can't you see how simple it would be for me to put a piece of paper out with all the names on it, for instance, and say, "Okay, Tao Sing, who should go in which group?" Sitting here, pencil in hand, expecting an answer and never an answer comes. And so I say, "Well, what do you think of this list, Tao Sing?" "Isn't that interesting?" Unfortunately, one of the games that I have chosen to play this time is the role I have been playing for you, a teacher. He will not tell me what to teach. He will expose many, many things to me, like he did for all of you the other night when he used his opening statement here when you were asking questions.

He is a brilliant man, and if you listen carefully to the way he answers certain kinds of questions, you can tell that he is not really answering that question. But he is making you think about it so that you will answer the question.

So as you go along with this kind of thing, keep control. I mean, do you realize what I can do? I have a fair amount of ability, okay? I can go home. Let's say I have been down here at the office. I can go home and sit down in a chair, kick off my shoes, and relax and get in a receptive mood and Tao Sing will pop in and I will say "Tao Sing, what have you been doing today?" Chatter! Chatter! Chatter! Chatter! Chatter! Chatter! Five or six hours later I am so sleepy that I have decided to go to bed. The next morning when I wake up, of course, you always have a little silence period. So, before you are up and stirring around and get all your problems stirred up in your mind, have a little silent period. But when I wake up and do that, of course, I will open my eyes and Tao Sing will be standing at the foot of the bed. So I say, "Tao Sing, what do you think we should do today?" Chompety! Chompety! Chompety! Chompety! And suddenly it will be noon. The one thing I want you to really remember is the thing that we talked about so much.

EXCESS IN ANYTHING IS WRONG! It is stopping you from living. There is a beautiful little poem, "This day when gone, will never come again." If you don't pay attention to days and use them wisely, you will find time slipping through your fingers like sand and you wonder what on Earth has happened. So keep control. Certainly, use your guides and teachers with every end. That's what they are there for. You will find very quickly, as I did some 25 years ago when I was about in some of your shoes, that there are certain questions that they will not answer. There are certain things they will not help you with. But it is up to you.

Rev. Bradley had a little statement she loved to use all the time. "It is said that the truth will set you free. If it will not work in your everyday life, be it truth or lie, it will not set you free." That is where you have got to espouse everything we have been talking about the last 14 weeks. What can you do with it? If you can't do anything with it, if it does not make you feel a little happier or a little more secure or give you a little more latitude to enjoy life, then chalk the last 14 weeks up to fun and games and do something else because it's got to mean something to you first. Otherwise, stop playing games.

I have told you that when you start your Wednesday circles you will have plenty to keep you going; I can assure you of that. I have got a number of advanced students here in the room that can say that I have kept them busy. The thing I am referring to here is that there is certain kinds of people that love to go to every psychic development class that is open anywhere. And they got into trouble. They get into trouble for a couple of very simple reasons. If you are really paying attention to what you have been studying here, you don't have time to go get someone else's ideas. I would never presuppose to be the finest in the field of psychic studies. I know the techniques used here at the Chapel work. We have got seven or nearly all seven, ordained ministers seated out there tonight that prove they work. So what can you do? The first thing you will bump into if you go to someone else's class. Let's assume you will go to, say, one of the churches in San Diego who are members of the National

Spiritualist's Organization. You will find they don't believe in reincarnation. I don't understand how they possibly cannot, but it's their privilege not to. If you are seated in a group like that, or attending a lecture of someone like that, don't challenge them. Don't challenge the teacher on the point of reincarnation. It does nothing but make you look like a fool. Remember another one of the little important quotations that most people don't know. "When in Rome, do as the Romans do. Or leave Rome." Very, very seldom do you hear the rest of that quotation; "Or leave Rome."

If you are fascinated by another teacher or a church organization or whatever, go. Go to some. My God, that is the least you can do. If it feels uncomfortable, don't try to convert him. Step back. Leave Rome.

Keep your goals. You have all set a lot of goals, I am sure. Some of you have set, in my estimation, relatively simple goals, meaning clairvoyance and clairaudience. Those will do simply by practice and by exposure to the techniques you will be using here. There are, of course, some important higher goals and after you reach those few levels you will find that there are many, many of those steps to take. But keep those goals there. Aim at them. They are important. You didn't put them there by accident. Very seldom, in fact, in your life do you plan anything by accident. Chance has not that much leeway. But keep at them.

Start your studies with a simple premise that you are going to learn how to do everything that we have talked about so far. Now some of you are avid readers, I am sure, as I used to be. I don't think I have read a book on psychic development from cover to cover for quite some time because you can simply end up filling your head with ideas, filling your head with techniques, which, if you don't put into practice, is so much trash. You might as well use them for heating the fireplace in the winter because they are not doing you any good. But if you will take one of those books, I don't care if it's our teachings here or some other book, but if you will take it and study it and do it, and then you are going to encounter something. But if you read it, put it on the bookshelf, and tell your friends "Yes, I have read so and so," and never use it, it won't do a thing for you. It sounds awfully narrow, doesn't it?

But it's true. Of course you can go back. If you want to go to the Judeo-Christian era when Christ was born he said the same thing. "Believe the things that I say and do the things that I do. These things ye shall do and even greater."

Stop and think a second. Here's a man that most of the Christian world accepts as the incarnate form of God. Here stands a young God saying you can do things greater than the things he did. If you want a good project, pullout your New Testaments and find out what he didn't do. I mean, it's a good study. Rev. Bradley made us do it. Like I said before, you all should be so darned thankful that she's not sitting here. Oh, the hours that I went over ancient Hebrew and Greek manuscripts. It was enough to kill me, but I guess they taught me something.

Okay, keep those goals. They are important. They are things to aim at. Don't go astray. It can be all kinds of fun and games. We will go into these two in just a second. There is a real fun way to go astray. The idea is to make use of what you have got.

You know, you are really quite spectacular creatures. Like I have said before many, many times, "You are the only one of you in the universe." Stop and think for a second. There is only one of you in the universe. That means you are worth something. We will use that as a way of control.

Among some of your goals (which I skipped over), of course, you know here at the chapel we can ordain ministers and healers, give you teaching credentials, and things of that nature. But I won't stand up here and beat our drum. I could say, "Hey, all of you are going to become ministers." But I really don't care if you do or not. I don't care if a single one of you gets your minister papers because my likes don't matter. If you feel that you are going to be a minister, then that's something else. Then I will help you. So remember what your goals are and go after them.

Okay, that inner knowing. We have talked about that before. You know what's right and wrong. I loved the way Tao Sing closed your talk the other night (I listened to the tape back in the office) "For some mysterious reason, you all know right from wrong. Why do you so often choose wrongly?" As you get to know Tao Sing a little better, especially in dark circles where he is speaking through me, you will be able to spot in the tone of his voice. A kind of pleading that he feels when he wishes for something very much. Just like he did here when someone asked him what was our major goal.

He said, "All you have to do is reach perfection." Here is the understatement of the century! But you know that's right, in fact.

You all have teachers and guides. Some of you know them already. Some of you will know them much better as you get into circle where you actually will be working in communication with them. I cannot even begin to share with you the thrill of having a high teacher step in and make their self be known and work freely with you. It is an experience that simply cannot be described.

Please don't be caught up with one of the things so many students do. I have got so many telephone calls, not so many now that the office is open because I just don't accept calls unless it's an emergency. Anyway, they will call and they will come to class and say, "I don't know what I did. I haven't seen my teacher for 2 weeks. I made him mad and he left." NO WAY! First of all, you are not going to make him mad. You can make him cry. In all honesty, I have to tell you that I have done that with Tao Sing. You will never make him mad. He will never step away from you for that kind of reason. The only reason he will ever leave you is when his work with you is done. Tao Sing will be with me until the day I cross over because of the arrangements we set up. All through your studies and your advancement, as you become more and more advanced at using your gifts, you will find high teachers stepping in for a specific purpose: to open your clairaudience, to open your clairvoyance; well, to help. You must do it; they can't, but they can help. And when that phase is finished, they will step away. So remember, you can't chase them away. I mean, just stop and think of the absurdity for a second.

At 9 years old, I was aware of the first teacher around me, a Jesuit priest that I lovingly called Padre. That man stuck through me through some of the most difficult things you can imagine. And probably one of the most difficult for him to swallow, being, of course, a Jesuit priest, was when I was a Mahayana Buddhist for 8 years. He never once stepped away from my side. Can you imagine what would happen if a group of Mahayana priests walked into a Catholic Church downtown? You cannot offend your teacher; believe me, you cannot. They are with you all the time and they will follow into every place in which they are allowed to follow you. They will not step across certain lines, but they will help you any way they can.

Okay, study groups. Certainly during this interim break I would recommend that you get together and chew the fat, compare notes, etc., etc. After we start forming circles, I would suggest that you have little circles at home, especially for psychometry. Remember what I said last time about forming dark circles. Don't do that until you know what you are doing. Study groups are very good because they allow you to share things on a very personal level which we cannot do right here with me sitting here and you sitting out there.

When we break into little circles, then you can. But individuals help each other. You can do it all yourself. That's why I became a Mahiani Buddhist because it was totally self-centered, self-imposed development. But it's a lot more fun to work with others. I think you will enjoy it.

Remember also the warnings I gave you last time. Please don't run around seeking converts. First of all, it's against the basic concept of the Chapel and the very things we teach. I think one of the most intriguing questions that has come up to me when giving private consultations more and more, is when a husband will come to me who believes in this philosophy but his wife does not. The first question that will pop out of his mouth is "Can you tell me some way to make her believe it?" And the reverse is true. She will say the same thing about the husband.

I have got one lovely lady who has been searching for old incantations to make her husband love her. Well, if she spent less time in old, musty libraries and more time at home, there would be no problem. Many times the solutions to your problems are right in front of you and you either don't see them because you will not see them or you don't see them because it hurts. Your guides and teachers will help work them out. But do not try to convert others. They must ask; and if they ask, then you are trapped.

If someone comes up to you and says, "I understand you have been taking such and such psychic awareness class," and starts asking you questions, make awfully sure you answer them. This will build the energy around your band. You will have teachers flocking to your side to help you answer questions and it is a beautiful, beautiful way of working.

Don't force a change. As I say, don't go out on the street corner and grab someone. It won't work. The Christians and their missionary activities tried that and almost every culture they touched was destroyed. You cannot force a change in thought. You must want it. That is why you are here. You will notice that 15 weeks ago, when this class started, there were no great big ads in the newspaper or great big bulletin boards in supermarkets.

You can't force a change so don't try to. You would not expect someone to try to make you change your viewpoint. Please don't try to make them change theirs. If they fight and get all upset, bless them and step away. Fighting never accomplished anything. I have a constant problem with some of the people who come door to door trying to convert us sinners. I really blew their mind in Pasadena one afternoon. I invited them in, with my Buddha and incense going, and asked them to sit down and meditate with me. That was the last time they came to my door. But nevertheless, don't do it. It doesn't work.

I want to get extremely serious for a second. I have touched this many, many times but I want to really stress this hard. The responsibility that you are going to have when you have accomplished easy use of these abilities, let us just say clairvoyance and clairaudience, you can find out things that they do not know about themselves because their mind has blocked them psychologically. That has got to be the most sacred trust you have ever held in the palm of your hand.

Remember what you are doing. You are not only reaching into their mind and memory, you may well be talking to one of their spirit guides or teachers who have been with them from the day they were born or before. Information you gain that way is fantastic. You will get a lot of exercise doing that. Incidentally, let me bring that point up. When we start sitting in little groups in psychometry circles and you are reading for each other, and someone says, "Hell, I think you are going to get a divorce," If it feels like "Hey, I think I will get a divorce anyway" say so. If it feels like something you don't want, throw it out. Learn to sort out what you are going to let affect you in your daily life. All the teachers who are working in circle will try to follow along to see what images you're getting, to see what instructions you're getting. Make sure what you are saying is valid as far as possible. But don't take these to the point of going out and killing yourself because someone says, "Two days from now you are going to be in real trouble." The entity who was talking might be so pious that spilling your coffee in the morning was real trouble. So stop and think about what's going on.

I don't want any of you comparing notes about what you found out about him or her. I made a note here about a quotation I thought was so great. "The most difficult thing about business is minding your own." Let that one soak in. It's so easy. I have heard fine accomplished mediums carry tales back and forth about people that they have read. As I say, it was just disgusting.

We have a staff of readers here who will give you private consultations if you call the office and I can assure you that anything you discuss with them will stay with them. They won't even tell me about it. But if they have a problem that they might think I can possibly enlighten them on, they might ask me a question. But I will never know who they are talking about. Even though I could psychically find out, I wouldn't because that is none of my business. So as you go along, remember what that responsibility is. It is a higher degree than any lawyer, any psychiatrist, or any doctor. Because, we talked on that subject many times before, you cannot lie to a competent medium. They might not know what the truth is, but they will know that you are lying. It will be all over your aura. So as you go along, don't let that make you afraid of them because we are all guilty of little "sins." After all, you probably learned something from every one of them.

Your responsibility is as far as you want to go. If you want to become a minister, we will lean over backwards to make you what we think are the finest psychic ministers in the United States, even in the world. It is not easy. I will tell you right now, we have some people who have studied for a long time and are paperless. We have some people who have studied relatively short times and are now ministers because it depends on ability.

Remember a long time back I warned you to not judge your development by the person you are seated by? When we start working in circles, please remember that. Especially you couples: men and wives, brothers and sisters, or whatever. Oh, that can start some beautiful family fights. It usually boils down to "He is going faster than I am," or "She saw that and I didn't." Don't do that. You are the only one that can handle it. As you go along, as I say, we will help you in every way we can. I think you will find the circles extremely helpful.

Advanced Lecture Series 1

Requirements and Trumpets

I. REQUIREMENTS
   A. Five minutes, morning and evening, of silence (meditation). This is not to be used for communication; this is stillness.
   B. Nine concepts or thoughts (affirmations).
      1. I am well.
      2. I am prosperous.
      3. I am greatly loved.
      4. I produce right meditation.
      5. I surround myself with a circle of right thought.
      6. I surround myself with a circle of right action.
      7. I am bathed in the light of perfection.
      8. I can reach the highest goals.
      9. I am needed in some work for which I am suited.
   C. Know and practice the "three R's."
   D. Be sure that you answer a knock.
   E. Never force your beliefs or thoughts on anyone.
   F. Remember: It is better to have never known, than to know and use it wrongly.
   G. Watch how you give a message. Do not give out all things to all people.

II. TRUMPETS
   A. Practice
      1. Your trumpet, your vibration.
      2. Talk to your spirit teacher, not to your trumpet.
   B. Trumpet Circles
      1. Aports, teleports, and fakes.
      2. Don't grasp the trumpet.

I want you to really remember some of the things that you have been asked and told that you should do. Let's really think about it. Ten minutes morning and night, because these are so important. If you miss it in the morning, don't try to do twenty minutes in the night. That's not the way to do it. Try to make it a habit, try to get into a habit. In those ten minutes, of course, I'm talking about that first five minutes when you would get comfortable, play with your spot, play with your flower, anything that helps calm you down, and end up with those last minutes striving for total stillness.

I want to pass on to you nine so-called concepts or nine thoughts to think about. These were given to me by Reverend Bradley, oh good grief–twenty-five years ago now, and they are just as true and right now as they were then. So jot them down and give some thought about them. They fall into that category of things that we express in extremely positive ways as being affirmations. All of these would fall into that category.

1. I am well. If you've got a headache, pretend you're well anyway. Someone in here sure has–hmm.
2. I am prosperous. We're all prosperous. (All the little subliminal snickerings are interesting.)
3. I am greatly loved.
4. (This is what you are supposed to be doing.) I produce right meditation.
5. I surround myself with a circle of right thought.
6. I surround myself with a circle of right action.
7. I am bathed in the light of perfection.
8. I can reach the highest goals.
9. A little longer one, I am needed in some work for which I am suited. Reverend Bradley changed that slightly when she gave it to us. The original is, "I am needed in some work for which *only* I am suited." She took the *only* out of it and just left it as first person singular, this way.

I usually recommend that you write these out and hang them by a bathroom mirror or somewhere like that so you can glance at them. You're not going to be quizzed on them or anything like that, but just put them there as a thought for the day. Take each one of them and use them as thoughts for the day. We haven't been giving you guidelines each week like you had during the actual lectures.

There are a couple of other things that I'll want you to remember–of course the three R's, which are covered here in Lectures VII, XI, and II. Be familiar with them; use them. They are the goals that will help you reach what you want to reach. We want to talk a little bit on some stuff that is going to be happening around you now that you are working in circles, now that you are learning to use psychometry and/or to give readings. Be sure someone asks you first before you butt in, and I mean that literally. It is sometimes very difficult to do, even for fine trained psychics, because many times we will see a situation where we can see the obvious answer. We can see someone is about to do something–to our eyes, stupid–and we can simply see with the help of their teachers or our teachers, how they can avoid it. If they do not ask, you be still. And this gets back again to one of the teachings of Jesu, "Knock and the door shall be opened." Same thing. Don't interfere. Leave it alone.

All of you have friends by now, who are extremely curious about what you are doing, if you haven't already told them everything. But never try to force someone into your way of belief, into your way of thinking. I have a number of people out of every class who come to me and ask me, "How can I make my husband or my wife believe what you're teaching us?" Well, you can't *make* anybody do it at all. If you try, you'll do nothing but make an enormous enemy. So don't do it. If they get curious–your friends, loved ones, or whatever–and ask you questions, answer them to the best of your ability and try to be open with them. But as I say, do not force them to change because they have as much right to… I've got a little man standing here beside me. I don't know what faith he is, but he's really chattering up a storm. He says, "Everybody's got just as much right to be as stupid as they are." Yes, I guess that's one way you could put it. Make sure on that point; don't do anything unless you are asked. Don't force your feelings, your thoughts or concepts, on anyone else. But if someone does ask, you must answer. Again, remember that. If someone comes to you and says, "Hey, what is so and so?" and if you know, tell them. If they've asked, you owe them as truthful an answer as you can give, as truthful an answer as you can give.

Then there's one little thing that we've talked about a long, long time ago, and I want to state it now, because as you start getting into some of this advanced work, especially Lecture II and III, we're going to be touching on some very important precepts and some very important powers. I don't like that word "powers," but that's exactly what it is. There's a little quotation that appears in Buddhist writings, Christian writings, Hindu writings, and Islamic work–all through almost all the so-called sacred writings–that it is better to have never known than to have known and used it wrongly. That is more closely quoted from the New Testament. It is interesting, how it appears all through all the philosophies. It is an incredible thing. As we get into some of these other techniques that you will be exploring in some of the next rounds of circles, you will see that there are ways that you can influence and can bring things about. But also, I want you to remember back to Lecture II, Spiritual Law, Right and Wrong. There are some high consequences to be paid for breaking some of those laws. Go back to your notes and think about what we talked about that night. It is extremely important and you can really cause yourself many problems by not being very, very careful.

Giving of messages is something that very few of you have done in circles yet, have you? Well, not extensively. We'll be getting into that more and more, especially after the next break, because it is one of those things that sharpens your psychic ability and it does so for a very good reason. Just as in the psychometry you've had and the psychometry you will have after tonight, you'll be able to have instant feedback, "Was I right or wrong?" A lot of people don't like that, and I'm really sorry that they don't. These are interesting displays of a particular ability, but you'd be surprised how many people don't want to be put in that position. For instance, behind me here are a bunch of envelopes that we used to use with numbers on them. You put things in them and pass them around the room. To me, this was always exciting and it was always something that I liked to do. It was something that Reverend Bradley made us do every single week, every time we came in. There were ten, eleven in her advanced class, and we'd walk in and there were eleven envelopes. The first thing we did was to play with those eleven envelopes and write down what each of those objects was. After while, you get pretty good at it. You get to where you can tell the difference. But you'd be surprised, if you go visit a medium downtown, or a medium someplace else, and hand them a sealed envelope and say to them, "Tell me what's in it." You'd be surprised at the reception you would get. They don't like to be challenged. Okay, that's a challenge. This happened to me many times, and I'll do my best. "Okay, I think there is chum, chum, chum." And if I'm wrong, so what? I did my best. I did the best I could.

This is something I want all of you to remember when you are giving messages, especially in circle. It'll be a little different when you are actually giving messages from the platform, but in circle, I want you to wait and get feedback, not fish for information. In other words, if I were to come to Rosita, "Rosita, can I step into your vibration?" This is asking permission, remember? Now if Rosita says, "No," let it go; back out. And I don't care, this can happen in your circle. What if someone in your circle has had a particularly upsetting day, and they would just as soon you not know what is going on or you not bother them. When you sit across the circle and ask someone if you can step into their vibration and they say no, honor it. Step back, find someone else.

Now, I can touch Rosita's vibration and I can say, "Right now I can tell your vibration is a little low. Have you just lost your job? Has your husband just left you?" And I can run through about eight or ten questions that will give me an awful lot of information, but that is not psychic working, not at all. About the only time, at least at Sunday service from the platform here, that you will hear us ask a question of someone is when we can't tell which part of a symbol is meaning what. Most of the time when I've asked, "Have you just come back from a trip?" it is because suddenly I am surrounded with baggage, and I can't tell if the baggage has just arrived or if it is leaving. That's a perfectly valid question, because then you can go from there and your teachers will fill in.

So as you give these messages, remember, to be wrong is almost as important as being right, if you pay attention to what your mind was doing when it was wrong. If you can see why you made the mistake, then maybe you won't make it again. And that's extremely important.

As you give messages, just out of courtesy, I would demand that you always ask permission. Out of courtesy, simply say, "Thank you," for them allowing you to invade their privacy. When you step into someone's vibration, you are stepping into their private domain. So either give them a blessing, say "Thank you," or whatever. Don't just (click) and go someplace else. So keep those little things in mind, and they'll be hammered away at you as you start actually giving messages from the platforms up here. Because you're going to be doing it! At least all of you who are going to go for papers will be doing it. I know you've heard me say it a thousand times (well maybe not in the last couple of months, because it's been quite a while since I've been up for an argue with you) but before that, I'm sure you've heard many, many times this simple little thing of practice makes perfect. I cannot stress that enough.

On Tuesday night and Monday night, we were playing with ESP cards. I assume quite a few of you have them, from what I've heard. I've got a different problem. I'll be perfectly frank. When I'm in the right mood, I'm pretty darn good. But about the last week, I've missed three or four cards out of the twenty-five, and it is driving me crazy. And that sounds, "Oh, listen to him bitch," but no–wait a minute, and this is what really blew my mind. I'm sitting here, pulling these silly cards off, and first I thought I was getting them mixed up, so I would take the card off the deck and simply hold it out like this. I look at it psychically, and it's a square. It looks like a good square, but it's a star. So I put the damn thing down, and the next one looks like a circle, lay it down, and it's a circle. Hmm. Why was I wrong that time and not this time? Good case. So as you play with your cards, pay attention to the errors. That's where you learn. You don't learn from your successes. You don't learn from your success at all. Watch the difference of what your mind does when you make a mistake, and then you can make enormous headway.

How many of you are still playing with your little PK pin wheels? Now, thank God for that. Next week I expect to see everybody's hand up. Remember how you made them? I'll tell you why. Because a little bit farther down the line, you're going to spend a night staring at a pie pan balanced on a pin, and you'd better be able to rotate it. Practice. Practice makes perfect.

Now that I've scared all of you thoroughly–you know I'm kidding! I'm not going to feed you to the lions if you can't move a pie pan. I might pound on you, but I won't feed you to the lions. Okay, there's one little other thing we want to bring up real quickly. Some of you have had a dark circle and a candle circle, and you know the difference in the two. That's obvious. When we start the new series of circles, you're going to be having circles, and a little later on a device called a trumpet is going to be used. Some of you, I know, know what a trumpet is. I haven't taken up knitting–this is just a trumpet. A trumpet is made of very lightweight aluminum and it has seams on it, like so. When you start using a trumpet, always make sure it is put together so the seams are lined up. The purpose for a trumpet is mainly threefold. A spiritual entity can build a voice box in the bottom end of the trumpet here, so it can actually talk so that those in the room can hear it with their physical ears. It works just exactly like the old fashioned phonograph. You know it had the big trumpet thing that came up. Look, (clicks fingers), see how much noise that made? I'm just rubbing my fingerprints across the end of it. This is the only reason it is used as far as communication is concerned. Indians like to pound on it. As you can see, this one has been pretty well had. Indians love to bang tables with them, to turn the table into a tom-tom and use this as the drumstick, tom-tom stick, or whatever. These are available here from the Chapel for you to buy. I would suggest that you not buy them now. Please wait until you get more familiar with dark circles and start actually working in dark circles, because I don't want you sitting at home at night with this on the table, saying, "Harry, talk to me!" There's more to it than that. If you're married, however, start discussing this with your husband at least surreptitiously right now, because the first thing you must do when you get a trumpet is to sleep with it. You have to open it all the way and put it in bed with you and sleep with it. Don't roll over on it or you'll have one flat trumpet. By now, I'm sure all of you know exactly why: so that the entities know your vibration on the trumpet. Pure and simple.

My little Indian, Tinitchcook… I have a trumpet of course that I've used for a long, long time, and he knows that trumpet very well. In fact, he bawled me out and made me take it home from the Chapel because a number of other mediums were using it here at the Chapel. One night I had it in Chapel on a Monday night, and Tinitchcook was standing beside me. Nothing else was happening, so I said, "Tinitchcook, hand me my trumpet." He said, "Where is it?" And I said, "It's on the table," so he walked over there and looked down at it, and I could see him looking at it like this, and he came back over to me and said, "That doesn't feel like your trumpet." I said, "Well, it sure as the devil is," so he picked it up and put it clear up in the ceiling; then put it back behind my chair and set it down. The point is, too many other people had handled it, and too many people had played with it. He didn't recognize it from the physical things that *I* can identify my trumpet with. So, you sleep with it, to get it used to your vibration, and then don't let anybody else play with it. Don't let your kids play with it. There are all kinds of old wives' tales about if you blow through the trumpet; spirits will never talk through it. That's just pure garbage. Don't believe it at all. It is simply a tool, simply a tool.

They're very old, of course. This is a thing that's mentioned all through the Bible, all through the Old Testament–the sacred sound of trumpets, the blaring of God's trumpets, the same thing. Only in that case, it was done in a synagogue instead of a séance at the Chapel of Awareness.

What else is there? It must be metallic for the same reason that your pinwheel must be metallic–because it is too easy for an etheric, either your etheric or a part of your etheric, to go through a piece of paper. It is very difficult for them to pick up or move a piece of paper. So, you make it out of metal just like your pinwheel is. If you do, a little further down the line, start using trumpets, there are several things you want to *not* do (let's go negatively first). Don't talk to the trumpet as if the trumpet is the entity. Don't sit there and say, "Hello, trumpet, talk to me." That's not going to work. Address one of your powerful guides or spirit teachers. Generally, if you want to start out in a good way, I would say, address an Indian. For some reason, Indians seem to have more fun with trumpets than most people do. Tau Sing would never even consider playing with a trumpet. Neither would Wanderer. Sir has picked the trumpet up and laid it in my lap a couple of times just to show me he could do it, and I think it was kind of like a condescending patting the dog on the head. Reverend Bradley will play with the trumpet; Tinitchcook plays with the trumpet. Remember those things. Address the trumpet by whoever is using the trumpet–not the instrument itself, but the entity. That is extremely important.

Try to remain calm. That's a silly thing to say. Most of the trumpets we use here in Chapel, we put a phosphorescent band around here, so you can see where the trumpet is in the dark room. But I can assure you, I don't care how much you have practiced, the first time you are sitting there and you see that band go, "Chk, chk, chk…" the whole circle is going to fall apart. It happens all the time. You can sit there on your hands, like this, and no way.

I'm as guilty of it as anybody else. At a big trumpet circle we had up in Denver, in the Temple of Harmony, there was a very powerful Indian, Tall Pine, who loved to play with the trumpet. We were in a room that was about a quarter the size of this one, with a ceiling almost as high as this one. It was a good old downstairs basement storeroom, that they had blacked out so we could have dark circles and trumpet circles. The trumpet had a band around the big end and around the little end so you could see both ends of it. The trumpet got up off the table (I could see Tall Pine of course, moving it) and he took it clear to the other end of the room. There were about twelve or thirteen in the circle, and the rest of the room was empty. The trumpet went clear down to the other end of the room, and lay there rattling on the wall. Everybody thought that was neat. I looked up and said, "Bring the trumpet back here," and it came like lightning, faster than your eye could even follow it, right straight at my head. I ducked! I got clear down to lay my head in my lap. And did I get reprimanded, because he brought the trumpet back and put it on the table and said, "Why did you duck? I know where you are." I said, "Well, yes, I know you know where I am. Excuse me, I'm sorry, I just didn't control myself." And the trumpet got up, went clear to the end of the room, and I thought, "My god, here it comes." I took hold of my knees and thought, "I don't care if that thing knocks out all of my teeth, and I'm not going to move an inch." It came again, sailing across that room faster than your eye could follow it, and it stopped, touching the hairs on the tip of my nose. Now, I might have flinched a few millimeters, but I'll admit that by the time it got back in the circle, I closed my eyes because I could see it coming. It stopped right there and just touched the tip of my nose, and came down to my lap and just set there, vibrating. So he knew where I was. This is the thing I want you to remember. In a trumpet circle, the trumpet is never going to bang you on the head, unless it is playful. Tinitchcook likes to do that. "Oh, this won't hurt you!" It won't hurt you at all. Most of the Indians we have had around here like to tap on knees. Anyway, it wouldn't hurt you even if it hit you really hard because it is very lightweight, so don't be shook up about it.

This of course takes energy, and this is why I don't want you to go home tonight, put it on the table, and wait for Henry to talk to you. It seems like it takes about three-quarters of the energy from Spirit and about a quarter from those in the circle, to move the trumpet. Generally they will draw it from the most adept in the circle. Let's say you've got a circle that has three competent mediums seated in the circle. Then that quarter of the energy will be drawn from them. It's probably not from the circle. It's just one of those convenient things.

There are two things that also happen with the trumpet, and you want to be very careful of them: aports and teleports. An entity can build a voice box, and it seems to occur about here. If you're looking in the other end of the trumpet when they do it, it looks like a little teeny blue cloud. If they're really putting energy in it, it's almost like you can see the cloud folding in on itself. Have you ever seen smoke coming out of a smokestack where it is rolling? That's what it looks like, but it stays put. It doesn't roll up and down. It just stays in one spot and the energy rolls.

Since they can put that kind of energy into a trumpet, they can also create aports and can also use it to transfer teleports. It can occur that a trumpet will come around the room and ask for your attention. The entity who is controlling the trumpet will ask your name, or whatever, and ask you to put out your hand. If you put out your hand, or both hands, the trumpet will come down from wherever it is, and sit on your hands. Then the aport or teleport, whichever is created, will roll down the trumpet and end up in your hand. It's a very spectacular thing, because it makes a hell of a lot of noise. I'm sure you can imagine it would. Here's a dime. (Clattering noise in the trumpet.) It can be heard all over a dark circle.

The only thing I say to be careful of is, while aports and teleports *can* come from a trumpet, everything that comes from a trumpet is not an aport or teleport. Trumpet séances are without a doubt the area where there is more fake and fraud than any other séance in the United States. I've gotten to the point that I will rarely visit one unless the minister will give me a private demonstration first, because I'm getting tired of it. I can see in the dark–I can see in the dark as well as I can in this room. It just breaks my heart to see some person playing around with something that, when properly done, is so very, very beautiful. I know of three trumpet mediums, none of them in California, who would meet with my approval. I have sat in dark circles with them and watched them work. You'll hear it everywhere.

We're coming into an area when all kinds of séances are becoming very popular. I would ask you to be very careful. Know the medium in charge. Know what it's about. First of all, if your trumpet circle costs you $25 a chair, tell them to go fly a kite. Someone is simply making money. If you pay say, $5 to go to a trumpet circle, I think that's fairly reasonable. If it turns out not to satisfy you, well, you blew enough to see a movie. Be careful of some of these others. I just recently received some brochures that we were supposed to have put up on the back bulletin board, of trumpet circles that are going to be held in this area in about three months, and I simply tore them up. They were $100 a chair. They were guaranteeing an aport and a teleport from your loved one and your high teacher. I think all of you know me well enough to know why I reacted the way I did.

So as I say, this is an extremely powerful tool for Spirit to use and it can also be a very powerful tool to fool you. Don't be fooled. Wait until you can see auras easily. Wait until you can *see* what is going on in a dark circle. Then, go to a trumpet circle. Now, if you do go to a trumpet circle, a materialization circle, or any of those other kinds, and you see that fraud is going on, don't break up the circle. Stay there and be a nice person, and then file your complaint with either the head of the circle or the head of the church group of organization that is supporting it. That's the only way you're going to weed some of these things out.

Trumpet circles are almost always total dark circles. There have been two people that have been able to do trumpets in not quite broad daylight, in a room with some light coming in, but subdued light. This has been thoroughly documented. Unfortunately, both of them are now in spirit and as far as I know, it has never been duplicated. There is a young man who, in his younger years, was a superb trumpet medium, Mr. Jimmy Gordon. I haven't seen him work now for many, many years, so I would not of course recommend him now. He did some experiments down at the University of San Diego in the gymnasium, where they put him out in the middle of the floor on a cot with a trumpet laying on his chest, and then dusted the whole floor with talcum. They turned out the lights. They were seated in the first two rows of the bleachers on both sides. The trumpet came to both sides and bounced on peoples' knees and shook and wiggled. As far as I know, no one spoke to it. Then it went back and stood at the foot of the cot. When they turned the lights back on, Jimmy was still in light trance, lying on the cot, and there were no marks or footprints on the floor at all. So it can be done. It is rare, but it can be done, that spectacular way where the trumpet is moving, like forty feet away from the medium's body. It can be done. But don't get carried away with it.

What else is on my little list? Oh yes, don't grasp the trumpet. If the trumpet comes to you and touches you, just let it set there. Someone else is controlling it. It's not going to fall on the floor. Don't grab onto it like this, because you'll scare the entity to death. That would be a little hard to do, but anyway, just let it rest there. The entity knows what they're doing, so don't take hold of it. The only time I would suggest that you take hold of it would be if an entity hands you a trumpet and you would hear the entity, through the trumpet, say, "Here, take this." That would be the only time. Do not act on a psychic impression or a clairvoyant/clairaudient impression of "Here, take it." Wait till the entity controlling the trumpet tells you directly.

Advanced Lecture Series 2

Avatars, Ava Rex Avatars and Archangels

I. AVATAR
   A. Extremely highly developed, complex beings. They are highly evolved and have mastered, after repeated reincarnations, all of the required goals. They have reached personal, spiritual perfection. In lieu of merging, they have chosen to remain in spirit to help mankind.
   B. They no longer need to go through birth or death.
      1. They can come back to the earth plane (i.e. project in solid form) to bring about a specific project.
      2. While in solid form, they require no physical sustenance. They draw energy directly from the universe.
      3. While in solid form they would not ordinarily have an Aura "C" but they can project one if they so choose, in order to protect their identity.
      4. Some "miracles" have been brought about by avatars.
      5. They are usually secretive.

II. AVA REX AVATAR
   A. A spiritual being who has reached perfection somewhere other than on the Earth plane. They manifest directly on spiritual plane of the Earth to work with open individuals, through spiritual channels, to help bring about a specific thing.
   B. They never manifest in three dimensional form, and they are sexless.

III. ARCHANGELS
   A. Spiritual beings, "messenger angels," who came into being out of the residual energy when the Earth was formed.

B. Collectively, they are the repository for the Akashic Record (the record of all thought, action, and deed–literally, *everything*–that has ever occurred on this planet.
C. They have never had three dimensional form, and they have absolute power.
D. There are thirteen in number. The first four will not judge an action, but will answer a specific request when the *incantations* are used. Be extremely careful what you ask for (i.e. know all of the ramifications of what you are asking for)!
E. The first seven archangels will answer your request, but only if it is your highest and best good.

The first seven archangels and their identifying color and direction:

Archangel Michael, Ruler of the West. Color: Blue. Main Duty: Progression and Protection.

Archangel Gabriel, Ruler of the East. Color: White. Main Duty: Understanding Wealth.

Archangel Raphael, Ruler of the South. Color: Green. Main Duty: Peace of Mind, Vitality, Consecration.

Archangel Uriel, Ruler of the North. Color: Gold (metallic) / Ruby. Main Duty: Perception, Psychic Sight, Ministration.

Archangel Jophiel (pron. Josaphiel). Color: Yellow. Main Duty: Illumination, Wisdom.

Archangel Chanael. Color: Pink. Main Duty: Adoration, Universal Love.

Archangel Zodkiel (pron. Zodakiel). Color: Violet (not purple). Main Duty: Invocation, Purity.

This evening we are going to talk about some very, very special kinds of creatures. I say creatures because some of them are very unusual. So this will be, as far as your notes are concerned, Advanced Lecture Number II. The things we are going to cover tonight are avatars, ava rex avatars, and archangels.

Probably the most difficult thing to comprehend when dealing with these kinds of entities, is sort of what you touched on when we talked about teachers and high teachers. Only here, we are dealing with entities that have almost unlimited power. In the case of archangels, this of course, is what the early Hebrews called "God" and by using certain kinds of prayer, their particular archangel brought about miracles that are described in somewhat fancy detail in the Old Testament. Often many of the miracles that we see today, or that are recorded especially by the Catholic Church, are the works of individual entities that we call avatars.

So let's start right there with the avatar. All of you are familiar with the name. We talked about it when we talked about spirit evolution. It is the one step away from perfection kind of position that an individual entity can attain. They are extremely highly developed. They have evolved here on the Earth plane through a whole series of incarnations, having reached all of the required goals. In other words, they have done everything that needs to be done to be a perfect being. They then have their choice, to merge at one with the universe, or to touch the Earth plane in any number of a very specific set of ways, and by that touching, bring about a specific thing that they are interested in doing. They say that it is in this group of individuals that we generally find the power mechanism of miracles, and that act between those people who are experiencing the miracle and the event itself.

There are, as of a couple of years ago, something like 16,000 of them, that have elected not to go into nirvana, but have decided to stay on the spirit side to, as I say, bring about something that they want. They can manifest directly on the Earth plane as three dimensional, physical entities. If you met one, unless you were extremely psychic, there would be no way of telling that individual from another ordinary evolving spiritual entity in incarnate form. There are two minor exceptions: one, they do not have to eat; and two, they are never born, nor of course, will they die. They will manifest directly in the way they want to manifest, if they choose to manifest in three dimensional form. In so doing, it's one of the keys that we find to a few of those that we know something about.

Probably the only one that we know a great deal about is the so-called healing priest of North Africa. This entity has been around for a long, long time, and he has repeatedly appeared at great distances within matters of very few minutes of each other. He is extremely secretive, as apparently are almost all avatars who take on a physical form. This particular one, as I say, we know a little bit about him because of a written record of some of the tribes that he has visited. The way he likes to manifest himself is to simply walk in off the desert at night, into the light of a campfire, and do those healings that need to be done. Rarely, if ever, does he speak. When the healings are done, he turns and walks back into the darkness, and nobody sees him again until there is another need for healing. This has happened, as I say, over great separate distances, with good descriptions of the individual. There would be absolutely no way that he could traverse that distance in that span of time, that short span of time.

As I say, we know very little about them. We know quite a bit about avatars that are in spirit and are acting as guides or teachers around different people, but we know very little about avatars who have appeared in three dimensional form. There is some confusion in this word avatar, because in the areas of India, Pakistan, Tibet, and that area, 'avatar' is simply taken to mean *teacher*. I know probably one of the questions that will pop into your mind is, "Is Babagi an avatar?" The answer is no, of course, because he was born of a mother and a father, and he will die. He eats and all those kinds of things. If he were an avatar, those things would not be true. They do not need those kinds of things. As I say, they don't need to eat, because they can draw energy directly from the spiritual field around them. This same kind of energy that you have felt in circles, or that you have felt in healings, is exactly the same energy, but at a different frequency. If properly used, it will sustain life, and it is one of those abilities that very high entities, i.e. avatars, have learned to control.

There is one other suspected one, a three dimensional form of an avatar, that was written up a few years ago. It was, oh, I've forgotten now, probably something like eight or ten years ago. There was a severe automobile accident in Manhattan, in New York, in which an elderly gentleman was pinned under a big section of the wreckage. Suddenly, beside the car, appeared a man wearing a brown overcoat. No one got much of a look at him, but he suddenly appeared by the car, with one hand reached down, and turned the car back over on its other side, taking all the weight off the old gentleman who was laying there injured. He knelt down beside the gentleman for just a few seconds and then the man in the coat walked back into the crowd and disappeared. A few seconds later, the injured gentleman sat up and asked what had happened. He had been miraculously healed on the spot and there was no evidence of injury at all, but laying ten feet away from him was a thoroughly mangled car. Okay. A great effort was put out in Manhattan, to find this lovely benefactor who did that miraculous thing, and of course, they found nothing.

Avatars in three dimensional form do not sit around saying, "Look who I am." They are way beyond that, way beyond that. But they do some very beautiful things. Those who work with various ones of us, in the living, work simply as very high spiritual teachers. And again, they do so because of their choice, not because you chose them.

An ava rex avatar. Only three of them are known to me at this point in time. They are very special creatures. They are spiritual beings who manifest themselves only in the spiritual plane of the Earth. Never will they take on three dimensional physical form, because they have completed all of their required growth on a different planetary system. So they are not familiar enough with our particular body chemistry, our particular nervous network, and it would be not necessarily to their advantage to be hampered in three dimensional physical form. It has never been done and Tau Sing says it will never be done. Certainly they would have the power to do it, because they could create any illusion they want. But they are here for very special purposes, and very specific purposes–to help illumine or enlighten a particular individual, so that that individual can share with someone else, something very, very special. The Wanderer, around me, is one of these. This is the one that I've talked to many of you before about–going on little trips and falling through star clusters, and things of this nature, to show me what could be done, pure and simple. So that I could share it with someone else. As I say, I only really know of two, and a third one will be known a little later around the Chapel, a little farther along down the line. As far as I know, the Wanderer is the only one that has worked through me certainly and the only that I've heard work in stage 3C trance. But there are two others, and the third one we will know, at his convenience, further down the line. I'm often asked, what did Wanderer look like on his other planet? What was his highest form of life? He guards that jealously. He will not let me touch that vibration at all. Those few times that people have seen him, he certainly looked humanoid, and I mean he's not some creature with snake hair or something like that. The only thing about him that is startling is that when you see him in projected form, he has no iris around his eyes. It is a thin, single line, with large, black pupils. What that means, or what you can infer from that, well, you can play the science fiction game and let your mind just run in circles. But for some reason, he has elected not to show me what he looked like.

The teachings that an ava rex avatar will give are always very abstract. They will call attention to ordinary mundane mental gymnastics or mental exercises that we go through. You will hear them–at least as I say, those that I know of–you will hear them say things that are not new, that are restating things that we have heard for the last 5,000 years. But they are things that they feel strongly enough to repeat, time and time and time again. I would say that 90% of my communication with Wanderer, certainly in trance, is on the subject of loving one another. It is *the* thing, the thing.

Now the third one, which is in a way the most exciting, is the archangels. And again just for definition, since we've defined the other two rather closely, let's make sure we keep archangels straight. They are totally spiritual beings. They have never had three dimensional form. In other words, they have never had an incarnation on the Earth, or as far as we know, any place else. They have absolute power, and I mean that in the absolute sense. An archangel can do anything it wants to do. Notice I said, *can,* not *will.* It has incredible power. There are thirteen of them, but we will only be discussing seven of them this evening. You already know a couple that we will not be discussing this evening. Beyond the seven that we will discuss this evening, I mentioned earlier that the god of the early Hebrews was an archangel, and of course that's Yahweh or Jehovah, or any of the other pronunciations that you want to put on the particular way of spelling it. There is another obscure one that you might run across in some writings, especially in black magic and these kinds of things, called "Jahaji." You will not be required to remember those, but just in case you are running along in some of your readings and you bump into one of them, you will know what they are.

Okay. I've listed them one through seven. I do not of course in any way want to insist that one is better than two, three less than two, and so on and so forth, because that's not the case at all. It's just a way to keep them straight. As I say, they are incredibly powerful. The first four, if you use certain kinds of prayers or incantations, will not judge an action. They will simply follow through and bring it about, which sounds bizarre, but this is why Yahweh worked for the Hebrews. When that particular nation wanted to destroy another town, or a village, or a group people, Yahweh did it, because he was commanded to do so by a very special technique known only to the high priests at the time. This is why we see this vengeful god concept coming off of these early Hebrew teachings. There is a little footnote here on one of my notes. (Someone else wrote up my notes from some of my other lectures.) Be extremely careful what you ask for. This is true. This is very, very true.

Let's look at these first seven. There are some funny things you're going to have to get used to right off the bat. Here's an entity as I say, of almost absolute power, and yet, an entity that has very sharp likes and dislikes. It is very difficult for me to comprehend Michael, Archangel Michael, liking or not liking something. I don't know how to equate to that. I would think that once we would have an entity on that level, personal preference would disappear. It has not. So I want you to write these things down; I will want you to remember them.

Let's take the first one, Archangel Michael. He is attributed to be ruler of the West. His color, blue. His main activities that he is interested in helping others with are progression and protection. Now I want to take a minute here to fill you in on what that means, what I've just said. The positions of the first four archangels represent the four directions of the Earth: West, East, South, North, as we go through them. The color is the color of a candle that you would use to pay homage to, or to acknowledge the presence of, one of these archangels. So in this case, Michael, being blue, if you wanted to sit down and have a cozy little chat with Michael, you would light a blue candle, set it in front of you, while you are facing West. Now, I know this sounds like mumbo jumbo and black magic, and I can see a lot of auras flashing. The only thing I can say is, try it, you might like it.

The things he is interested in are as I say, self-explanatory: progression and protection. Protection, of course. Those of you who will be able to touch his vibration, which is a very interesting challenge in itself, will almost always find him carrying a sword, living up to the image that all of the artists have painted. Or is it the other way around? The artists really did see Michael, and painted him with a sword. Which came first, the chicken or the egg? I have seen him, I think, only on one occasion when he did not have the sword. Once you identify the vibration, there's never a question in your mind which it is. He almost always carries a sword, and he almost always carries it point down. So, the first thing you might see (if you see him) is you will see him standing there like this, and at first you'll think it is a cross. It will come up here, and here is the handle, and here is the cross member. At first you'll think it is a heavily jeweled cross. It is very beautiful. But then you will notice that there is a brilliant white silver blade hanging down from it: one of the ways you will spot him.

The next one is another one that you are familiar with. The first series of these, the first three, of course you are familiar with because they are from the Bible itself. The next one is Gabriel, Archangel Gabriel, Ruler of the East. His color is white, and his main duty, or his main activity, is understanding and wealth. I mean wealth in the way like cash, greenbacks, gold coins–wealth in the absolute sense. Same thing holds true there, like I used in the example of Michael. Gabriel, I think I've seen him once when he had his trumpet. But here again, it is one of these things of living up to the image of the Hebrew nation. Gabriel will blow his horn and the graves will open up, and everybody is going to get up and go do something. Well they've already been up and doing something for a long time, so he's not going to blow his horn. But, to make it possible to identify him, he may carry that.

Incidentally, all archangels appear masculine. Sorry, women's libbers, but that's simply the way it is. I think we can see why, and it's the same reason why we see so many of the high teachers around people as male. You've got to remember from the point in time they're coming from. When each of you come back, with the power to be someone's high teacher, especially the women's libbers, then you can project as a woman and will be *listened* to. Notice the difference? A subtle difference, but a very real one. And to me, most archangels look very Greco-Roman, very Greco-Roman in dress. Simple robes, or elaborate borders around the center, something like this, but they're very interesting creatures.

Number three, Raphael, Ruler of the South. His color is green, and he is interested in doing a lot of things: health (health of mind and body) and peace of mind. In some of the Hebrew writings there is a distinct difference between health and peace of mind (I think we tend to lump it together). Raphael's is health, peace of mind, vitality, and consecration. He will assist anyone in the consecration of holy ground, setting up a system in which things are to be consecrated. This is one of his activities.

Number four is one that used to be in the Bible, but you'll have to find it now in the Apocrypha. When they threw out the Apocrypha, they threw out Archangel Uriel along with it. There's an interesting thing that happened there too, and I'll touch on that in just a moment. Uriel, Ruler of the North. His color is gold. I'm talking now about metallic gold, not yellow. Metallic gold, and ruby. So if you happen to find a big ruby, you can carve a chalice and put a candle in it, and you've got him. It's not quite that bad, not quite that bad. That's why incidentally you see all the beautiful little red votive candle holders, representing ruby. His main duty is perception; psychic sight; and ministration–the carrying out of duties, to help you carry out something that is expected of you or that you need to do. As I say, the interesting thing about this is that about the time that Uriel was thrown out of the so-called Holy Scriptures was the first and only time that Holy Rome fell to invaders, and they fell by an invading army that came from the North. Isn't that interesting?

Incidentally, and I hope some of you will do research along this line, you will find many of them spelled differently. The answer to this is a simple one at first, till you try to figure it out yourself–there are no vowels in Hebrew. So any place you see a vowel in these things, you could use any other vowel. Only the consonants are there. It's a very interesting thing to research, especially when we get down to some of these more obscure ones. But Michael is Michael, Gabriel is Gabriel, Raphael is Raphael; we know those.

Uriel is a very beautiful individual. Here's a good place to give an example of using a particular kind of prayer or incantation. Incidentally, they are extremely specific. You are not going to accidentally bump into one. But let's just assume for a moment that you found that little prayer or that little incantation, and commanded Uriel to give you psychic sight. Okay, now that sounds good. All of you are sitting here hoping to be psychic and hoping to see clairvoyantly. What happens if suddenly you had it one hundred percent of the time, three dimensionally solid, to the point that you couldn't tell which is a real person and which is an entity. Now, would that be a desirable gift? Okay. So that is why, as I mentioned before: be extremely careful what is requested, because it may have some side effects. There's a good example. Yes, I want all of you to have psychic sight, but not all the time, and not all the time three dimensionally solid clairvoyance. You'd go mad in very short order.

Now we're getting to some more difficult ones. Number five–and many of these are pronounced as if there is a missing "a"–Josaphiel. It is really Jophiel, but it's almost as if there's another "a" in there when you hear the word spoken. His color is yellow–this time yellow-yellow, not gold, but yellow. His main activity is illumination and wisdom. He generally works very, very closely with Uriel, because of the psychic sight and this kind of thing. The two are often associated together.

Number six, Chanael. Color, pink, and of course you can imagine what his duties are: adoration and universal love. Anyone who picks pink for a color, should have that. Number seven, another difficult one, pronounced as if there is another "a," Zodkiel. To pronounce it, you would put an "a" between the "d" and the "k." The color is violet, and I mean violet–I don't mean purple. It is so funny, in all the old writings concerning this particular archangel; they draw a real sharp distinction between purple and violet. When you see him or see his color, the field around him reminds me of–you know the glow around a Christmas tree bulb, that you can't focus on? That deep purple, radiating glow? (Yes, Reverend Bradley.) That deep violet, radiating glow? It's that kind of a color, very self-luminescent and very beautiful. It's not purple at all. His main duties are invocation and purity.

These last three, if you want to go find things about them, you'll have to go back to some of the very obscure writings in Hebraic literature. The first three, of courses, are from the standard Bible. Uriel–you can get information on him and his activities from the Apocrypha, those missing books of the Bible. These last three, you'll have to do some scouring around. If you're really interested in looking up some more about them, I would suggest Fuller Theological Seminary, or one of those kinds of centers where they would not only have the material, but also a librarian who could translate for you, who could read you materials on those particular things. There used to be a little booklet out, and I haven't seen it for twenty years, in which it listed all of these little angels on separate pages, gave pictures of them, and had beautiful little write-ups to them. It was a small book, about yea big, a square. I don't know where mine got to; you know how books disappear. So that happens. If you ever run across it, it's printed in England, and it's called <u>Messengers of God</u>.

Incidentally, you'll find them referred to in the Bible that way, as messengers from God, and that's exactly what they thought they were. This is where this whole thing of angels having wings came from. Sometimes Michael, I think just to satisfy our curiosity, will appear with wings on his back. I don't think I've seen any of the others with wings. In re-translating, for instance, early Hebrew, "...and he flew to his master." Now, I could say you "flew" to the front of the room and you wouldn't visualize suddenly sprouting wings and flapping up to the front of the room. Yet so many people get caught up on exactly what the words say. "He did fly." In reality the original Hebrew was simply moved or move. He went from here to there. But it sounded better. Some of our older artists said, "Hey, isn't that neat?"

Archangels, cherubs, seraphim–there's one more. Oh, angels! They have wings, they're nice. Some of them will project it that way. I've seen a little entity play Cupid, and look just like Cupid, a little fat naked baby with wings, but simply to humor several people that we had in circle. I'm certain the entity didn't run around that way all the time. He had many more important things to do than that.

Here we've touched on, without a doubt, the most difficult group of entities to comprehend or even to understand. They are very powerful, as I say, every one we've talked about here are. If you had to put them in order of power, of course archangel is going to be first, ava rex avatar is going to be second, and avatar is going to be "low man on the totem pole." But they're an incredible group, and as you work more and more in your own development, and when you really get into very specific details, you're going to start bumping into references to these, and this is why I wanted to bring this out, so that you would be familiar with these.

The first four archangels, in fact all of the archangels, have visited with people who are either teachers or students here at the Chapel. Incidentally, please don't get caught up on a trip, and I know it's a very easy trip to get caught up on. I can assure you that if I wanted Michael to be standing behind me, he would, and he would do it simply to please me. Now, that doesn't mean that I'm some super kind of creature that could ask Archangel Michael to do something and he would do it. So especially those of you who are healers, because many of these archangels are very powerful and they love to work that way–don't get jealous because you saw someone with Michael around them.

Michael was a constant companion of Jesus and was his major source of power for all the healings that Jesus did. It goes with involved spiritual forces. Jesus was an ordinary healer too. Remember the definitions of the two kinds of healings? He could do both. So remember, you're going to see them from time to time. As far as I know, none of the seven archangels have restricted themselves to an entity, as Michael did during the life of Christ. (Tau Sing, thank you.) Tau Sing agrees wholeheartedly; they have not. They are simply here to help in any way. That's what I was saying back when we started this, a few minutes ago. This incredible sensitivity, that they would help because they love to help is something that mankind has become almost so callous about. We always see people helping, "Because of...," or "If I do this, I'll get this." Well, here are some creatures just like your high teachers, who are doing what they are doing because they love to do it, and that's a pretty sobering reason for doing anything.

Response to a question from the audience. If they want to talk to you, they will be the most clairaudient, the most clear clairvoyant images you will ever receive. There will never be any doubt in your mind. I can see Tau Sing as well as I can see the two of you, but when Michael decides to step in to call my attention to something, it's as different as night and day. I think part of it is, when I see Tau Sing in three dimensional form, he looks like you. He looks like light is reflecting off him. I can see his robes; I can see the highlights in the folds of the robes, just like a lot of you can see objects clairvoyantly. But when an archangel steps in, they are self- luminous; they simply glow from within. They don't obey any of the natural physical laws that we would think of light and properties, not at all. And they're very beautiful. You'll never forget one.

Advanced Lecture Series 3

Meditation, Trance, Astral Projection, Soul Travel, Bilocation and Thought Projection

I. MEDITATION
   A. Meditation Stage I
      1. Stillness of emotion (a state of thinking tranquility).
      2. Observing thoughts as they cross the mind, but not reacting emotionally.
   B. Spirit communication occurs at a level that is somewhere between Stage I and Stage

II. Meditation.
   A. Meditation Stage II
      1. Stillness (silence) of the mind. You are not aware of things around you with the exception of touch.
      2. At the deepest level of this stage, sounds do not bother you.
   B. Meditation Stage III
      1. Total silence (total oblivion to all three dimensional sensation and thought).
      2. You're always alone. Spirit is not allowed to interfere.
      3. Very deliberate act. Cannot accidentally slip into Stage III meditation.
      4. Must set biological clock to come back, or will be gone indefinitely.
      5. Taught as a form of mind control in some Buddhist monasteries.
      6. Some say it gives you an ability to rebuild vital energy, but so does Stage II.

7. For a Spiritualist, it is not of much use because there is no communication while in it, and it accomplishes nothing.

III. TRANCE

A. Trance Stage I
   1. A receptive state very akin to communication level (between Meditation Stages I & II). Very receptive to spirit thoughts and impressions.
   2. Receptive state allowing automatic writing.
      a. When doing automatic writing, do not read as you go along, or you may "color" with your own thoughts.
      b. Know who is working with you.

B. Trance Stage II
   1. Kind of trance used in inspirational speaking.
   2. You are aware of what is going on but make no effort to control it.
   3. Spirit is impressing upon you with thoughts of what to say.
   4. You may not remember what is said.

C. Trance Stage III
   1. General Definition: Relinquishing total control to an entity. A conscious, deliberate act; it cannot accidentally occur. There may be a voice change in this stage of trance. You can end the trance at any time.
   2. Stage 3A
      a. Stepping slightly aside–listening to what is going on.
      b. You cannot change what is being said unless you re-enter your body, thus ending the trance process.
   3. Stage 3B
      a. Usually will leave the general vicinity and perhaps visit several areas. There is no specific destination or purpose.
      b. Essentially, you are unaware of what is going on with your body. However, you may be aware of

loud sounds or your physical body being touched and it may cause you to come back.

4. Stage 3C
   a. Will travel to a specific place for study and/or investigation. Usually, the destination will be the choice of your teacher, but with your consent.
   b. You will not be aware of sounds but you will still be aware of touch.
   c. Highest form of trance. (The only true example of pure possession, but it only occurs with your permission.)

IV. ASTRAL PROJECTION
   A. An ESP phenomenon
      1. You can guide and control where you are going, to some extent.
      2. No control over time.
   B. You are always alone.
   C. Generally occurs spontaneously during light sleep, but does not interrupt rest.
   D. Can learn to remember.

V. SOUL TRAVEL
   A. A Spiritual phenomenon.
   B. You are always taken by a guide or teacher.
   C. Always occurs during deep sleep (not during "REM" time).
   D. You will probably not remember what occurred until the information gained is being used. However, you might recall the start of the experience only.

VI. BILOCATION (Absolute Law: non-interference with any living thing)
   A. General Description: A deliberate will of the mind. The etheric body is used and goes elsewhere. The physical body is at rest, not sleeping. In the controlled phase, the body can appear as dead.

B. Bilocation I
    1. Merging into a physical, non-living object, to investigate and experience that object.
    2. This is required of all Buddhist novitiates.
C. Bilocation II
    1. A change of form. The etheric body is made to match *exactly* the shape and vibration of another life form.
    2. Non-interference is absolutely in play at this time. If the host senses you, you must withdraw at once, or you will be withdrawn by your high teacher.
    3. Plants: easiest type to match. You may feel the sap running through you.
    4. Man: should *never* even be attempted as it is total invasion of privacy.
D. Bilocation III (the most beautiful)
    1. The etheric body is projected in solid form.
    2. It can be seen with the physical eyes.
    3. Time out of the body is unlimited.
    4. You pre-arrange location.
    5. During this time out of body, the aging process is drastically slowed.
    6. Bilocation III with Bifurcation: After projecting out of body, the etheric is split into at least two duplicate forms which then go to different locations in solid form; very difficult to do with control. (Jesus did this more than once.)
E. Bilocation IV
    1. A group, working harmoniously, can be taken as a unit to a place in time, to observe.
    2. Go back in time only, by use of the Akashic Record.
    3. Under Spirit control of very high teachers.
    4. Used as a teaching technique.
    5. Amenterret says a group will be going back to Karnac, 1475 BC). The group will recognize Don Schwartz at that time.

VII. THOUGHT PROJECTION

A. General Definition: The deliberate projection of images by thought, either from yourself or from a spirit teacher.

B. It may seem like bilocation, but it is not.

1. The way to tell the difference: In thought projection you will always be aware of your physical body.
2. There is no deliberate stepping away from the body.
3. There is a difference between thought projection and all forms of bilocation. Avoid delusion by knowing this difference...!!!

Tonight we are going to dive into a little more of the advanced stuff that you will be using especially when you start working with, what should we call it, more exotic psychic phenomena. We are going to run down through a number of things. Terminology is important so that you will know what you are experiencing and so that you can understand what the teacher means when they tell you what you are experiencing. We will go through this as quickly as possible because I want to be done by 8:30 so that you can get into circle. I think we will have plenty of time to cover it. Some of it, of course, you are already familiar with. There are a number of terms that you have heard me use many times, and probably your teachers in class have as well. So, let's look at major divisions of things around you that have to do with advanced psychic activity.

First of all, let's look at meditation. By now you are all able to meditate perfectly, no problems at all? (A smirk and a twinkle of the eye) It falls into three categories:

Meditation Stage 1—

Stillness of emotions. A state of thinking tranquility. This is a state very similar to some of the forms of Transcendental Meditation. It is where you are simply letting your thoughts run and you are not emotionally reacting to the thought itself. You are also not analyzing the thought per se, but allowing the thought to simply flow from one thought-form into another. So remember, Meditation Stage 1—stillness of emotions.

Meditation Stage 2—

Silence of the mind. This is the one that you have been diligently working with. You are not aware of things around you with the exception of touch. When you first start working in Meditation Stage 2, you will be aware of sound. As you get better and better at it, you will no longer be aware of sound. A very slightly altered form of Meditation Stage 2 is that stage in which Spirit is able to communicate directly with you. You will recall that we have talked about going into meditation and then instead of coming all of the way back up, just come part way back up to awareness and this will open you to Spirit communication. Many times we hear people use phrases like "in my meditation I talked to Tau Sing". That is not actually true. In Meditation Stage 2 you talk to no one. After meditation, then comes the communication. So there is a subtle difference, small, but very important.

Meditation Stage 3—

Total Silence. Total Stillness. Total oblivion to all three dimensional things around you. Sight, sound, touch, temperature, and everything else. You are completely alone. And it is the only time that in this whole, wide universe that you can be absolutely alone. It is an extremely rare stage of meditation. I don't believe that there is anyone outside of a monastery who practices it with any regularity at all. First of all, because it is too dangerous. Second of all, it accomplishes nothing other than it convinces you of your ability to be in control. To enter Meditation Stage 3, you would set your biological clock inside you; let's say for 20 minutes. You would simply start slamming down all the switches that allow you to communicate with the world outside or the Spirit world, either one. All is gone. In a session sometime ago, someone popped up with a definition-it is a total turnoff. And that is exactly what it is. It is a turnoff to such a degree, that none of your teachers will interfere with it. Case in point - let's assume that you were seated at home and practicing Meditation Stage 3. You set your biological clock for 20 minutes and 5 minutes after you have entered stage 3, your house catches fire and burns to the ground. You would burn to death, and never be aware of it. Your teacher could not step in and awaken you or warn you that something was coming. You literally lock yourself up. I have seen this demonstrated in my younger years when I was a Mahayana Buddhist especially in Hawaii. We had several priests who would demonstrate this for us and it is a very dramatic thing to see. Two little things that occurred that will always register in my mind as long as I have a mind to think with, was the young priest sitting down and going into Meditation Stage 3. Then one of the junior priests walking up beside him and firing a 45 automatic into the mat right beside him. The gun was about two feet from his head. He didn't even flinch. His aura was about one-eighth of an inch away from his body. (It closes down into a protective mode, as you know, during meditation.) But when he came back from his Meditation Stage 3, his ears were ringing so badly that he could hardly hear. The nerves got the impact of the 45 going off. If you have ever fired a gun like that, you know what a hell of noise they do make. But it would not register on his conscious level because he had completely turned everything off. The other thing, which I was involved in at least once, was with the same priest again. To teach us this, he would go into that stage of meditation, seated in the temple or one of the meditation rooms. He would sit cross-legged with his arms folded in his lap, and we would pick him up by his buttocks and his knees and carry him outside and set him by a bush, so that when he came up out of his meditation, it gave him quite a surprise! We didn't get reprimanded for it, which is surprising.

I have never touched Meditation Stage 3 at a deep level at all. I think that I have tapped the edges of it. I do not feel comfortable with it and I will not teach you how to do it. There are some special steps involved and I would not teach you how to do them. I think that maybe the only place that this would be advantageous–and I thought about this just recently when the airplane crashed back east–if you knew the airplane was going to go down; it might be real handy to be able to pop into Meditation Stage 3. Then if you did die, at least it wouldn't hurt! So there may be an application for this special technique after all. Unfortunately with these sorts of things, when you turn off to that degree the sensitivities of your body, you are wide open to anything. Someone could come in and shoot you because they have nothing else to do, and you would never know it.

So, those are the three forms of meditation that you will bump into. These definitions are of course, Buddhist. The type of meditation that Christ was referring to is of course Meditation Stage 2, to be silent and go within. But these are the three that you will bump into.

Now we come to a very fascinating topic and one that all of you are going to be excited about and will be playing with down the line, and that is the various kinds of trance. Now, there are a lot of kinds of trance and there are a lot of kinds of people who work in trance–or what they call trance. Again, we are going to fall back on some of the Buddhist definitions of trance because they can be easily defined and they can be detected, one stage from another.

Trance Stage 1—

A receptive stillness, very closely akin to Meditation Stage 2, where you are receptive to spiritual thought and impressions. This very often happens when one deliberately sets about to communicate with a teacher and they will step into your vibration very lightly, very delicately, but you are aware of *their* thought processes instead of yours. This makes a very beautiful form of communication. There is one altered form of Trance Stage 1. Tau Sing lists it simply as:

Trance Stage 1A—

Receptive stillness, just as in Meditation Stage 1, but allowing automatic writing. Now, this is one of the problems with automatic writing. You are not deep enough into trance so that you are certain that you do not interfere with what is being written. There are a few precautions that you should always take if you want to work with automatic writing. Never read what is being written. Wait until it is finished and then read it, because if you start reading it, it is so easy for your mind to put in words or concepts or phrases. In that shallow form of trance, you will not know which is which. There is absolutely no way of telling which is truly Spirit and which is influenced by you. I am personally against automatic writing because I feel that it does not give you enough control. Certainly if you are interested in automatic writing, make certain that you know and are familiar with the entity that is writing through you. Don't let it be Joe Blow from somewhere! Find out who it is. Certainly make absolutely sure that you know who it is before you would alter any of your plans or suggest changes to other people, as if it is coming from an enlightened Spirit. It is very easy to electrically manipulate muscles, to change writing. It is very easy to do this in Trance 1A. Make sure you know who you are working with in Trance Stage 1A. I think one of the best and well, gee, one of the very few times, that I have even done any automatic writing that was successful, was in Stage 3, but we'll get to that in a moment. But in this form, it was when Amenterret, one of Donald's teachers, was talking with me about the differences between hieroglyphs and Coptic. I had a phrase from a book that I was very curious about, so I asked him what the pure Coptic form of that would look like. He asked me if I knew what this stage of trance was and I said, "Yes of course." So, I sat down with a felt-tipped pen and he wrote two beautiful lines of Coptic through me, which of course I could not read. He wrote it very, very beautifully and then translated it for me. But that's what I mean. Know who you are working with in all forms of your psychic work.

Trance Stage 2—In this kind of trance we see inspirational speaking. One of the things that you are going to have to watch very closely is that the person who is doing the inspirational speaking is totally aware of what is going on, but makes no effort to control it or to change it. You are not outside the body. You are simply here but letting someone else do the work. Again, it is a very difficult form of trance to control because you are still too involved with what is going on. If the person who is speaking inspirationally through you says something to offend you or upset you it will snap you out or you will change what is being said. Of course, that is no good. But this is one that you will see where people are speaking inspirationally whether they are on a platform or simply speaking to one another. Inspirational speaking can occur many, many times. In fact the place that you will generally spot it is when someone comes to you with a problem or you are discussing something with someone and suddenly you say the right thing at the right time. Then a few seconds later, you think back and you wonder why in the devil did I say that? You were just right at the right point and the information could be given to you to help that other person with their problem.

Okay, by far the most important form of trance is:

Trance Stage 3—

Relinquishing total control to another entity. This falls into three categories. You will notice that the three categories are degrees of letting go.

Trance Stage 3A—

Stepping slightly aside. You will be listening to what is going on. In other words, your body will be in a state of trance and you will be standing nearby in the same room, observing what is going on. You will hear what is going on, but you will not have any control over what the entity is saying.

Trance Stage 3B—

Again, you go into trance and you are free to drift to see different areas and different scenes. It's like a pointless wandering. It's actually a lot of fun. You are just floating around in a lot of clouds or bushes or trees or whatever. It is a very relaxing form of trance that we see quite often.

To me and to the high teachers, at least that I have discussed it with, the last form (Stage 3C) is the most beautiful and the most perfect form of trance.

Trance Stage 3C—

You are in trance and the biggest part of you is gone. You go someplace to study, or to look at, or to investigate a particular object or subject. In my case, when Tau Sing is working through me, I go to the lamasery at Doc Tau Lu which is in southwestern Tibet. It is a very beautiful thing because while my body is sitting here and Tau Sing is talking to you as students or whomever he is talking to, I can be studying and learning other things myself. This is a very beautiful form of trance. One of the ways that you can easily spot it is that you will be totally unaware of what has been said when you come back and you will not be aware of your body at all during the trance. In my case, apparently in Stage 3C my breathing slows down. I have noticed that in all of the hundreds of tapes that I have of my trancing, when I come back from Trance 3C the first thing you will hear is me exhaling and then inhaling as if I am almost out of air. You will find me taking one big, deep breath. So there's sort of a transitional stage. It is a beautiful thing and it is one of the things that all of you who are going to be ministers and mediums should strive for. Stage 3C is the most beautiful form of spirit communication there is as far as using a physical body is concerned.

Now I want to touch two other things that are very similar. Like I mentioned in Trance Stage 3B, you are free to drift around and see things. The first is:

Astral Projection—

There are three things that I want you to remember about Astral Projection.

First of all, it is an ESP phenomenon. It has nothing to do with Spirit or spirituality. It is purely an ESP phenomenon. You can guide and control where you are going to some extent with the exception of time. There is a very funny thing that happens in astral projection concerning time. A couple of years ago, there was a lot of excitement because the Russians were training spies to use astral travel so that they could come and spy on the White House. Well, they can spy without astral projection, but that's beside the point. With astral projection, it won't work, because you cannot determine the point in time that you visit a place. If you want a good book on the subject get Sylvan Muldoon and Hereward Carrington's book, The Projection of the

Astral Body. It is relatively old; I think it was originally printed in the 1929. It is by far the best on the market. Muldoon was one of the finest astral projectionists that there is. Or was–I think he is in spirit now. He did a beautifully detailed study. One of the things that he bumped into all the time was this problem with time. Carrington would want him to go someplace, for instance they were going to have a party at Buckingham Palace, and so Muldoon would lay down on a cot and project to the ballroom there, hoping to bring back a list of who the people at the party were. When he got there, he would find nobody there. So then they started snooping around and they found that he had arrived at sometime in the past. The party hadn't started yet. There was no way to control that point in time.

There is also some work that the Air Force did, referred to in The Sacred Mushroom by Andrija Puharich, and they found the same thing. They tried training spies using ESP and they would assign certain things for them to go look at when they did astral projection. For instance, the headlines and the date on a newspaper down on the corner, and things like that. They never were today's date. They were always in the past. It seems as though if you get more than about (at least in my case) if I get more than one hundred yards away from where my body is resting, time starts slipping and it slips very fast and we don't know why.

Secondly, you are always alone.

Lastly, it generally occurs during light sleep but does not interrupt your rest. Most of the time, when you are aware of astral projection, it is just when you are waking up. You may awaken with a start. You will jump because your etheric body hasn't quite gotten back into you so that your conscious mind registers it when you wake up. You can delegate it as kind of a sightseeing thing. I have some pet places that I like to go to for my astral projection–one is the Zabriskie Point in Death Valley; the other is just north of General Sherman in the sequoias at Giant Forest. Surprisingly enough, when I project to those two locations, which I do quite regularly, I am always there at either 10:00 in the morning or 2:00 in the afternoon regardless of what time it was when I went to bed. I can tell this by the angle of the shadows from the sun. It is a funny routine. Sometimes it's a little disappointing, because I would like to watch the sun come up in both of those places but so far I have never made it, astrally projection-wise.

But remember these things–it is an ESP phenomena, you have no control of time, you are always alone, and it always occurs during light sleep. The reason I want you to remember those three things is because we are going to talk about another thing that is almost always confused with astral projection and for a lack of a better term we will call it soul travel.

Soul Travel—

Here again we have three things that I want you to remember about it.

Soul travel always occurs during deep sleep.

You are always taken by a guide or a teacher and you will be aware of him. You will be aware of his presence.

You will very likely not remember what you studied. The point of soul travel is to supply you with the information that you will need at a later time when you might not have time to grab the information quickly enough to use it.

Remember, soul travel always occurs during deep sleep. You are *always* accompanied by a guide or teacher. You may remember starting to go somewhere with your guide or teacher, but exactly what you did will escape you. So you will generally not remember it.

So keep those two things separate, astral projection and soul travel. They are entirely different. If you watch as you start to experience these things, time and time again, you will begin to spot that subtle difference.

There are a couple of other "biggies," and one of them you may not be familiar with at all. But, again they are things that are an awful lot of fun. They are called bilocation.

<u>Bilocation</u> —

You can see by the term what it means: simply being in two places at the same time. In all forms of bilocation there is an absolute spiritual law in action: non-interference. I will touch on that a little more heavily when we get down to a very critical form of bilocation.

First of all, by simple definition–bilocation is a deliberate will of the mind. The physical body is at rest; it is not sleeping. Notice the difference–it is at rest but is not sleeping. In the full controlled phase, the body can appear to be dead. The etheric body is used and goes elsewhere. Bilocation really falls into four categories. There are only three that you can do anything about directly.

Bilocation 1—

Merging your etheric into a physical, non-living object to investigate and experience that object. This is required of all student Buddhists, to merge into a stick of incense and identify it. You can merge into a piece of wood, a candle, a stick of incense. When you get good enough–a candle flame which is very exciting! If you think any of you have had fun trips on acid or anything else, wait until you bilocate into the tip of a flickering candle sometime–that is an experience! As I said, this is a test required of all Buddhist monks. They put up a whole series of incense sticks, some of them having fragrance in them and some of them not having fragrance in them. They ask you to bilocate into each stick, and to identify what the fragrance is, and you had better be right.

Bilocation 2—

These get more difficult as we go. A change of form. The etheric body is made to match exactly the body of another life form–a bird, a plant, a man, an animal, whatever. Non-interference is strongly in play at this time. If the host senses you, you must withdraw at once. Not to be melodramatic, but if you don't withdraw, your teachers will make sure that you do! And that is not the best way to end Bilocation 2, believe me. So remember that if you are sensed, you must back out immediately. A plant, of course, is the easiest. The first thing you will notice as you merge your etheric into a plant is that you will feel the sap or the water in this case, running up your body. It feels like you have stepped into a shower where the shower head is on the floor and you've got this stuff coming up past you. It is a beautiful feeling.

It is very difficult to bilocate into animals. I've succeeded with a red-tailed hawk. We live out by Lake Val Sereno overlooking the lake, quite high up. One afternoon I was lying out there getting some sun on the veranda and this huge red-tailed hawk was flying around. I thought, "Oh, how neat!" So I quickly went through the various steps: I identified a match, locked in, and suddenly I was with him. And was instantly disappointed! Because of course I was thinking in terms of the exhilaration of flying and feeling the wind sailing by and wiggling my feathers and all this, but all he was doing was hunting for a mouse or a lizard. He was not aware of flying at all! When I got back, and almost in tears when I related this to Tau Sing, he said, "Next time when you go walking downtown, will you be aware of walking? Or will you be thinking about what you are going to go do?"

Well, I interfered with the hawk. He flew out over the lake and towards the tail end of the lake, I wanted to go back over and see what the marshes look like from up there. Now, I have built a lot of model airplanes, so I thought that all I would have to do is just tip this one wing tip and we will just pivot around. I did it; he sensed it and he collapsed his wings and we fell, tumbling. I let go and disengaged as quickly as I could. He recovered and took back off shaking his head and feathers and everything else, and I got thoroughly reprimanded by Tau Sing for doing such a dumb thing. The whole problem is that you interfere with their nervous system. You start changing a command that their nervous system didn't give and it really fouls them up. He literally forgot how to fly for just a few seconds. If I hadn't gotten out, he would have crashed into the ground and killed himself, pure and simple. But I got out quick enough that he spread his wings and was able to come back up. He stayed away from our house for a long time. He and his mate are back now, but I leave them alone; I don't pick on them.

I bilocated using form 2 into a friend of mine's body one time to see what it would feel like. Tau Sing warned us not to match memory networks or thought processes. So it was only a partial matching as far as the body was concerned. It felt okay; it felt kind of like my body. He is thinner than I am, so it felt tighter, but part of that was because I did not let my head match into the rest of his. The reason for that for all of you who play with Bilocation 2, even you husbands and wives or lovers–don't play games! I don't care how much you love one another, there are things in your mind that are private and are very personal. Neither one of you as lovers or husbands and wives, really want to know that. So it is best not to play with Bilocation 2 with a human form. There are some places in some very advanced forms of healing where it can be used. We only have some sketchy notes on that. But we will have to go into those at another time. The most important thing to remember is that non-interference is at play and if you do not step out when the host senses you, you will be taken out. As I said, it is a very rude way to stop Bilocation 2.

Bilocation 3—

This is the most beautiful thing that there is. It is almost total etheric projection. The body is at rest, seemingly dead. The etheric body is projected in a solid form and can be seen by ordinary physical eyes. The time you can be out of your body by using this technique is unlimited. Surprisingly enough, from all of the information that we have from the Eastern philosophies and monasteries, the body does not age during this time. It is in, as close as possible to, a state of perfect suspended animation. The projected etheric body will even have an aura C. So it is very difficult to spot one. You prearrange your location where you want to project into. For those of you who have read <u>Life and Teaching of the Masters of the Far East</u> by Baird Spalding, Emil and Josh use this technique all through it. I think it is Emil who puts his body under a bush and he is gone for several months; he comes back and they have to scrape away the leaves and whatnot to get him out. While there are a lot of things in those books that are not exactly as they really happened to Baird Spalding himself, many of the things are true and accurate. I think that the thing that is so disarming about it is how casual they are about things that seem miraculous. It is only because of our narrow sight, that we believe it is.

I have used Bilocation 3 a few times. I am diligently working on it so that I can project down here because there is a form of Bilocation 3 which is called Bilocation 3 with Bifurcation. In other words, you would bilocate your etheric form out, make it solid, divide it in two, divide that and make four, and here would be four Genes standing here! Then I could hit all the circles during class, and have lots of fun! It has only one big drawback. As you put them all back together, you are suddenly going to have four sets of memories that all occurred at the same time. What your mind would do with that I'm not real sure.

Response to a question from the audience about clothing during etheric projection. Your etheric body doesn't care if it has clothes on it or not. It is one of these things in Bilocation 3 that I have succeeded with: I have been naked. I scared the devil out of one observer and got scolded for it. I get scolded very often in some of these advanced things! My first attempt at Bilocation 3 was to simply bilocate, walk into my tropical fish room, and reach up like I was going to feed the fish. Because then if they could see me, they would all come to the front of the tank which would mean that I was in solid form. And they did. 150 fish came to the front of the aquarium expecting me to feed them. Then a little later on when I got a little better control of it, as I was doing some stuff in the Akashic Record work, there is a certain book in the Vatican Library that I wanted to see. So I projected to the Vatican Library and found out where the book was, but I did not look around carefully enough. I thought the place was empty. So, I came back, went through the whole routine again, went into Bilocation 3, and bang–I was standing next to this desk on which the books were located. Suddenly I sensed someone behind me. I turned around and here knelt a poor little Catholic priest with his cross out in front of me, screaming prayers. There I stood in my birthday suit and I am certain that he thought Satan himself had simply just appeared! I got thoroughly scolded for it because you are not supposed to do those kinds of things! That was a gross error on my part. I should have sensed his vibration before I did it. But, so help me God, I did not. I did not spot him at all.

Bilocation 4—

It is extremely rare. It has only been done one or two times. The reason is this–it is always done under the guidance of a high teacher where a group of people are taken back in three dimensional form to observe a scene in the Akashic Record as it really occurred, so that they can simply be part of the scene and observe it. It can only be done with a group that is working in total harmony. It can only be done with a group who has mastered Bilocation 3. It can only be done with the help of a very high teacher. So that is something that a lot of us can aim for. The first three you can learn to do by simple exercise and training. Those are requirements to even allow you to approach Bilocation 4. Bilocation 4, of course, since it involves work with the Akashic Record, can only be done in the past because in the Akashic Record, the future does not exist. You can go into the past. In fact in my notes here, Tau Sing told us some time ago that one of the things that Amenterret wanted us to do, was to elect a special group to go through these things so that he could take us back to Karnac in 1475 BC. The group would be able to recognize Don Schwartz, one of our healers here at the Chapel, in his lifetime at that time. That is one of the things that we would like to do, but we have a lot of homework to do first.

Now this next one is one that is very difficult to pin down. I want you to listen very carefully to what I say.

Thought Projection—

The deliberate projection of images by thought either from yourself or from a teacher. It may seem like bilocation but it is not. The way to tell the difference is that in thought projections you will always be aware of yourself, the real you. In other words, if I bilocate and try to step into those flowers, it would be, of course, Bilocation 2 because they are alive. I can imagine what it would be like. To feel like a leaf, feel like a white petal, and so on and so forth. But at the same time that I am doing that, I am aware that my buttocks are sitting here on this chair. If I did Bilocation 2 into those flowers, I would not be aware of this body at all, or the light bouncing off of these papers in my eyes–not at all. I would be that flower. In our next lesson, we will learn the steps to start Bilocation 1. The thing that I will want you to watch there is to be aware when you are no longer aware of your physical body. This will give you a hint that you are there. The same thing holds true in the advanced forms of Trance 3A, B, and C. You will not be aware of you seated in the chair. I know this is one of the things that I have scolded Tau Sing about. If I don't really pay attention, if I were to just sit down here, and speak to you and if his influence was strong, I would sit in a lotus position. Well, years ago I had the cartilage removed from my left knee, so if I sit that way, for twenty or thirty minutes, I can't walk until I have everything back into position and going again. So, if I go into trance in a seated lotus position, my body won't know that my knee is throbbing and giving me all of the signals ("Hey idiot, straighten me out!") and this kind of thing, because I am not there. But then when I come back, I have to pay the price. So I have learned to get comfortable first. Remember how I have harped on getting comfortable for all of these things? Especially in these–trance and bilocation–be sure to be very comfortable first.

We are going to break now so that you can get into classes. Give some thought to this. You will have some questions next time. I know we have covered a lot of material. The only reason that I covered it fast is because especially in the next series of classes you are going to be working with some of these things in class. I wanted you to be aware that when you are sitting there going into meditation and Rosita says to you, "No, you only touched Stage 1," you will know what she means. Or if you have gone in and you are working on trance and someone says, "No, that was Stage 3A," you will know what it was. That way you can judge your own progress and your own development and gain ground faster. So file it away, jot down some questions and we'll dive into those next time. Let's take a break for about ten minutes and then end up in class.

"The student and the teacher are the same.
The student never stops learning and the teacher
who grows will impart his growth to his students…
This is the pathway:
Meditation…
Practice of skills…
Display of skills…
Observation of one's true level…
Total absence of delusion…
Learning to live with your newly developed sensitivity…"

From Tau Sing

Doc Tau Lu by Tau Sing, tranced by Rev. Eugene C. Larr

February 12, 1976. Good evening, ladies and gentlemen. It is again a great privilege to talk to you, but may I first explain that I am fulfilling the request made by this entity, that I place on one tape a brief history and outline of the formulation of the Green Jade Priesthood, and their building and guiding of the lamasery at Doc Tau Lu.

The history of the Green Jade is lost almost in antiquity, for its earliest beginnings predate the written history of mankind by thousands of years. By consulting the Akashic Record, it is possible to see how each of the original nine, that constituted the formation of the Green Jade, explored in their various countries and various studies. They mastered many, many traits that were later to be considered the symbols or significant points of the most high. But to bring it into one concise package, it would be most apropos to start the story in 1017 B.C.

At this point in time, nine members of the Green Jade assembled together, three in spirit form, the others in three dimensional reality. They decided among themselves to make a retreat in which could be stored the guidance and knowledge of those great teachers of that day, as well as those great teachers that would come on the scene as time passed slowly by. They worked diligently to lay out a design of the core structure of the buildings that are now, as you know them, Doc Tau Lu.

It was made in a very remote area of the planet in that southwestern part of the country that you now call Tibet. The reason for placing the lamasery in such a remote area is twofold. One, the beauty, serenity, and tranquility of the setting is almost beyond imagination. And the other, of course, is to isolate it from those wandering people, both past and present, who would not understand what the lamasery was doing and could do it much harm. For it has been said, "A man who does not understand beauty cannot stand to have it around." It was decided to build the lamasery on a large plateau with a steep cliff dropping to the north, beyond which could be seen some of the highest mountains on the earth's surface, many of those some of the finest examples of glaciated peaks known anyplace in the world. But I digress. Many times we experimented at controlling matter. The nine working together had mastered completely the imagery and formation so that rock, both granite and limestone, could be easily handled. The nine decided on what you would call a floor plan and proceeded to work on this core structure. The nine working together completed the core in a little over twenty hours by sheer mental exercises.

Once completed, the lamasery was a thing of beauty and, of course, it was added to as time goes on. But it became apparent that some protection must be placed around the lamasery. And so, by using mental energy, a screen was erected that would make the lamasery invisible to those who would view it without psychic knowledge. This screen is erected some ten feet from the outer walls of the lamasery itself. When it is in place, it renders the lamasery quite impossible to see.

The screen is not erected at all times, for I'm sure you realize that personages as high as those of the Green Jade can detect the presence of a visitor or intruder long before they would be in sight of the lamasery. In fact, it is quite easy to detect a single person within a radius of thirty miles of the lamasery itself. When someone comes within that detectable area, it is easy to analyze, to see. Will they be potential friend or potential foe? If the latter is the decision, the screen is erected and in no way will they be able to see the lamasery at all.

It is still in operation and is used many, many times. There are nine priests, not the original nine of the Green Jade, but–how could you say–student priests, whose job it is to erect the screen when they are directed to do so. Usually, the screen need only be used for short periods of time, for there is very little travel in that part of the world.

After the lamasery was built, over the next two years much time was spent in contacting those persons, both in the three dimensional world and those on a spiritual plane, to invite them to join and to partake of our mission. You may find it interesting to know that during the eighteen days that actual decisions of invitations were made, many refused to join. Many of the personages, though they were quite high, had decided that possibly there would be some more efficient ways of managing our goals and declined to join, either as Green Jade, or as students to grow into that plane and level of awareness that is required to become a true Priest of the Green Jade.

I would have to point out, that at this point in time you must remember that most of mankind lived a very primitive sort of life, and it is only today, with the modern conveniences, that man seems to have advanced. But alas, he has replaced true awareness with instrumentation, which in most cases has done more to shackle him than to set him free. Many people did come to Doc Tau Lu to work, to study, and to build a reservoir. But knowledge would be given to the world and to those students who were earnestly seeking. At that time, it was decided that the maximum number who would be members of the Green Jade would be 333.

Doc Tau Lu was added to in structure as time went on–some of it, of course, by actual manufacturing with the use of three dimensional hands. Other sections of course, were added, as was the original core structure, as mental exercises for those who attained the highest realm of awareness.

We postulated three rules that were to govern those at Doc Tau Lu. The three rules were necessary to maintain a degree of harmony and love that is absolutely required for the fine advances of the individual man. Those three things you have been told many times by this entity, for they are of extreme importance.

The First Rule is moderation in all things, which you are all very familiar with.

The Second Rule is non-interference. Each has his own pathway and will work his way along that path, diligently and quickly or more slowly, depending on how he handles the mental framework within which he is working.

The Third Rule is that there would be no distraction of any kind. This one sounds rather simple, but I am sure that you can see that it is linked closely with *Number 1*, for distractions cause disharmony, and this makes rapid advancement almost totally impossible. But as time walked on, we found that only these three were required, for living within this framework one can develop high and develop most quickly.

Much time was to pass by, while all those of us who lived and worked at Doc Tau Lu, both in spirit form and in the three-dimensional, strived to not only perfect ourselves, but to help those whose needs came to our awareness.

It was then many years before a young man appeared on the scene, that all of us at the lamasery knew was going to be one of those bright lights that would illumine all of mankind. He was born of a royal family, but at a tender age knew that the life of leisure was not the pathway of understanding; there was something more. You know this individual as Gautama, the Buddha. He worked for many years, both in conjunction with some of us at Doc Tau Lu and, of course, in seeking his own pathway. It was not a new pathway. It was not a startling revelation, but a refinement of a pathway that mankind has known for a long, long time.

The entity that you know as Sir, who is a member of the Green Jade, realized that Gautama Buddha was going to be one whose knowledge and guidance we would require at Doc Tau Lu. So he incarnated to be raised nearby to become Ananda, the favorite pupil of Gautama, the Buddha.

Buddha, as you know, lived a long time as sages go, and when he finally crossed over he joined us at Doc Tau Lu and continued his work in designing techniques and processes by which man could be liberated from himself and become more at harmony with the world in total. He developed very quickly, becoming a Green Jade Priest and has now gone on to merge as one with the universe. But he has left behind a priceless record of techniques and details that we will give to those students at the appropriate time, when they are most needed. They are held in reserve here at Doc Tau Lu and at a retreat in Ceylon, and in the appropriate time will become known to the world.

Some years again passed by and many people visited Doc Tau Lu, both in spirit and in real form. Finally a young priest came to our awareness. He was a student of Gautama and worked long diligent hours at translating and transcribing many of the writings that were given by Gautama, the Buddha. Then, in the year 342 BC, he was asked to join the lamasery. You know this entity by the name of Gene. He is working today at a project that he has tried many, many times to teach others, to open their eyes and see. If we were to look at his long background that he has played this role, we would have to say he has failed many, many times. But he is still persistent and he will bring much understanding as time goes on.

Many of you have been at Doc Tau Lu in various forms, and when the time is right you will be told and you will be most surprised.

The other in the group that you know very well, the one that you call Don, has been at Doc Tau Lu many times in spirit and three dimensional form, but he is more closely associated with a retreat similar to Doc Tau Lu that is located in North Africa, where his teachers have worked with him for thousands and thousands of years. But he is a student of the Green Jade and, upon reaching his higher point, will identify with Doc Tau Lu. I have deliberately left out many, many persons who have come and gone at Doc Tau Lu, for as I say, when the time is right, such knowledge will be given to those that might find it interesting.

Again, many years were to pass by before a great teacher came on the scene that was to leave a lasting record. There are many, many teachers whose material is safely filed away at Doc Tau Lu that you know nothing of. As time goes on, some of this scholarly work in archeology will reveal many great teachers.

Many of their words and thoughts are so familiar, because many have said the same things. But as I say, many years were to pass until another bright spark appeared on the scene.

This was the one you know as Jesu Christi. He worked diligently in his early life, and as he moved into manhood and began to teach what he knew to be the truth and the way, it is interesting to see how he developed. Many of his early teachings were more or less colored by the upbringing of his family and the traditional religion that surrounded the area at the time of his birth and for the first many years of his life. I've seen that he would be on the scene and would be a most appropriate one, reincarnated as one of his disciples to walk at his side, to both learn and to help in any way that I can.

As Jesu Christi became more and more aware, he knew that he must contact a greater number of people than those in the few simple villages that he visited, and he sent many into the world. Many of these that he sent were Green Jade, and some were very important, for if you will consult some of the biblical texts, you will find references to those who were working miracles. Six of these were avatars, in the absolute sense of the word. Because of Jesu Christi's early teachings, most high entities who would appear around him to act as guides would come in the form and shape of what you would call *angels of the Lord*, for these he would accept. But as time goes on, he developed his awareness to a keen point and then knew what it was all about.

Again some time passed by, and then in the year about 500 AD Mohammad came on the scene directly from Doc Tau Lu, for he was a Green Jade and he enlightened a great many. Some of his truths have been greatly misunderstood, but at the core of them will be found that great single understanding that appears in the teachings of all great men. And as time goes by, scholars will link the teachings of not only the three I've mentioned, but of many others, and will see running through them a golden thread of knowledge, a golden thread that is the same thread, although spoken in many different tongues and with many different flourishes, depending on the culture in which the words were spoken.

As things now stand at Doc Tau Lu, there [are] sixty-three Green Jade Priests. Fifty-nine are men and four are women. This group is extremely powerful and could give a great knowledge to the world, as if it were presented in a blinding flash. But this would be interference. And so, following the prime directive, only those who knock will find the door opening, and only those who seek will find and know.

Many, many times, various members of the Green Jade and others, who have developed on their own a high developed awareness, have tried to impress the world with the simplicity of the proper path, and like this entity have failed time and time again. For the last thousand years, very few of the Green Jade have reincarnated. Those of the Green Jade who are avatars have done many, many things, some of them recorded in other religions as miracles, and in the context of which they were presented, it would be most appropriate to call them that.

I myself have been, as you receive this information, a member of the Green Jade since its foundation. And while I have not, of course, as yet reached perfection, I have not a long way to go. For the edification of this entity, I would tell him I have five more steps to go and I will wait for you, Gene, and we will take them together.

There are many things that man must learn. Most he already knows but does not practice. But to complete the concepts and drives that [have] made Doc Tau Lu what it is today, I would step slightly into the future.

The goal of mankind has been expressed by many, many people. Some have expressed it in strange ways and strange words, but they all say essentially the same thing. The goal of mankind is to become totally aware and to walk the earth as a god. He can do this and in time he will reach that exalted position. At that point, also, the history of the lamasery at Doc Tau Lu will be finished and its work completed, when all of the students have become Green Jade Priests, so that the lamasery is then inhabited by the 333. Our work will be finished, and the lamasery will be able to be discontinued.

It would be dissolved back into the basic components of the surrounding itself. For when that time is reached, there will be total harmony with all mankind obeying the simple directive of loving each other. As things stand now, man spends much time wallowing in his own misery. If he would but stop and wallow in his own concepts in things of beauty, what a different world this ball would be.

The works of man have gone endlessly into tangent directions that do not lead directly to his own spiritual highest and best good. But if man will stand, open his eyes, and see the beauty of life that can be his. But what does he see most often? Suffering, anguish, and struggle.

The great longing of mankind is to be free. We here at Doc Tau Lu sit waiting for that call, for we will answer the cry of those who suffer, those who are filled with anguish and dread. Those who do not understand what they are about need only knock and the door truly will be opened, for when you seek you will know. And having once known, you can move at rapid paces toward that time when you, as an individual, will be free and know the story.

But if all of you will practice and learn to knock at the right door and actively seek, you will know. And then, when that great day has come, the universe will be truly at your very fingertips.

Good evening…

A Day in the Life of Jesus

Part 1

Good morning, ladies and gentlemen. Please excuse me while I remove my sweat-creating machine. Summer is a really bad time for me. I have always thought we should move the Chapel to just slightly above the Arctic Circle. For some of you who may be aware of it, I just returned from an extended trip to Mexico, collecting orchids and swimming, and doing all kinds of fun things.

We always bump into the same problem of language. While Spanish will help you a great deal, some of the Indian dialects, characteristic of the area, are spoken. They are beautiful people–diminutive, small, truly beautiful; nothing like the Spanish or Mexican at all, but beautiful in their own way.

When I arrived home, I found a joke in one of my magazines I thought was most fitting. A mother mouse took her children mice for a walk and suddenly there was a large dog. The mother mouse backed up and said, "Ruff, ruff, ruff, ruff," and the dog ran away. The mother mouse simply said, "Sometimes it helps to know a second language." I think that certainly holds true when we are out of this country. Well, we had a beautiful trip and I am glad to be back. I feel like I brought the heat with me, but hopefully it will cool down as we go on.

Over the last many months, I have been talking about many sections of the Bible; trying to impress you with the beauty of the man Jesus. Not his saintliness, or godliness, but his true self as an individual human being.

There is a technique we use in certain spiritual studies that allows us to see an event as it happened. It allows us to see the event in real time as it is actually happening. It is called the Akashic Record.

A little while ago, I casually asked one of my high teachers if I could actually watch a day in the life of Jesus. What did he really do? I found very suddenly that I had to be very specific because there were many days where they did nothing. They would sit around and swat flies and dangle their feet in the stream and basically discuss the things that you and I discuss all the time. Then about a month ago, I bumped into a section of one of the days that I want to relate to you this morning, for it gives several lessons and it gives us an insight as to what this man was really like.

As you know, I normally do not read from the podium unless I am reading the Bible itself, but it is very important that I get across the words as they were really said. I am going to read directly some of the information. The information we obtain from the Akashic Record is exactly what they are saying. It is like walking among a three-dimensional laser projection. It is as real as this room. You can hear, you can smell, you can sense temperatures, literally everything, as if you are really there.

The major drawback it has as an historical data-gathering mechanism is that it happens in real time. To actually go through what I am going to give you this morning, is a total of something like nine hours spent in a light form of trance, simply watching what is going on. I was popping back and forth, of course, not in a single setting, but over several months' period.

Some of it happens very quickly and with diligent work with your teachers, you can literally replay the tape. It is almost as if those of you who have recording machines and you want to see something, you have to rewind the tape and watch it again. You will notice that you will overshoot many times what you actually wanted to hear, because you don't have a counter. So you would overshoot and this is beautiful because it gives you verification of what you received before.

I would like to give you Part I of A Day in His Life.

I appeared on the scene, late evening, watching them as they were walking along. It was Jesus, Peter, and James. They were walking along the road and it was getting dark. The road was simply a wide spot where there were few plants growing. Wandering up the floor of a valley, and wandering up ahead, you could see where there was a stream. It was beginning to get dark and there was a grove of trees. The three of them walked into the grove of trees, and I believe from looking at the trees, they were olive trees. However, the grove did not seem to be laid out geometrically like we would see an orange grove today.

What did they look like? Jesus was about my height, or maybe a little taller; dark brown hair, almost black, coming to about his shoulder, full beard, rather neatly trimmed, close to the face. His eyes were quite sunken, his cheeks quite hollow. We would call him on the thin side definitely. His eyes were incredibly beautiful, rich dark brown pupils with dark brown irises. His irises were so dark brown; he almost looked as though he had no irises at all. His forehead was quite high; his hair combed back; large nose, characteristic of the Jewish people.

Peter was more built like me, stocky, on the heavy side. He was older than Jesus, I would guess, because there appeared to be some gray at the temples of his hair. His hair was shorter, cut very unevenly, like he had simply taken some out and cut if off. You will recall he was a fisherman and so he was probably in the water a great deal. He would keep his hair cut short to keep it out of his face, to keep it out of the way. As I say, he was a heavier man, stockily built, more round in his face, with the same dark beautiful eyes, not as deeply sunken or set as Jesus' but a very, very beautiful gentleman. Older as I say, I believe.

James was younger than either one of them. This is James who was Jesus' brother. He was much younger, thin, tall–taller than either of the other two. His hair was long and hung down longer than the others; it hung down his back at least three or four inches longer. He also was on the thin side.

What were they wearing? They were wearing the typical dress of the area. When Don and I were in Egypt, we saw them all the time–called galabiyas. It is a single long shirt-like sack that has a collar that comes around and is open to about the mid-chest. It has long sleeves that are very loose and open, fits loosely around the waist, and falls clear to the ground.

Their sandals were thongs with a single toe loop that the big toe went through. The sandal had what looked to be a small bit of leather that tied up over the top of the foot, that came from underneath to hold the thong on the foot.

All three carried with them what I would loosely call a blanket. It was a piece of material about six feet long, coarse woven of a natural color, a whitish brown kind of color. The galabiyas were all light brown, not the startling and beautiful stark whites, blues, and reds we see in the paintings of some of those older artists. They carried this blanket, if you would call it, over their shoulder, folded many, many times so that it hung down a long ways on both front and back. Peter, on his other shoulder, was carrying a bag. It looked like leather, roughly sown, and in it they carried their food stuffs for the three of them.

As I say, it was getting dark, and they walked into the grove of trees and sat down under several trees, whose branches mingled together. Peter took out of his bag some dried fish, and some flat bread. The bread reminded me of pita bread, like we have today but I don't believe it actually had a pocket in it. It was not hard and stiff like unleavened bread, but was soft and would remind you a great deal of a thick flour tortilla. The small fish were dried fish about three inches long, which they either ate one at a time or rolled up in the bread and ate together.

They then laid their blankets, if you would call it that, down on the ground, and laid themselves down so that their upper torso was on the blanket. They pulled the blanket up over their face and left a little air hole for air to come in, and went to sleep. At this point, watching the Record you could simply sit there and watch them sleep for the next six hours or so, but this is not too productive so I stepped away and picked up the scene about morning time.

They awoke at first light. The sun had not come up. The light was in the sky. They walked over to a small stream and refreshed themselves–mainly washing their feet and their legs, their hands and their faces. Meanwhile they were talking of all kinds of things. This is one of the things that really impressed me. How you would write down what Jesus said and the way we would say it today is important because they talked about all kinds of things–the bugs that kept crawling in and out of their hair, the temperature of the coming day which they agreed was going to be hot, how nice and cool it was the night before, and the little village they were heading for, which appeared to have no name. I tried to pin down even thought form images of a name for the village. It was a small place, a few hundred inhabitants, so it did not have a name per se. After cleaning themselves up, they sat down under the trees again and had breakfast. They once again had this flat bread, with dried fish and what I believe was dried figs. They were dark brown in color and shaped about like this, and they each had a small handful of those with their fish and their bread.

So using that as an introduction to the scene, I was curious to see what they were going to talk about that day–why my spirit teacher had chosen that specific day and that specific time for me to observe part, at least, of a day in his life.

As they started walking, James pulled his galabiya up on the left side. He had a rip in the left side of it and he was trying to fix it. He picked up a small stick and he was pushing the small threads through the coarse material and tying them on the back so the threads did not stick out and look all bunched up.

Jesus was watching this and asked, "What are you doing to your robe?"

James said, "There is a tear in it and I am trying to mend it so I will look properly dressed when we meet the people of the village."

Jesus replied, "But James, do you think the outward appearance of yourself will properly teach the people?"

James stopped and asked, "But if I do not look my best, what will they think of me?"

And Peter answered, "Don't you remember what Jesus said about being known by your works. It is more important to do, then to be looked at."

Jesus reached down and picked a flower. There were flowers growing all over the place, wild flowers. This one looked like a poppy. It was red and had a purplish-black center with a lot of fine yellow lines going around the black center, flanked by the red. He reached down, picked the flower, and held it up between the three of them. He said, "Do you see this flower and how beautifully it is dressed? It does not sow, nor does it spin cloth, yet it is dressed in clothes more beautiful than the richest man can possess. Why do we consider it beautiful? Can you clothe it and make it better? It is at it should be. Perfect as it is. If you are perfect, it matters not what clothes you wear for what you are, is what you are."

James then looked at the ground and said, "Then why did the priest of the tabernacle go about so richly dressed and jeweled?"

Jesus replied, "It is not the outer cloth that announces a man. If he is a good priest, his robes will not make him better and if he is not a good priest, the finest robes will fool no one. Remember, it is what is in the bottle that matters, not its shape or color. Listen and remember, beware of the wolves who dress themselves in the innocence of lambskins. Listen with care and rightly hear. Look with care and rightly see. Do not be deceived by sight or by hearing. You must see and hear as it really is. Those men who deceive others begin by first deceiving themselves, and they know of their deception, and have a reward of the same kind."

That is profound and it is heavy. It is one of those things that we can see how it fits into many of the things we read, especially in the Aramaic text of the Bible. But how difficult it would be, assuming that James or Peter wrote it down thirty years later, to quote those passages. It would be almost impossible. I went through them several times, to make sure I had them right word-for-word because some of it does sound a little strange, but the message it gives is far too obvious.

They continue to walk along the road, talking of all kinds of things. A small grasshopper jumped on the side of the galabiya that James was working on and he brushed it aside and they laughed about the grasshoppers eating the plants in the field.

I think to end this session, my teacher guided me to a beautiful scene just a few moments later. They were walking along and they stopped under a big tree to listen to a bird. It was a large tree and had heavy shade and they listened to the bird as it sung its greetings to a new day. That is Jesus.

Part II

So glad you could be with us this morning. I want to continue with Part II of A Day in the Life of Jesus. For those of you who were not here for Part I, the technique I am using is stepping into the Akashic Record which is a record, or a library, of everything that has happened on the face of the planet from day one to this very fraction of a second. With the help of your high teachers, you can step back into it and watch it, like a three-dimensional motion picture, complete with sound, sense, touch, and feeling–everything about it.

The only flaw in using it as an historical source of documentation is that it is in real time. In order to see this one day in the life of Jesus, it has occupied the better part of four months, doing a small bit at a time because it is very difficult to go into that degree of trance and stay there for twenty-four hours–to actually walk along with them all the time. In doing this, I have tried to back up and actually replay the Akashic Record tape, if you will. Most of the time, I would overshoot it to make sure I was at the same location at their point of time, because other than a few very spectacular things that occurred, one hour of the day was very much like any other hour of the day.

As you recall last time, they had been walking along a road on the way to a small town, the name of which, I cannot locate in the Akashic Record. It simply may not have had a name since it was a small village of maybe a couple hundred at the outside. They had last stopped under a large tree and listened to a bird. It was morning and they continued to walk up a small road that was about six or eight feet wide. Along the road to the right was a small intermittent stream.

As I mentioned last time, I am going to refer to notes constantly. In fact, when I am quoting I have simply written it down in long hand because I do not want to misquote things that I heard. They were written down within minutes after I heard them so there is no question about me forgetting what was said.

As I say, they were walking along this road. It was hot. There was a wind blowing from the forward left and they walked along talking about all kinds of things, just like you or I would talk about.

Next time you are downtown walking along, find two people and walk beside them and listen to what they are talking about—maybe about Aunt Agnes or Uncle Harry. It may be about the flats she had on the morning before–a constant chatter of rather irrelevant material. So I was amazed when I heard their discussion of a grasshopper that landed on James' galabiya, his clothes, and as he flicked the grasshopper off, they commented about how far it could fly or how fast it could hop.

These are very profound things, you see... (chuckle, chuckle). So we are walking along this pathway, or roadway, and an older woman came from the side and saw them. She was carrying a large basket of dates that were covered with a square cloth that hung down on four corners of the basket. She was carrying the basket over her arm. She recognized Jesus, and walked up to him, uncovering her basket, and said, "Oh Rabbi, please have a few dates and give me your blessing." I quizzed my teacher to ask him how she knew to call him Rabbi. My teacher said that it was because she had heard that he had given lessons on the steps of the temple and no one was allowed to teach or preach from the steps of the temple, or on Holy ground, unless he were a rabbi.

So she recognized him; she had seen him before. Jesus turned to her smiling. She knelt down. He placed his right hand on her head and with a quizzical smile on his face, he said, "My blessing be with you all your days." She rose, said nothing, and smiled at him. She gave each of the three of them a handful of dates and went on her way. A simple little interlude but it had a great deal of beauty to it.

They walked along eating the dates and they talked about the dates extensively. Some of the comments were clever so I wrote them down. Incidentally, as they were eating the dates, they would take the pits out of their mouths and squeeze them between their thumb and forefinger hard, to see who could pop them further away, like you and I have done with cherry pits and any other kind of thing you can think of. As they walked along, finally Peter said, "These are real sweet. I think they are sweeter than the dates were last year."

James replied, "Yes I agree, the grains of sweet are larger, or at least I think so."

Then Jesus popped up and said, "They say it depends on the amount of water they get. The more water, the better they do. Too much water and they don't do well at all." Jesus continued to say, "It is just like living, too much of a good thing can also be bad for you. Thinking or doing must be done in moderation, not too much good, not too much bad. It is that balance that makes a good life."

Peter stopped walking and they all stopped. He looked back at Jesus and said, "But how do you tell the difference between good and bad? It is easy in some activities to know the difference but in others, it is very difficult."

Jesus again was smiling. Incidentally, Jesus smiled a great amount of the time. He was a happy man at this point in time, at least. Jesus turned to him smiling, and said, "You must hurt no one. Do whatever you like as long as it hurts not your fellow man, and be sure to count yourself in those who you must not hurt. Help others when they need helping so they in turn can help you when you need."

They walked on along the pathway. James had finished fixing his cloak. As you know, he was tucking in frayed threads so it would look good. When he finished it, he said, "How far is it to the town? Will we be there before dark?"

Peter said, "Yes, we should be there by mid-afternoon." It appeared that they ate no lunch other than the handful of dates that they had. Incidentally, the dates were not the huge ones like we see today. They were small, about the size of my thumb. The pit seemed to be quite large in proportion to the fruit but it was obviously sweet and they obviously enjoyed them.

They talked of many things as they walked along and they finally finished their dates. They walked over to this small stream and, pulling up their robes to the waist, they tied a knot in it to hold it up and waded into the stream about halfway to their knees. They left their sandals lying on the ground beside the stream. They washed their hands and splashed water on their faces and ran their wet hands through their beards and through their hair. Then they came back, shook their feet a few times, retrieved their sandals, and continued to walk up the road.

Ahead of them, a young man was seated on a rock on the side the road. His left shoulder was bandaged with a soiled cloth. Blood stains were easy to see. His left arm hung down limply at his side. James walked quickly ahead to the man and asked, "What has happened to you?" The young man looked up and told of a fight that he was accidentally involved in. Jesus listened. Peter stopped and stood listening to what the young man was talking about as he described a sword cut across his upper chest on the left side. It had gone clear to the bone. He said that a good man had helped him, had treated him the best he knew how, and had bandaged his arm. The good man said that his left arm would never be useful again.

Jesus looked at him and said, "Do you know who I am?"

The young man said, "No, I don't think so."

Jesus said, "I am the promised one. I have come to bring truth to a wayward people."

The young man stood up and he was wearing a simple skirt that was tied around the waist and hung down to just above the knees. He said, "Oh yes, I have heard of you but this is the first time I have ever seen you."

James turned to Jesus, touched him on the side, and said, "Can we do anything to help this poor man? Without the use of his left arm, his life is going to be very difficult."

Jesus turned back to the young man, placing his left hand on the young man's right shoulder and asked, "Do you believe I can make you whole?"

The young man said, "I don't know. I have heard what others have said you have done, but if you could try, I would be most thankful."

Jesus stepped closer to him, undid the bandage which was tied at the top of the shoulder, and let it drop. There were five stitches through a very deep cut through the major muscle that controls the forward motion of the arm. Jesus reached down with his teeth and bit through those threads and pulled them out. The man started bleeding again of course, slowly at first and then increasing. Jesus turned, stepped behind the young man, and pulled him up against his chest with his right hand over the bleeding wound on the man's chest. Blood ran between Jesus' fingers and hand. It ran down his arm, as well as running down the side of the young man.

He slowly moved his hand back and forth across the upper chest. The blood stopped flowing. Jesus reached down and wiped his bloody hand on the man's skirt and then using just the three center fingers of the man's hand, he reached up and slowly ran his fingers along where the cut had been. It was now closed and appeared as a very long red line. He rubbed it a few times and again placed his hand over the wound and held his hand still. Then he took his hand away.

The blood was dry. Through the dried blood, you could see a normal, healthy, hairy chest. There was no line, no crease, and no hint of any error. Jesus closed his eyes and gave the man a simple blessing. "Go, my son, with the knowing that you are whole. May my blessing go with you all the days of your life."

The young man was startled, absolutely nonplused. He didn't know what to do or what to say. He looked up, tears streaming down his face as I am sure you can all imagine. He leaned forward and kissed Jesus, muttering, "Thank you, thank you, thank you." He stood there smiling through his tears, moving his left hand and swinging his left arm, as the three turned and walked away.

They had walked a short distance when James turned to Peter and said, "By the grace of Jehovah, did you see what Jesus did?"

Peter, looking at the ground, did not raise his head and said, "Yes I did. There is so much to think about. This man is much more than you or I understand." They took a few more steps and Peter stopped. "He is truly the one that was promised." He turned and looked at Jesus, just for a moment, then looked back at James and said, "He is like a god walking among us."

Part III

Good morning everyone, indeed it is a lovely time of the year. The temperature is below 80. As you have noticed from the bulletin board, today will be the third part of a little project I set for myself many, many months ago: namely using the Akashic Record of one of my high teachers, Tao Sing, to watch an individual day in the life of Jesu Christi.

Several things surprised me at first because we picked several days to simply watch and see what was going on and for an enormous number of days, nothing went on. They simply walked around, had a good time, ate the fruit, and ate the food people gave them as they walked along. As I really looked at it, I thought where did the writing come from for the New Testament?

I mean, they spent one whole day walking up a stream with their bare feet and their little cloaks pulled up, walking in the stream and laughing along the way at all the people they would joke with and have a good time. It is a little difficult to see a day like that and then imagine what we have created in our image of Jesus–to watch them take off their clothing, bathe in this river (small river), wash their clothes, lay them out on a rock to dry, lay in the sunlight to dry their bodies, and sit there stark naked, spouting words of wisdom.

It is a little different picture than we usually get of Jesus in his snow white raiment and his royal purple robes. His robes incidentally were not even white, they were kind of an off color brown, like a tan, and they were very clean. As you know in so many areas of the holy land, water is a scarce commodity, but this time of year there were streams. Almost every day they washed themselves and/or their clothing which is quite different than ordinary Arabs did at that time, or even today.

As you know in the first two episodes; it sounds like a commercial for television, doesn't it? We were discussing Jesus, Peter, and James. Toward the end of the day, we meet Andrew and right at the end of the day, we meet John.

As you recall, Jesus is about 5 foot 10 inches, with dark hair and dark eyes. His eyes are so brown they are almost black, so it is difficult to see where the pupil stops and the iris begins. He is quite sunken, on the thin side, very prominent cheekbones, very high forehead. His hair comes down to about shoulder length and of course he had rather dominant features of the Jewish ancestry. Peter was stocky, older.

Oh yes, how old was Jesus at this time? Mmm, well, it is hard to say. I would have dubbed maybe thirty.... Somewhere between late twenties and early thirties, but it is difficult to tell just by looking.

Peter was a lot shorter, stocky with gray hair. As you know, he was a fisherman so he was in and out of the water a lot of the time. His eyes were also dark. His face was fuller and rounded, not as sunken as Jesus'.

James was the youngest of the three. He was thin, a little taller than the other two. His hair was brown and pulled back, hanging about three or four inches below the shoulder. I never could see what it was tied with–if it was tied back with a type of a ribbon or band of material, or if it was simply the way the hair was wrapped around itself. It was very difficult to see.

Andrew was about the same age as Jesus and about the same size and shape. He walked with a slow gait and it looked as if his right leg was slightly stiffened. He had dark hair, dark eyes.

John was younger than Jesus and we will meet him at the end of today. John was younger I say, and very well built and very strong. Obviously a very hard worker and yet he was very sensitive; a very sensitive man who loved Christ very much and is called the beloved disciple. He is the one who is with Christ much of the time in a very close way. It is quite obvious that Jesus confided in John. Jesus talked to him apparently about things the rest of the disciples were not privileged to know, so it is interesting to bump into him as we go along this route.

As I did before, I will continue to read many parts. As you know, I normally do not read lectures here at Chapel, but it is so important that the words be given as they were spoken, and not as I might interpret what I might have said under the same conditions, so I will read much of what I will tell you.

Last time, Jesus did a very spectacular healing on a young man who was cut across the chest. It surprised Peter and James beyond imagination. They continued to walk along the road, still talking about the healing of the young man. Finally after some time, Jesus turned to them and said, "Why do you marvel at what I have been teaching you to do? You have seen me heal before and you know I have said that you can do the same thing and you must do it to spread the teachings. Is it possible you still doubt?"

Peter spoke up, "Oh no master, we do not doubt you at all. Yes, we have seen you do all the deeds but I am not sure in my own mind that I am worthy to do the things that you do. I have not led a perfect life as you have, and therefore, I must cleanse myself to be worthy of such great things."

Jesus stopped. He turned to Peter and said, "Peter, are you not worthy of cleansing yourself? If a garment is dirty, it can be washed and made clean again. How can you wash your heart?"

And Peter said, "I have been working on that, been working with myself every day by thought and by prayers."

Jesus smiled and said to Peter, "How long will it take to wash away something you only think is there? Remember that the fire and fear will go out, if you do not feed it. You are as you are. You are worthy of great works or I would not have chosen you."

Peter said, "Thank you master, I will do all that you would have me do."

Jesus stood there for a little bit and then finally he raised his eyes and said, "The words fade quickly and are lost; action and doing leave a lasting sign."

They went on walking. James popped up and said, "I am beginning to see and understand. It is as you have said all along. We harm ourselves from within and if from our goodness we can help others, then we can also help ourselves."

Jesus said the lines we all know very well. "Yes, physician heal thyself. If you cannot help yourself, why think you can save the world? But be of light heart; there is time and I have much to teach you."

A side, subtle footnote there. The moment he said that, there was change in the vibratory feeling of Jesus. It was as if he had said something that was not quite the truth; as if he stepped across some funny little invisible line. It was a strange feeling, a strange feeling indeed.

They walked on to the small village. It had a small synagogue, a simple square building with steps in the front of it. There were probably 200 homes, mud brick, neatly kept. The town was clean and neat. They went to the synagogue and sat on the steps. A number of people began to arrive and many brought food with them. It was fruit and bread and some kind of dried meat that looked like jerky. It was a red meat. It was not fish like we have seen him eat until this time. There was a wineskin with a very dark red wine. They drank the wine, not from beautiful crystal goblets but from very short cups made of clay that were fired but not glazed, so they were porous cups.

After a while, a large group of men had assembled around the steps. A few women were standing against the far building, and were sitting on the ground on rugs, back out of the way on the side of the circle of men, probably totaling about 100 to 150 people in all.

As they began to be quiet, a young man worked his way through the group and approached Jesus. "Master, I am late but there were so many to tell about your coming. Bless me for I am so glad to be here."

And Jesus said, "Bless you Andrew, you have done well. My blessings are with you at all times."

Andrew leaned down, kissed Jesus on the cheek, and sat down on the steps about three feet away from him. Jesus moved up a few steps, three or four steps. He did not stand up. He just scooted up the steps, like you would normally do, and then began to speak.

As you have been told, then he lapsed into various sections of that part of the Old Testament called Leviticus that is concerning law and punishment. I jotted down all that I could of course, and put a lot of it on tape, but I could not find it in the sequence that we find it in Leviticus, so either he was paraphrasing or drawing on different parts randomly. It is quite a big book. As you know, it is part of the Torah. All the teachings were there but they were not in the order we find them in Leviticus in the Bible.

He finished speaking, poured himself another glass of wine, took a couple drinks, and simply sat there. One of the men who were standing by said, "Yes Rabbi, we judges know the law but you have been heard to say, 'Judge not, lest you be judged.' How can we keep order and uphold the law if we do not do our job as judges?"

Jesus said, "You are mixing thistles with figs. I speak of your worthiness as a child of God. You speak of man's law. The law you administer, and the one I have just repeated to you, is the law. I now say to you, do your judging with a cup of compassion for surely you know that all killing is not murder, nor all sins are damnation. Look into the heart of the man accused. Do you know why, do you know how his guts feel? When you truly know of him, then you must judge and judge him under the law, but your judgment is only of this world."

Jesus continued, "There is an inner judgment and only he can judge himself."

The standing man repeated, "Rabbi, what should we do to a man who has wronged but we cannot prove his wrong-doing?"

Jesus said, "If you only think he has done wrong, be of great care. Your thoughts are not his, nor do your thoughts make him a wrong-doer. If he is a wrong-doer, he will punish himself and dearly so, for in his own heart he does know the truth. He will judge and sentence himself, often times more severely than you. You can only take his life; he will destroy his life and his very soul. Each man knows of what he is made, and knowing it, what will create his actions."

Jesus stood up and bowed at his hip. "My blessing be with you, not only this day, but all the days to come."

The four of them walked back down the road that they came up earlier. They walked along and talked about a lot of things. It would be very difficult to write down everything that happened in that period of time. He stopped to scratch a mule–an ass–and to brush the flies that had collected around the mule's eyes. He brushed them away. They stopped to look at fruit stands and almost every time they stopped, the owner of the stand would offer them some. Jesus would always say something or give them a blessing or something of this nature.

But if you wrote down everything that was said, I am sure you can all imagine this. Write down every word you say in a twelve hour day. You would have an enormous volume. As I watched all these things going on, the thing that really hit me was how you would decide of all the things he said in every day, which were real teachings or which were funny little analogies that you and I all come up with, every single day? So it is interesting, as I watched everything they talked about, to pick and choose what to write down.

They were very curious and aware of what was going on. Andrew talked about his going ahead into the town to let them know Jesus was coming. It was very late in the afternoon and they turned aside and went up a small hill. Once over the crest, they came down into a small valley of a grove of trees and prepared to make camp for the night. They spread out this thing they carry, that I call a blanket. It is called a waddee. It is like a narrow long blanket. Anyway, they spread it out and talked idly about various things. Then Jesus said, "Let us give thanks for the day of reward." They bowed their heads and as I watched their thought forms, each was reviewing the actions of the day. In the forefront of Peter's mind was the healing of the young man.

Jesus said, "Now let us be still and seek peace."

They all sat there with hands folded in their laps. Jesus' mind went a total blank and the intriguing thing when I touched it–it felt like I was totally engulfed in a slowly rotating, swirling purplish grey. It was like an enormously deep, shimmering, slowly swimming, swirling motion. It was a beautiful feeling and I would have liked to have stayed there forever but since these are in real time, they stopped their meditation time after about ten minutes. That is as close as I could figure.

Jesus said, "Find a leaf that feels right to you and we will do our practices." Each man picked up a small leaf from the ground. They were about an inch long and about a half-inch wide. I think they were dead olive leaves from their shape. They laid the leaf in the palm of their right hand and they started staring at them. Peter, James, and Andrew started staring at their dead leaves as Jesus watched. Peter could make his leaf wobble but the other leaves remained completely still. By 'wobble,' I mean the leaf was lying in his hand and the leaf would just flop back and forth.

Jesus held out his hand on which a similar leaf was resting. It slowly rose, wobbled a few times, then floated a few inches above his palm, and then froze absolutely still in mid-air. All of them looked at this and then all of them looked back at their leaves. I think some of us know how that feels. Jesus smiled and then looked at them. At this point in time, it was almost as if there were tears in his eyes. But he said, "You must try with more dedication. It is control of the mind that allows you to use the power that is all about you. You know many of my words but still have not applied their action."

Andrew said, "But master, we will learn what you are teaching us, but it takes times to make us truly know."

And Jesus said, "When the talome is gone, it is difficult to remember its fragrance; still yourself now so you will not have to rely upon memory."

I looked up the word 'talome.' It is a desert flower that is extremely sweet. In fact, it is described to be sickeningly sweet. Apparently it belongs to the lily family and blooms only once a year for a very short period of time. So what Jesus is talking about is quite obvious.

They looked at him and then looked at one another and wondered what Jesus was saying and what he really meant. James started to ask directly when a young man entered the grove of trees. Jesus got up and met him. They walked arm in arm back to the group. They exchanged greetings. It was John. John had a large bundle of food which was distributed and they sat about eating and talking. It had grown dark as they prepared for sleep.

John was massaging Jesus' neck and back and there were tears in Jesus' eyes. John leaned forward and kissed him on the cheek and Jesus said, "Oh John, how can it all be finished in time, and the time flies so swiftly."

John said, "They are learning and you must not be so hard on yourself: as you have said, you are following a path that was laid down a long, long time ago. Be happy in the knowing that they all love you. And you know that I love you over all things under heaven and earth." Jesus lay with his head in John's lap and very, very softly sobbing, went to sleep.

We talk about the things that Jesus showed and taught us, and yet, why we don't follow it today? And so I end this series of lectures with a simple footnote. This is how Jesus lived, and tried to teach. What he taught, we all know, and still we do not truly know how to live each and every day.

Through the Eyes of the Buddha

It's interesting the topic that I chose this morning, Through the Eyes of the Buddha, because that topic was chosen several months ago. In the meantime, I was very pleased and happy to take a short trip to Hawaii for a couple of weeks. Arriving at the hotel, rummaging through the drawers, I opened a drawer and here, sitting side-by-side, were the Gideon Bible and this little book, The Teachings of Buddha.

I thought how interesting that the hotel management would be concerned enough about the hotel visitors that come to his hotel, that he would represent two of the most important teachings that the world has ever known, those of Buddha and those of Jesus, the Christ. They worked very, very well together to tie into my topic for this morning. I'm going to try to refrain from comparing the two teachings. It's a temptation and I do it all the time, but I'm going to try not to. I will let you see the similarity, where you see the similarity, and let you pick out what's going on by itself.

A couple of weeks ago we had a session here at the Chapel in which an entity was speaking through me in trance, an entity we know as Tau Sing, who in his last lifetime was a Chinese Tibetan Buddhist. One of our ministers, who is very interested in Buddhism, asked Tau Sing, "When was Gautama, the Buddha, born?" I very quickly received it in Sanskrit, which I jotted down and it meant absolutely nothing to me. So I asked him to please translate it into our understanding today, and using our calendar as a zero point, if you would. It turns out (and I love the Sanskrit phrase, the whole Sanskrit phrase) that it would read like this:

> *5:20 a.m., April 12, 557 B.C., amid the singing of birds and the opening of day flowers.*

Beautiful combination and it is this kind of thing that we find all through the teachings attributed to Buddha. Incidentally, only about six to eight percent of the teachings have been translated into English. It is incredible! There are, well–we can't call them volumes because they were written on plaques of wood or on strips of palm fronds, and they stack them up. They don't bind books like this (the ones you see) at a Buddhist retreat. They are stacked up and tied together. And there are tons of them that have not been translated.

Do we have any original words of Buddha? Just like we know in the case of Jesus, none of the writings were written in Jesus' time, but what about Buddha? Do we have any there? 500 B.C. is a long time back, and unfortunately the answer is no. We have some that are probably very, very close for a simple reason. His teachings were incredibly sensible, incredibly obvious. There was no cloak and dagger; there was no hidden meaning. They were simple observations that are obvious to everyone in this room, as they were obvious to his own people in his own time.

Let's talk about this gentleman, Gautama Siddhartha, who was to become the Buddha. As I say, he was born April 12, 557 B.C. in the morning, of a woman like you women who are seated out here in front of us. She died a short while after his birth, a matter of a few years, and so he was really raised by a surrogate mother in the castle. He was born of royal blood, a prince–a prince that could do anything that he wanted to do. He was surrounded by luxury; there was no limitation. No limitation of what he wanted–food, money, people, position, music, pleasure–simply at the touch of a finger. His father (the king) was given a message by a wise man that this young boy was going to grow up, forsake all the known values, and be a leader of mankind. This scared the father, of course, because he wanted his son to grow up, become the ruler, and to take the throne, when the father died. So he really started protecting Gautama from all the things outside. In fact, he had a very high wall built around the courtyard of the temple and around the yard in which Gautama spent most of his time. But even there, things began to occur to Gautama that looked strange. A gardener was digging out in the yard and dug up a worm. A bird immediately flew down, grabbed the worm, chewed it up, swallowed it, and flew away. Gautama's first thought was, "Do all life forms harm other life forms?"

Finally after many of these type thoughts, his father, in order to distract him, gave him a bride. He was married and he lived in the castle confines until about his 28th or 29th birthday. He had one child by his wife. Then he sneaked out one day and went into the city. He met an old man who was lying on the ground moaning and groaning because he was going to die. And Gautama said, "Is all life suffering?" He went on a little farther, and met another old man, who was being consumed by some kind of disease (from the description it sounds like leprosy). This hit home even harder. "Is all life disease, pain, and suffering?" Then he remembered that when his child was born, his lovely wife was in pain and suffering. "Is all birth pain and suffering?"

And so, only a short while after his son was born, he decided that something was wrong in the way he was looking at the world, in the way other people were looking at the world. So he stripped from himself the royal garments and went into the world to find the truth. He studied with many so-called wise men. I want you to remember that the Buddha came on the scene in India when there were a lot of other philosophies going on. It was not like walking out of the wilderness with something brand new, not that at all. So he studied with a number of ascetics to see if he could find the true secret. One of the ascetics insisted that you starve yourself, so he almost starved himself to death, and that didn't give him that feeling inside that he really wanted.

Finally he decided it had to come from within himself, that no one else outside could prepare a pathway and make him walk along it. He had to go inside and see the relationship as it really was. So the story goes that he sat down under a bodhi tree and demanded of the universe that it pay attention to him and that he see the reality as it really was. After some period of time, it occurred. He saw the relationship between himself and the universe, and the universe and everything else around him. He reached what we now call enlightenment, and he began to be called the Buddha. 'Buddha' means nothing more than *Enlightened One*, someone who has beheld the truth, and in this case began to teach it.

He had many followers, and unlike some of the other philosophers of his day and later on in history, he lived a long time. He taught for something like 45 to 47 years. So he had a long time to get across what he was trying to teach. And what he was trying to teach was rather startling because it was simple; it was direct. It was taking away the concept that there was a god up there somewhere who would forgive you your sins. You had to do it yourself.

Most philosophies, including all the Western ones, look at yesterday, today, and tomorrow as a straight line, going from here in that direction. Buddha saw it as a closed circle: yesterday, today, tomorrow. Because as you move to tomorrow, your today became yesterday, and the day after tomorrow is now the future. So he saw it as a closed loop, closing up upon itself. It was in the shade of the concept of the wheel of dharma, the wheel of pain if you would, the wheel of being born, living, and dying. Pain and suffering, unless you look at it a special way.

I'm going to read a number of things from two books, the new one that I'm just enjoying, and an old one that has been out of print for a long time, Nyogen Senzaki and Buddhism and Zen, by Suzuki. It has some pertinent questions, the kinds of questions that we ask ourselves all the time. I will touch just a few of them, because they are the kind of thing that you wonder about. What does a Buddhist worship? What does a Buddhist believe? The words believe and worship are unfamiliar to any Buddhist. They do not believe, because they understand. And they do not worship, because they practice what they understand.

Is Buddha an Oriental god? The answer is a definite no. He was a man who simply achieved enlightenment, and his teachings are to guide you to the understanding of the universal law, to give you enlightenment. If Buddha is not a god, then there must be a real god above us–do Buddhists believe in god? If you use the word god in the poetic expression, of a universal law, the answer is a resounding yes. If you imply by the term some personal existence apart from the universal law, then the answer is no. There is no remainder in the mathematics of infinity. If the universe and god are one, then there can be none left over. A god not of this world is a false god, and a world not of god is unreal. All things return as one, and one operates in all.

What is the mind? Was it the mind given by god in the very beginning? His answer was, "Judge fairy tales or legends for yourself." If there is no personal god, then there can be no one to create mind. The mind is an endless chain of three processes: craving, acting, and discontent. These cycles produce unhappiness. And on, and on, and on. We can see part of the problem in his concept–as you know, he did not appreciate women early in his life because he felt that men who lust after women suffer pain. Now let's step away from our hierarchy of teaching and look at that. It's true, isn't it? If you guys have a girlfriend and she doesn't do exactly like you want her to do, it hurts. If you women have a boyfriend and he doesn't do exactly like you want him to do, it hurts. Pain and suffering are centered between the two sexes and it's a strong drive. How do you avoid it? You avoid the contamination, in both directions. It's a little difficult. But in answer to that–why is it difficult–the truth is perfect and complete in itself. It is not something just newly discovered; it has always existed. It is one of these interesting comments, that as we try to define things, we get into trouble. If you start looking at how to study, how to do them, it becomes one of these things that you can reach for, but not quite attain.

Why is it difficult to do? It is difficult to do because it requires the control of mind. It is the only thing that is required. A Tibetan Buddhist wrote the following words, "Greed, anger, and ignorance. These three stand as obstacles to the way of deliverance. They prevent us from growing as the roots of couch grass prevent the growth of useful plants. But I know that among the mighty mountains of my native land, there are men and women who can bear witness in this very lifetime, that they have attained the supreme goal and tasted the ultimate deliverance. One must not expect these enlightened ones to come and live with us worldly ones, whose most serious actions appear as the play of small children." Interesting. An abstract way of looking at things. I think this is so apropos of today, especially with television. Some religious workers build a brisk business by selling people on the idea that their sins can be wiped out by another. Those who speak such untruths in this world, be they bishop or archbishop, reverend or right reverend, are making a hell for themselves, right now.

How do we get around it? How do we achieve what we're after? That is one of the beautiful things about this little book–it is very practical. It's the Japanese approach to Buddhism, and therefore leans heavily on Zen as well. Some of the things that you are supposed to do are kind of fun. Your suffering is my suffering. Your unhappiness is my unhappiness. You cannot be alone, for we are all one. How do you achieve this inner knowing? You first train yourself to be kind to all animate forms of life, to avoid the sin of killing a living creature, and then to wish that all people might know the blessings of a long life. Train yourself to avoid the sin of stealing. Train yourself to avoid committing adultery. Train yourself to remain free of deception. Train yourself to avoid duplicity. Train yourself to avoid abusing others. Keep yourself free from idle talk. Aim at an ideal. Train yourself to be free of greed and to do only virtuous deeds. Train yourself to avoid anger. Train yourself to avoid ignorance. Train yourself to be still. The four noble truths, which we've already outlined, are simple, and they're something that we must learn to do. Right view (some of you will recognize some of these)–right view, right thought, right speech, right behavior, right living, right effort, right mindfulness, and right concentration. These are the eight noble pathways.

How are you going to do them? We can go on and on with some of these things. But what is it? Take a definition of each of them. The eightfold path refers to those I just read to you. Right view includes what? It is a thorough understanding of truth, to believe in the law of cause and effect, and not to be deceived by the appearance of desire. Right thought means a resolution not to cherish desires of greed or anger, or to do any harmful deed. Right speech means avoidance of lying words, of idle words, abusive words, of speaking with a double tongue. Right behavior means not to destroy any life, not to steal, and not to commit adultery. Right livelihood means to avoid any life that would bring shame to any man. Right effort means to do those things diligently and in the right direction. Right mindfulness means to maintain a pure and thoughtful mind. I think to sum up his major view of the world; it is that it was suffering and pain. The way to get away from the pain was to eliminate delusion, to eliminate those things that we wish were so.

There's a beautiful little teaching. One night, many years ago, a blind man was visiting a friend, and was offered a lantern to carry home with him. "I do not need a lantern," he said, "Darkness and light are the same to me." "I know *you* do not need the lantern to find your way home," his friend replied, "but if you do not take it, someone else may run into you. You must take it for your own safety." The blind man took the lantern, but he had not gone far before someone walked straight into him. "Look where you are going!" exclaimed the blind man, "Can't you see this lantern?" "Your candle has burned out," the stranger said. "Always be sure your candle is burning, both for your own safety and for the safety of others around you."

Thank you.

The Bible, a Study

Introduction—The following is taken from a transcription of two lectures that Rev. Larr gave on at least two separate occasions over the years. This one was recorded in August of 1981. The lecture was given to students at the Chapel of Awareness, so the tone is informal and Rev. Larr doesn't stick to a strict outline or format. Because of this, in editing, we have removed a number of Ah's and Umm's, as well as places where he repeated himself or was thinking out loud and then changed subjects abruptly… i.e." but we'll get back to that later…."

Rev. Larr was a very intelligent person, who as many very intelligent people do, thought a lot faster than his mouth could keep up with, and his spirit teachers would often give him information that would change his course. His lecture style was always relaxed and somewhat informal and this drew the listener in until you were almost mesmerized. His breadth of knowledge and experience always added to his discussion of any subject. The Bible was no exception.

We have taken the liberty to annotate for the reader the passages that he is referring to, if he didn't mention them directly. He had on the lectern at least three books that he was referring to or reading from: The King James Version of the Bible, The Lamsa Bible, and a supplementary book that was published with the Lamsa Bible called Idioms in the Bible Explained, by Dr. George M. Lamsa.

Note for pages referring to Dr.Rocco Errico. He studied under Dr. George Lamsa, the translator of the Lamsa Bible which is a direct translation from the original Aramaic text. He has written a number of books and articles in reference to the process of translating the Bible and the problems that it has created in the final meanings of text.

Note for page with four comparative religious studies books mentioned. The set of books that Rev. Larr is referring to is not completely clear. If memory serves us, it was published in the 1970's and was popular at that time. A search has not turned up this set to make reference, so we are assuming it is out of print at this time. We would direct the reader to two very fine alternatives, The Religions of Man and the World's Religions by Huston Smith.

Hopefully we have been able to keep an honest transcription of this lecture series for the reader and that Dr. Larr's humor and intent are kept intact. It's a warm and balmy August evening, you have on your sandals, a soft Hawaiian shirt, and a comfortable pair of shorts. The windows to the Chapel are open and it's summer in Encinitas, California. Sit back and enjoy.

The Old Testament

Good evening, everyone. (From the students, "Good evening") What we are going to be doing tonight and a week from tonight is analyzing, looking at, and trying to get an understanding of this book (The Lamsa Bible) or this book (The King James Version of the Bible), whichever you want. This one (The Lamsa Bible), I prefer, and we will get into some of the reasons why.

Probably nothing has been written that affected Western man as much as has this accumulation of stories, fables, laws, and folklore, known as the Holy Bible. Why is it Holy? I think I have relayed to some of you that you could get into some real trouble by harming this book in any way and I, like a great many of you people when you study something, love to underline. It wasn't too many years ago when I was studying at the Fuller Theological Seminary and I was busy doing things like this (he shows a page in his Bible that has numerous underlines and notes in the margins), making marginal notes, crossing words out, and adding words in… and a lovely, little old grey-haired lady came over, I think, with full intent to commit mayhem, and gave me a great blasting because she knew I was going to straight to hell because I was defiling God's book. Well, I am sure that it doesn't take much logic to see that God is a little more concerned about a lot of other things other than what I would do with pieces of graphite or ink on the pages of a book that I bought for a few dollars.

To look at the Bible in a very real way, at first, is going to sound very negative, and I don't want it to be that way. The Bible is *not* an historical textbook regardless of how badly a great many of our devout "Christians" would like to make it. In order to study the Bible as a whole, we have to look very, very closely at, of course, the concept of the Jews, both today and in the past, because a major part of this book is the doctrine of the Jewish religion. [It's the part] from here forward, (showing the Old Testament within the Bible he is holding).

The New Testament, that part that we consider the keynote of Christianity, is really a rather minor footnote to the laws, regulations, and rules as set down in the Old Testament. To just give you an idea of why that is, remember that Christ was on the scene a relatively short length of time. Some of the later estimates show that his actual preaching was maybe a little over a year, maybe as small as fourteen months. Not too many years ago, everybody was sure it was at least three years and maybe a little more. But such was not the case and they found this in some very beautiful detective work done in a very interesting way. They simply went through the New Testament, especially the first four books, and fed into a computer all of the things that indicate seasons: when certain things were in flower, when certain crops were harvested, when certain plants were planted. Then they fed that information into the computer along with an ordinary climactic chart of the area, and how long was it? It comes out to be 13.7 months. Whether or not the gospel is to be relied upon that closely, we don't know. Certainly in the New Testament–Matthew, Mark, Luke, and John–none of those men actually wrote those books.

We always have visions of Matthew sitting here, pen in hand, ballpoint or otherwise, scribbling down in some strange looking script, and believe me it was. The written script of the day was Aramaic. If you have ever seen Aramaic writing, it is a mess. It really is. And because it is a mess, it has created a great many problems. In the New Testament we have had a little bit to back it up, because Matthew, Mark, Luke, and John are saying the same thing, supposedly. They miss some very important points. If you take a chronology of those facts and those details that the authors agree on, you are absolutely certain they are talking about four entirely different occurrences. The Old Testament is even worse and the Old Testament is the one that has caused all the problem in the Western world. It is because Jesus did not come as a prophet. He did not come to the House of Israel to foretell coming events.

If you read it very carefully, he does very little predicting. The fall of the temple in Jerusalem, his own death and resurrection, even that is not prediction but simply a restating of what the Old Testament prophets foretold would come about. Today when the modern form of Christianity is called Christianity, we should in all likelihood call it 'Paulism.' Paul, who never knew Christ, who never studied with him, who never met the man on a one to one basis, makes up the biggest share of the New Testament and it is on that basis that we have founded the religions of Christianity today and all of its variations.

But let's look at the Old Testament. How old is it? We are looking at the first five books; those books purportedly written by Moses. Here again, you know darn well he didn't write them. Moses, if he existed, was very likely illiterate; 99% of the people were. This is why there were scribes in those days who would write down things of princes and kings and records of a town. What kind of time are we looking at?

Well, that whole group of people were nomads. They moved around the desert, similarly to the Arabs of not too many years ago. They were Semitic people, of course, and they literally lived by migrating from one area to another. One of the big centers of population and centers of knowledge, of course, was Egypt.

So a big part of Genesis and Exodus is referring to Egypt and the things that went on there. As close as we can figure, these wandering tribes were out there, moving from place to place, gleaning information, folklore, and knowledge from everyone else at about 2000 BC. Well, 2000 BC puts fair advancement in the Egyptian empire. Saqqara was built, the ruler of the North and South had united the country, and they had begun to expand. It was only much, much later that anything at all was written down by these nomads. Up until this time as these nomads met along the way or their trails crossed, they sat around the campfire and told stories. They told stories about their heroes and their concept of God.

They touched many people–they touched Egypt, Babylonia, and Assyria. In many cases, you will find the lessons and teachings of Genesis and Exodus especially, almost as if they were borrowed from another culture. As you look at the whole series of events, the earliest scrap–the earliest piece of Old Testament that we have–is on a small piece of leather and it was written in 220 BC. That is a relatively short time ago. It is thought by most scholars that the actual writing down (putting these stories, legends, teachings, and laws into writing) happened somewhere around 800–600 BC and they were being written in Aramaic and in an old form of Hebrew. They are difficult to read and we will get into some of the problems of translating these things as we go along.

I want first to kind of pin down two characters that make this book, the Old Testament, possible. The first, of course, is Moses. Here is the center, the focal point, the real messenger of God, if you would. The message was given to him to give to the chosen people of Israel, not to you and me. It sometimes comes as a little shock, but if you read, especially in the Hebrew versions of the Old Testament, and read carefully, you will find that there is going to be no one in heaven except the chosen people. The rest of us are just going along for the ride. Now, we can't say that's wrong because remember what the Old Testament was trying to do. It was trying to unite a group of people that had been violent nomads almost all of their generations. What about their generations? How long ago did it start? Well, we have some fair evidence not found in the Bible but in some of the Babylonian writings that certain areas were inhabited at about 1000 BC. But then a lot of other things fall into place and we start having trouble, because when you start reading, especially Genesis, you bump into some things that are difficult.

There is the story of Joseph who goes to Egypt, for example. He is an extremely brilliant man who becomes the favorite of Pharaoh, and he takes with him a small community of (we would call them) Jewish people, Israelites. They set up several villages in Egypt. If you read the story as presented, Joseph is an extremely important person from the standpoint of the Egyptians. He saves their lives several times in a row during drought, by planting fields in a different part of the country. Incidentally, I brought a map along to kind of clarify some things. Every time you hear about Joseph clumping off into Egypt or Moses going over there to see what's going on, we always visualize the Nile Valley. No way! It's difficult, I am sure for you to see from there, but, this is Egypt. You will notice here is the Red Sea, the Sea of Galilee–and all of the Holy Land is under the rule of the Egyptians. This is under the reign of Thutmosis [III] about 1450 BC. So you see, if the tribe was over here on this little sandy hill, and Joseph went into Egypt, he did not go over to the Nile Valley. He simply climbed over the mountain and he was in Egypt.

Now this upsets things, because we have all of these visions of this young man (and old man) having lengthy conversations with Pharaoh and then he goes away into the land of Canaan to plant more crops. Then he goes back and talks to the Pharaoh and this happens a number of times. The distance from Canaan to Egypt is about 800 miles of trackless desert. If he existed, did he ever actually go to the palace of Pharaoh which at that time was in Luxor (Thebes in the old title) which is actually in the Nile Valley? We don't know. Did he bring grain in from the outer reaches where he and his Hebrew followers had planted it, and then save the lives of the Egyptians? We don't know.

In the book of Genesis, as you read it along, finally his father dies and then finally he dies. These were some remarkable people. They are not just like you and I. Joseph lived 110 years. If we follow the normal dates, as given in the King James Version of the Old Testament, it means that Joseph lived through the reign of three pharaohs. I wonder why there is no mention of Joseph in the Egyptian text? Here's a man who outlived three pharaohs, who saved the nation–the whole nation of Egypt–two or maybe three times. Very peculiar.

In the text, it very clearly states that he is buried in Egypt and this is one of the reasons I wanted to show you that map. '*So Joseph died being 110 years old. And they embalmed him and put him in a coffin in Egypt.*' (Genesis 50:26) Our good Jewish and Christian friends have literally torn sections of the Nile Valley, the Valley of the Tombs of the Kings, and especially the Valley of the Tombs of the Princes apart to find his tomb. Well, with the map I just showed you, he might be buried beside the Red Sea. He might be buried beside the Dead Sea. At that time, that was Egypt. We have no idea where it is, but we do have a problem. No one has found any cross references to his presence in Egypt. If the biblical account is true, there certainly should have been a lot said about him.

To make matters a little worse, after we get him out of the way, we have Moses coming on the scene. You know the classic story. He ends up in the little boat of reeds sailing on the Nile and is rescued by a group of maidens and nursed by some Semitic woman (we don't know who). He was raised in the court of Pharaoh and became the pride, almost a prince, of the Pharaoh. Ladies and gentlemen, that's absolutely impossible. There was probably nothing more sacred to the Egyptians than the genetic line of ascension to the throne. No unknown child, and I don't care who or what, would have been able to achieve that exalted position as first son of a ruling Pharaoh. It would have been the Pharaoh's son, period, or no one else. Moses grew up and did a lot of things. If we follow the Old Testament account, he created plagues, destroying enormous sections of Egypt. He touched the Nile and made it run red as blood, for days. He brought on plagues of locusts. Okay, yes, there are plagues of locusts, but it rained all kinds of things. The ground caught fire, lightning flashed out of a cloudless sky, and the first male child of the whole valley died. All of this was going on because God had told Moses to go back into Egypt and bring his people out of bondage.

Was there a Moses?

If we go simply by the historical record we would have to say yes, there was a Moses, and he was a funny little fellow running around with the Semitic people going from place to place to place. Did he visit Egypt? Probably that part of Egypt that is now the Holy land. Did he visit the Nile? Did he do the miracles that are related to on a purely data basis? We would have to say no. Some of the things that he did are well known tricks performed by Egyptian priests and fakirs–turning staffs into snakes, things of this nature which sound great and bizarre. But if they happened and especially if they happened in the reign they believe Moses was there, namely the reign of Ramses II, it would be absolutely inconceivable that his name would not be some place either on statuary, on the walls of temples, or certainly within the tomb of Ramses II itself. And it is not.

So what do we do with it? We don't do anything with it. Whether or not Moses was in Egypt, whether or not Joseph was in Egypt, has nothing to do with what the Old Testament is talking about. The main key of the Old Testament is an understanding of a way to live: the law, the Ten Commandments you are all aware of. But there are dozens of others. We will get to some of those in a little bit. There is, incidentally, a very common thing, in the Eastern world that you and I would call exaggeration, but it is referred to as amplification so it is a little tamer. Like if I were to tell somebody how many people were here tonight, "Oh, there were over 200–we had a great turnout!" It sounds better that way. If there were three, maybe I would stretch it to only 75. So maybe the man, Moses, did visit parts of Egypt. I doubt seriously if he ever saw Pharaoh. Ramses did go into what is now Palestine during a war with the Assyrians, so he might have been seen then. But if Moses sat down and discussed things with

Pharaoh, and brought about and did all of these miracles that are reported, they should have been reported from the Egyptian side. And they are not.

But what else did he do? First of all, to really look at the Old Testament, we've got to step away as I say, from the historical novel, and we've got to look at it certainly as a teaching, certainly as a way of life, and certainly as one of the most spiritual books ever published. I know several people who say that some 80% of this book is psychic; I would like to say that about 95% of it is psychic. Most all of the things that occur are revelations. They are spirit communication. They are inspiration. Because of that, there are some very clever things that happen farther into the book. How do you tell when something psychic is happening in the Bible? There are some real keys and I've made a list of some of them:

Dreams, of course.

A vision involving a prophet who is dead.

The Lord is speaking to someone.

They saw it in a vision. That is obviously clairvoyance.

The person felt as if they were being carried by spirit to someplace to observe something. We all know what we would label that here at the Chapel: astral projection.

The Spirit of the Lord had touched them and given them some information.

An angel appeared unto the observer.

Any conversation between a spiritual angel or god has got to be relegated to the level of spirit communication in the very sense that we use it today. Most of us don't run around talking to Jehovah, Yahweh, or Allah, but it could be done. I don't know if we would find out anything new or not but it certainly could be done. But this kind of communication is what both of these volumes or both sets of these books is based on: spirit communication.

So why, towards the end of the famous passages from the book of Exodus, in which Moses delivers God's law unto the

Israelites, do we get the comment that, '*Thou shall not suffer a witch to live?*' (Exodus 22:18) First of all, let's back up and look at the word 'witch.' It's not witch at all in the sense that we think witch–a pointed nose and a wart, a pointed hat, on a broomstick, and the typical Halloween thing. No, it is really a sorcerer, or sorceress. The classic spiritual definition of that is 'someone who will make someone do something against their will; and over which they have no control.' Gross interference. We would teach the opposite of that here at the Chapel. It was done for a very simple reason. You've got to remember that in this period of history, even clear up until after Christ's birth, certainly, they were very superstitious people. And it is very difficult at times to draw a line between superstition and religion.

'*An eye for an eye and a tooth for a tooth*' (Exodus 21:24) has been quoted a hundred times. And yet, it is not quite the way the Aramaic people looked at God. In fact, it is very, very difficult to define God. We bump into this problem of limitations. This, incidentally, is why in the work of Mohammed the word is never used in any kind of a definitive discussion or writing. It is the Lord God. They don't define him. All-knowing, all-understanding, all-forgiving, yes, all of those things are simply assumed. But the word 'Allah' itself from Aramaic, or now from modern Arabic, has no translation. There is no way to simply give it a title. We use God, Father, all of those variations interchangeably. The words do us a disservice because they are limitations. They are limitations.

Let's get back to another point; there is another problem. In the Old Testament, in order to make things work out time-wise, because we are looking at several thousand years that have to be accounted for before the birth of Christ, we have some key points. As I mentioned, Joseph theoretically went into Egypt about 1700 BC. So we have to use up everything from the creation to about that time. So how are we going to do it? Well, we are going to start with creation and we are going to let Adam live 930 years. That's pretty neat! It gives him enough time to have lots of children! His third son lives 912 years. His fourth son lives 905 years. And his fifth son lived 910 years. So by the time we get down to Joseph and Moses, the poor children died in infancy! They died at 110 and 120. One of the most interesting in that whole group was Enoch, the fourth son of Adam. He only lived 365 years and instead of dying and being buried, he simply disappeared. He found favor in God and disappeared before their eyes. It is interesting to put the footnote to it: in the concept that we use in spiritualism, he was the first avatar. I wonder if the incarnation that they are reporting in the Bible was really a birth or simply a materialization to carry out something he wanted to do? We will never know.

The biggest problem is trying to interpret what is really being said. For example, there is the story of Jonah being swallowed by a big fish. Great! We know that anatomically that would be impossible. To be swallowed by a fish, and certainly, to live. There have been a few fish swallowings reported, and I love some of the Bible scholars who go all out to try to prove this.

There is one report, believe it or not, of a man being swallowed by a basking shark. A basking shark is a very, very large shark. Well, he's as long as this room is wide, certainly. And he has a huge mouth, because he eats plankton. He has a pretty good sized throat, too. So a man could get in. Now I don't know how they were going to verify this, but they had a native off of Cape Town that got swallowed by one, so they harpooned the shark and pulled the young man back out again, and he lived. He was badly scarred because of digestive juices and his hair had been bleached to kind of a straw yellow instead of the black that it had been. So what is Jonah doing sitting in the bottom of a whale carrying on a conversation with an archangel? Well, one has to kind of look at this in a different way, and it's the same way that you are going to have to look at 90% of those kinds of things in the Bible. They are teaching a lesson, and they are teaching one main lesson: obedience to God. This is why we see so many of these stories that look so strange.

I think the thing that has done the most to destroy the true validity of the Bible itself, is some of the big manufactured movies from MGM and the rest of them. *The Ten Command-*

ments, Land of the Pharaohs. In *Land of the Pharaohs*, they had Joseph build Cheops' big pyramid. Well, that happened before 2000 BC, but he didn't come on the scene until about 1600 BC. Difficult problems. If you watched any of the late night shows, you know, what are they called? *Famous Men of the Bible*? It's atrocious! However, the scripts could be incredible if they would take the *real* stories and look at them and really study them.

If you really want to study the Bible, I would recommend this one, of course. This is the Lamsa Bible, a translation from the Aramaic text. The reason I recommend this is that it is taken from a manuscript that was written about 700 AD, plus or minus some years, and has not been changed. Every other Bible you pick up has had some horrendous changes in it. This, of course, is a King James Red Letter Edition. I won't bother to rattle them off but this is an interpretation of an interpretation, of an interpretation, of an interpretation–through nine interpretations. It was translated from the Latin and from the Greek to this one.

When you compare it to the Aramaic, and undoubtedly the original writings were done in Aramaic, there are many places they don't agree. And you wonder why. I think one of the most disappointing things is when you look at some of the groups of people who got together and decided this or that belonged or did not belong in the Bible. There have been several of those lovely little get-togethers. They threw out, of course, the Apocrypha, a set of books that goes between the Old and the New Testaments, somewhat bridging the gap between Isaiah and the birth of Christ. I'm a little unhappy with that because when they threw them out, they threw out the archangel Uriel, which was kind of a nasty thing to do to the poor guy. But if you read, and read carefully, you will notice some interesting problems. Imagine you were a scholar back about 100 AD You are trying to put together the Old Testament and you've got armloads of scrolls, and I mean *armloads of* scrolls. And so you start putting them together. I want to read to you a section just to show you what happens. It's the same thing we see happen in the New Testament when we have four people telling the same story. They don't tell the same story, and they don't tell the same story on some very important points. Let's look at Genesis. Incidentally, the start of Genesis is almost exactly the same as the ancient Babylonian story of creation. It is also extremely close to the story of how Amun, the high God of Egypt, created the world. It is common that you will find a great many cultures (I don't like to call them primitive cultures because all of these are appearing at about the same time as these three bigger cultures). All of them have very similar stories about the creation. But there is something here that many people overlook when they read the Bible.

> '*God created the heavens and the earth in the very beginning. And the earth was without form and void; and darkness was upon the face of the deep. And the Spirit of God moved upon the face of the water. And God said, "Let there be light," and there was light. And God saw the light and that it was good; and God separated the light from the darkness. And God called the light Day, and the darkness he called Night. And there was the evening and there was the morning, the first day. And God said, "Let there be a firmament in the midst of the waters, and let it divide the waters from the waters." And God made the firmament, and divided the waters and they were under the firmament from the waters that were above the firmament; and it was so. And God called the firmaments Sky. And there was evening and there was morning, the second day. And God said, "Let the waters that are under the sky be gathered together in one place, and let the dry land appear," and it was so. And God called the dry land Earth; and the gathering together of water he called Seas; and God saw that it was good. And God said, "Let the earth bring forth vegetation, the herb yielding seed after its kind, and the fruit tree yielding fruit after its kind, wherein is their seed after its kind, and upon the earth," and it was so. And the earth brought forth vegetation, the herb yielding seed after its kind; and God saw that it was good. And there was evening and there was morning, the third day. Then God said, "Let there be lights in the firmament of*

> *the heaven to separate the day from the night; and let them be for signs, and for seasons, and for days, and years. And let them be for lights in the firmament of the heaven to give light upon the earth," and it was so. And God made two great lights, the greater light to rule the day, and the smaller light to rule the night; and the stars also.'* (Genesis 1:1)

Now, much later in the game, he creates the sun and the moon. Incidentally, the reason he did that was because they were fighting Zoroastrianism, which of course worships the sun as did the Egyptians. This was written in this way to show that their God, our good old Hebrew God, could do it all without the sun–and we'll put the sun in there as an afterthought. So if you want to call the sun the Sun God, that's really neat, but we didn't need him to create the world. Okay?

Now we go through the fourth day and from the water we bring forth living creatures, but I want to skip over some of these because there is one neat thing I want to point out. We are at the end of the fifth day and on the sixth day he is trying to decide what to do next.

> *'Then God said, Let us make man in our image, after our likeness; and let them have dominion over the fish of the sea, and over the fowl of the air, and over the cattle, and over all the wild beasts of the earth, and over every creeping thing that creeps upon the earth. So God created man in his own image, in the image of God he created him; male and female he created them.'* (Genesis 1:26)

Okay, so now this is the end of the scheme. *'And God blessed them, and God said to them, Be fruitful, and multiply, and fill the earth, and subdue it; and have dominion over the fish of the sea, and fowl of the air...'* and so on and so forth.

Then Adam starts about naming the plants and stuff. Incidentally, the Garden of Eden is a very real place. It is very well defined by the regular King James Version, so there should be no mystery as to where the Garden of Eden is. We'll get to that in a second. But notice what has happened here. By the sixth day we have created everything; we have man and woman. We haven't defined them by name as Adam and Eve as of yet, but we have man and woman created in the likeness of God. And then look what happens. He rests on the seventh day. So he blessed the seventh day and sanctified it. Then in Genesis 2:7,

> *'...the Lord God formed Adam out of the soil of the earth, and breathed into his nostrils the breath of life; and man became a living being.'*

Were there two creations?

> *'And the Lord God planted a garden eastward in Eden.'*

Eden is located between the three rivers that are named out here. Of course, they are in the Tigris-Euphrates Valley, so it is pinned down very well. He gave Adam, of course, dominion over all of the plants and things of that nature and the rivers that flowed in and out. Incidentally, there's a little problem in Genesis 2:12 with this one river called Havilah. In this river of Havilah there is gold and it is good. There are also beryllium and onyx stones. I can assure you that nobody knew of beryllium back at that time. So here is the kind of confusion that comes into the biblical texts. There is absolutely no way that the Aramaic could have had a word for beryllium. It was a word coined by Europeans when they found the element and that was a relatively a short time ago. In the King James Version it is not spelled that way. It is spelled bdellium. Now the 'llium' is a common ending that is used for stones, gem stones, and this kind of thing. So it would be very interesting to go back and to see what the original Aramaic was that allowed the Aramaic to call it beryllium and the King James to call it something that we have no idea what it is.

Okay, so Adam is giving the names to everything, and the names of the beasts, the wild beasts and the animals of the air and so forth, but Adam was found without a helper who was equal to him.

> *'So the Lord God caused a deep sleep to fall upon Adam, and he slept; and he took one of his ribs, and closed up the place with flesh in its stead; And of the rib which the Lord God had taken from Adam he made a woman, and brought her to Adam. And Adam said, This is now bone of my bones, and flesh of my flesh; she shall be called Woman because she was taken out of Man.'*

Hence the name. Same question again, were there two creations? Probably not. It simply means that in this particular set of verses from Genesis there was more than one author. Not just Moses–someone else. Of course, as I said earlier, Moses didn't write it. But he told this same story to enough people, and some of the people remembered the story one way and some of the people remembered the story the other way. Again, does it make any difference? No, it really doesn't, because the whole thing of Adam and Eve and the Garden of Eden is a parable. It is showing obedience to God.

It's funny, but all through the Old Testament if you read it very carefully, you have God pitting himself against himself. Certainly in things like the creation, and the devil and temptation. In the Garden of Eden, what would be more tempting than the tree of knowledge, the tree of good and evil? But you can't touch that apple... why? Any psychologist or psychiatrist is going to tell you that that's going to be the first thing you do, is touch it. Just like Dr. Erico, in a lecture he gave recently, used the analogy of wet paint. It takes a great deal of will power not to touch what is behind a "Do not touch wet paint" sign. Same thing. Who led who to the fall? Did Adam force Eve to pick the apple? Was it an apple? I doubt it very much. There aren't any apples that grow in the Garden of Eden, at least today, and there are no records of them back then. There was a funny little fruit that is similar and it is related to an apple. The apple, of course, occurs in Western Europe and so it would be funny to find one clear down there. But the whole point of this part of the story is to give you an excuse or a reason, especially you ladies, as to why you should suffer in the process of creating something as beautiful as a child. It is from this that many of the organized churches have taken the concept of 'original sin,' which is very, very sad. There is certainly nothing more innocent than a newborn babe. You may remember, if we go on into the New Testament, some of the comments that Jesus makes about children. If they are conceived in sin and born in corruption, Jesus would have had nothing to do with them until they had grown to adulthood or at least into maturity, and had proven their worth. All of it is simply not true. It's a parable.

Were Adam and Eve cast out of the Garden of Eden? No, it's part of the story. Did Cain slay Abel? I don't know. He probably did; they were violent people. These kinds of things went on all the time. Another point–Cain slays Abel and then hides. They are fully aware that here is an omnipotent and all-powerful, all-knowing, all-seeing God–and Cain is hiding? Okay? He gets found of course. It's like playing hide and go seek with an adult when you are only two years old. He gets found, and he is given kind of an option: to be killed himself or leave, so he goes into the land of Nod and takes unto himself a wife. We have no idea where that woman came from if we follow the Genesis story. The only offspring there could have been were from Adam and Eve. That meant he married his sister, which is against Hebraic law. Incidentally, that union, Cain and his wife, went on and found favor in God and started another set of cultures that is implied, at least, in the Old Testament. There are big problems, of course. One of them is population. Remember, when a lot of these early interpretations were made, they thought that the earth started on a certain Sunday in October, 4004 BC. Now, if they are going to put Moses on the scene at about 1700 BC and they are going to have the wandering tribes running around about 2000 BC, they only had 2,000 years to populate the known earth. That's not enough time. In order to do it, we have to have had these first eight or ten people living to the tune of 900 years so they would have enough time to have enough families and have enough babies and groups, to populate the world. It was because of that mistaken idea that we have problems taking the stories as fact.

Here again is one of the problems in studying the Bible. You cannot use a book to prove itself. A great many Bible scholars say, “Oh, the Bible is true. Look, it tells about this city and that city and this visitation and that visitation.” Okay, let’s step away from the Holy Scriptures for a minute, and look at a modern American historical novel in which famous names are used, names you and I know. Towns and the names of cities are used that may or may not be there now. Just because the author has used some things that he is familiar with, you cannot use that historical novel as fact. You must get verification outside it. There is almost no verification outside of the Old Testament. We have a few–King Solomon, of course. We know who he was. The mysterious things, such as they knew where Nineveh was–well, why not? They were traveling people; they had caravans going from the Dead Sea clear over into the Tigris/Euphrates Valley, down to the area of Babylon. They traveled back and forth from what is now Baghdad, and those kinds of places. So of course they knew where these cities were. So when they wrote their stories about the poor man riding on the camel, the camel dying, and the man walking all the way hundreds of mile to get to Nineveh–great, sure it’s true because the old people knew that Nineveh was there. Now the archeologists come along and they dig and they find a city–“Oh look, Nineveh was really there! That proves the Old Testament is true.” No, it simply proves that whoever wrote the Old Testament traveled around and happened to visit Nineveh. Simple as that. I doubt very much if Enoch fell off of his camel and walked without food and drink for forty days through the desert and ended up at Nineveh. It would be pretty hard to do, unless God was feeding him.

And God did feed them. When the whole tribe left Egypt, God sent manna from heaven. You know that word? You will have no idea what that is, unless you have done some research. If you read the text carefully enough (Exodus 16:13), you will notice that they found this white, crusty material under the bushes. They were starving, and when they tasted it, it was sweet. Because it had a texture like bread, they used the Aramaic word that means ‘bread,’ sweet bread, and they ate it. Guess what it was? It was the exuded droppings of the insect we know as aphids. For those of you who raise flowers, if you have aphids on a plant, you will notice that the leaf will get shiny below where the infestation is occurring. Lick it next time. It is pure, sweet sap of the plant that the little insect was feeding on. This was their manna from heaven. And of course, if we follow the text, it saved their lives.

I just wanted to point out one thing here with Enoch, because it's kind of interesting. Here was another one of these men that had enormous control.

> *'Enoch lived sixty and five years, and begot Methuselah; and Enoch found favor in the presence of God and three hundred years after he begot Methuselah, he begat sons and daughters; and all the days of Enoch were three hundred sixty-five year; And Enoch found favor in the presence of God, and disappeared; for God took him away.'* (Genesis 5:21)

This is one of the very few places in the Bible, where someone does not die and get buried, because he was a very special individual.

Another thing that I won't harp on because most of you are students and you've heard me harp on it, is Noah's Ark, the Kraft Cheese box floating out in the bath tub. The measurements given in the King James Version are accurate, as far as the Aramaic version is concerned. Again, you've got to look upon it as a story to show obedience to God. Noah and God were very good buddies; they talked a lot. But God was unhappy with some of the other things going on. Now, there are a few things that people forget.

> *'And Noah and his sons and their wives, went into the Ark because the waters of the flood were rising, the clean animals and the unclean animals and the fowls and everything that creepeth upon the earth. They went in two and two with Noah into the ark, males and females, as God had commanded Noah. And it came to pass that after seven days, the waters of the flood covered the earth. And in the six hundredth year of Noah's life, in the second month, and on the seventeenth day*

> *of that month, on that very day all the fountains of the great deep burst forth, and the windows of the heavens were opened. And rain fell upon the earth for forty days and forty nights. On that same day, Noah (and all of his children) entered into the ark with every beast that creepeth….'* (Genesis 7:6)

And so on and so forth repeating the whole thing again. This would be a little hard to do. The Ark was simply not that big. A cubit is about 18 inches.

> *'And this is how you shall make it: the length of the Ark shall be three hundred cubits,'* (300 times 18 inches). *'Its breadth shall be fifty cubits, and the height shall be thirty cubits.'* (Genesis 6:15)

It was not all that big a boat. But nevertheless, it had one window, so that they could look out, and so that later on he could let out, as you recall, a raven first, to find out if land had appeared. The second time he let out a dove and the dove came back with an olive branch. Where on earth did the olive branch come from? But as you know this went on and on and on for forty days and forty nights. The ground was all covered with water and then finally the boat came aground on a range of mountains just north of the Tigris/Euphrates Valley. It may or may not have been Mt. Ararat. Then the water dried up and here we start all over again populating the world with Noah and his sons and daughters and so on and so forth. Notice, once again, incest running rampant through the Old Testament–something that is really not the thing to do if you follow the Mosaic Laws.

There is one part that I think shows most beautifully the concept of how superstitious and religious these people were. We have the water going down and there are still clouds in the sky, and it is a very precarious thing. Noah is wondering–can we get out of the ark? Look, there are still a lot of clouds around. What's going to happen? Suddenly he saw a rainbow in the sky, and he decided, aha! That's a good omen. And you bet it was a good omen.

> *'God said to Noah, "This is the sign of the covenant which I make between me and you and every living creature that is with you, for perpetual generations: I set my bow in the clouds, and it shall be a sign of a covenant between me and the earth. And it shall come to pass, when I bring clouds over the earth, that the bow shall be seen in the clouds; and I will remember my covenant, which is between me and you and every living creature that is with you of all flesh; and the waters shall no more flood to destroy all flesh."'* (Genesis 9:12)

They had no idea what a rainbow was. No idea at all. In fact we didn't know–intelligent, scientifically advanced people–didn't really know what a rainbow was almost until Isaac Newton. Why is the rainbow formed? It is a reflection of sunlight and droplets. Yet if you read this story carefully enough, some of the parts before this that I didn't read to you, you must assume that there had been no rainbows before that point in time. That's a little hard to believe. I am sure a cave man standing beside a waterfall to take a bath saw a rainbow without clouds in the sky. So here again, we are seeing these people who had an enormously rich culture, but who were filled with fear and foreboding. They were trying to justify and to understand some of these basic laws of nature. I can clarify that even better by going to the front of this book [the Lamsa Bible]. There are some things that show the differences between the original Aramaic meanings and the later translations. If you get a copy of it, it is interesting to look at. This is the Aramaic word and the meaning of the word as it is interpreted both ways. A couple of them I like very much. I won't even try to pronounce the Aramaic word, but here is a word and it is exactly the same, except this one has two dots under it and this one only has one dot under it. So this is like you're writing a word that has an 'i' in it and in one word you put one dot above the 'i' and in the other you put two. Unfortunately it makes a big difference. With the one dot it means 'ungodly.' With the two dots it means 'babies.' So you can see that you have to be very careful about how many dots are there. In fact, Dr. Erico, who worked with Dr. Lamsa translating the original text, made the candid comment that probably fly spit has changed more of the meaning of the original text than anything else! But let's just look at some of these; they are kind of interesting. Here is a funny word that looks very much the same. The King James Version interpreted it as 'wrestled,' as if to tussle with someone.

> *'And Rachel said, With great wrestling have I wrestled with my sister.'* (Genesis 30:8)

What on earth does that mean? So, if we were to take it from the Aramaic, it makes a little more sense.

> *'And Rachel said, I have besought the Lord and pleaded with my sister.'*

This is a lot easier to read and it makes a lot more sense. Another one is in Numbers 25:4 and the two words in question again are a question of whether there are two dots above or one dot above. Two dots above, it means 'chiefs;' one dot above, it means 'heads.' In the King James Version,

> *'And the Lord said unto Moses, Take all the heads of the people, and hang them up before the Lord against the sun.'* (Numbers 25:4)

If we look at that in just the ordinary way, we've got Moses running around there beheading everybody, and hanging them up in the sun. But if we take the Aramaic,

> *'And the Lord said to Moses, Take all of the chiefs of the people, and expose them before the Lord in the daylight.'*

He was mad at what the chiefs had been doing, so he wanted them exposed in the daylight. Isn't that a term we use today? "Let's shed a little light on the subject." Same thing. Not chopping heads off and hanging them up in the sun!

Let's take another one from Deuteronomy 27:16. Same word; in fact it really looks the same. In fact, right now I don't see why they are different. They look exactly the same… oh no, one's got a longer tail on it. Okay. The meaning is to 'revile' or 'radiance.'

> *'Cursed be he who setteth light by his father or his mother.'* (Deuteronomy 27:16)

And *'Cursed be he who reviles his father or his mother.'*

Let's find some others–'venom' and 'wine.' Another one is 'sin.' What is sin? I ran into some others in some of Dr. Erico's tapes. If you are going to be a sinner, what are you? It means you slip. You miss the mark. You don't quite make it. How about 'poisons?' Are you going to run around and drink poison? No, you are going to 'gossip!'

In the New Testament, Jesus said,

> *'You shall pick up snakes in your hands and they shall not bite you.'* (Mark 16:18)

We've got people in this day and age who die every year because they are trying to live up to that with copperheads and water moccasins and rattlesnakes. It simply means 'enemies.' It is Aramaic for enemy. Jesus is giving instructions to his disciples before he ascends to heaven.

> *'And they will handle snakes; and if they should drink any poison of death, it will not harm them; and they will lay their hands on the sick, and they will be healed.'* (Mark 16:18)

How about the concept of 'a full heart?' It's funny; the first time I ran across that, I knew what it meant. 'Full' translates as 'free, released;' that kind of thing. Another one that is a little harder to catch is 'bowels.' May your bowels be moved. Sounds like an ad for Exlax! But what it means, if you will stop and think, all of you that have clairsentience will know that meaning exactly. To be moved by love or intense feelings. Have you noticed that? When your lover kisses you, your innards go all like that! Of course they do! And you can interpret that in many ways, in several places in the Old Testament.

> *'My beloved put his hand by the hole of the door, and my bowels were moved for him'* (Song of Solomon, 5:4)

We had better look carefully at what that word means.

Here we have another one in Samuel. It can mean 'sinful' or 'wheat.' In the King James version,

> *'And they came thither into the midst of the house, as though they would have fetched wheat; and they smote him under the fifth rib.'* (Samuel 4:6)

In the Lamsa version, *'And behold, they came into the midst of the house; then those sons of wickedness took and smote him in his abdomen.'* Makes more sense.

There are several very, very beautiful ones. Here's a good one. In the King James,

> *'As thou knowest not what is the way of the spirit nor how the bones do grow in the womb of her that is with child... '*

Interesting point–when you are reading King James, anything that is in italics, has been added; it is not in the original manuscript. Anything that is in parenthesis is a marginal footnote and is not verified. In this one, the 'nor' is not supposed to be there. Just let me read it as if those words were not there.

> *'As thou knowest not what the way of Spirit, how the bones in the womb of her who is with child.'*

It doesn't make much sense. But in the Aramaic it reads:

> *'As you do not know the path of the wind, and the manner of a woman who is with child.'*

Interesting. Women with children are strange people. They certainly are.

But this is the kind of thing that you can really study up on. They only give one example in Matthew 19:24, which is one that I think all of you now know. There are many others. I think Dr. Erico said there were something like 1,200 of these that they have found in just their casual translations. In the King James Version,

> *'And again I say unto you It is easier for a camel to go through the eye of a needle... '*

In the Aramaic, *'Again I say to you, it is easier for a rope to go through the eye of a needle... '*

This paints quite a different picture. In this case, it doesn't really change the meaning per se, but some of them really do change the intended meanings.

I want to get into the Ten Commandments because this is probably the thing that causes more trouble. The Ten Commandments are not only in Genesis, of course, and in Exodus, but they are in all the rest of the books too. Let me just find one set. The ordinary Ten Commandments, I think we all kind of agree with and that's probably the way it should be. It is very old law, the Mesopotamian Law of Hammurabi; some of you will remember that. It undoubtedly predates some of this [the Bible]. Compared to Trial by Ordeal, building the Tabernacle and its Laws and Ordinances, believe me, the Ten Commandments is duck soup. One of the problems is this. You have to read the whole set of the five books of the Old Testament to find out what the penalties are, for these kinds of things. In Exodus, of course the first one is,

> *'Thou shalt have no other gods before me.... Honor thy father and thy mother. You shall not kill. You shall not commit adultery;, you shall not steal; you shall not bear false witness; you shall not covet thy neighbor's house; you shall not covet your neighbor's wife, nor his manservant, nor his maid servant, nor his ox, nor his ass, nor anything that is your neighbors.'*

They were very strong with this, and remember why. They are mobile people. They are moving around and if you had possessions, that was your whole thing; all that you had, you carried with you. And so you are not supposed to take things away from someone like that. Then if I'm going to kill anybody, that's obviously a capital crime. But what happens if I don't really honor my father and my mother?

'He who strikes his father or his mother shall surely be put to death.' Capital crime.

'He who steals the possessions and sells them or it is found in his possession, he shall surely be put to death. He who curses his father and mother shall be put to death.' You're going to get rid of a lot of people!

'If two men quarrel and one strikes another with a stone or his fist, and he does not die, but is put into bed with the injury: if he rises and walks in the street with his staff, then the one who struck him shall be acquitted.' So you've got to wait a while to see if you killed anyone or not. Except that he will pay for the loss of time, and the physician's fee.

> *'If a man strikes his servant, or his maid with his staff and he dies under his hand, he shall surely be punished. But if the victim is well, after a day or two, he shall not be punished for it is his property. If two men quarrel, and strike a woman with child so that she miscarries and yet no mischief follows; he shall surely pay a fine such as the woman's husband will lay upon him, and he shall pay as the judges that determine. But if any mischief does follow, then he shall give life for a life.'*

The mischief they are talking about here is another story a little farther along in the book, where a man came upon a woman who was pregnant, and knew it was wrong to have intercourse with her while she was pregnant, and so he caused her to miscarry and lived with her so that he could make love to her for days and days and days. They stoned him to death. Which might be okay.

Then of course, the classic one, an eye for an eye and a tooth for a tooth. A hand for a hand and a foot for a foot. A burning for a burning, a wound for a wound, and a slap for a slap.

> *'If a man strike the eye of his servant, or the eye of his maid, and injures it, he shall let him go free for his eye's sake. And if he knocks out the tooth of his man-*

servant or the tooth of his maidservant, he must let him go free, for the tooth's sake.' I wonder how many slaves pulled a tooth here and there along the way?

Then there is an enormous thing that goes for several chapters and I won't bother you with it, but,

'If an ox gores a man or a woman that he or she dies; then the ox shall surely be stoned and its meat shall not be eaten; but the owner of the ox shall be blameless. But if the ox were known to be in the habit of goring in the past and its owner has been warned, and he has not kept it in, and it kills a man or a woman; the ox shall be stoned and the owner shall be put to death.' Interesting... and it gets more and more complex. I could give you some here that are all the classic ones that you know; you are not supposed to make love to an animal. Whoever lies with an animal will surely be put to death. Whoever sacrifices before idols shall be put to death and utterly destroyed. You shall not harm a widow or an orphan. And on and on. So the whole problem boils down to, like I say… I can't kill anybody. If I slap my father, that's also going to get me killed. What is the least sin I could create and get away with it? Because everyone thinks that way–there have to be some loop holes. There are some interesting loop holes. But there are some laws that are incredible, including the things you can eat and can't eat. There is some very good and sound ecological advice in Exodus 23:10. '*For six years, you shall sow your land and shall gather in the crops thereof; But the seventh year you shall leave it fallow.'* Interesting! Good reasoning behind it. Then he goes into talking about the celebrations of special times of the year. In Deuteronomy 5 we are heading through the Ten Commandments again, but there are a couple here, later in Deuteronomy that I thought would be interesting to bring out.

'...and you see among the captives a beautiful woman, and you desire her, and would have her for yourself as a wife.' (Deuteronomy 21:11) That is, a captive–a slave. The troops have gone off and drug a lot of people back and you see one that really touches your fancy.

'Then you shall bring her to your home and into your house; and she shall shave her head and pare her nails; and she shall put off the clothes of her captivity and shall remain in your house, and mourn for her father and her mother for a full month; and after that you shall go in unto her, and be her husband and she shall be your wife.' Interesting.

'If a man has two wives, one beloved and the other hated, and they have borne him children, both the beloved and the hated; and if the firstborn son would be hers that is hated; then it shall be, when he makes his sons to inherit his property, it is unlawful for him to make the son of the beloved wife firstborn before the son of the hated.'

This goes on and on through enormous numbers of pages. Law after law. If you crucify someone by hanging them in a tree, you are not supposed to leave them in the tree all night; you're supposed to take them down. If you see that your enemy's ass or ox has fallen down by the wayside, and you turn your eyes away from them, you are an abomination in the sight of God. You should have run and told the owner. It shall be unlawful for a woman to wear the clothing of a man and unlawful for a man to wear the clothing of a woman for they shall both be an abomination in the sight of God. You cannot trim the corners of your beard, and you may not cut your hair. We could go on through this forever; it goes on endlessly. There are the things you can eat and the things you cannot eat. You can't wear red. You are not allowed to wear clothing that are two kinds; if you are wearing cotton you cannot wear a woolen garment, and if you are wearing a woolen garment you cannot wear a cotton garment as well. This whole thing came from when they built one of the sacred places for the Torah to be stored in an ark. There was a ladder going up to it, and at this time of the history, they did not wear undergarments. So they made some stringent laws about standing at the bottom of the ladders, so you could not look up under the undergarments. When you went up the ladder, there was a proper way to hold the back hem and the front hem, pulled up to your navel so that your privates could not be seen as undressed. So we had peeping toms even then, and they were well known.

I love the bumper sticker that I saw recently, "The Moral Majority is neither." I like that! But it's true, if we were to take some of the teachings of Christ, about his concept of the church and his concept of money. I know an awful lot of big religious organizations that are in trouble. I am sure that you all remember Mark 12:17,

> *'Render unto Caesar the things that are Caesar's and to God that which is God's.'*

In the New Testament there is no set tithing. In the Old Testament it is given as ten percent and then it's a sliding scale, so that you can adjust it accordingly.

But back to the basic laws. We all know that you are not supposed to kill. Incidentally, in one set of the original Aramaic, I noticed in here that Lamsa used 'kill.' In the other one it is "Thou shalt not murder." It's a subtle distinction but an awful big difference. If you accidentally kill a man, it should not be as heavy a penalty as premeditated plotting of a murder. As you heard from some of the stuff we have read, that is their interpretation as well.

Then there's the problem of harlots. Incidentally, one of the biggest shocks to me is in one of the very famous stories of the New Testament: the stoning of the whore in John 8:7. Jesus is supposed to have uttered those famous words,

> *'He who is without sin among you, let him cast the first stone.'*

That is in none of the original manuscripts. That story was apparently added to the Aramaic about 700 AD, but is in none of those that date about 300 AD. So again, a story that sounded good, it sounded like something Jesus would say, was added to make a point.

Those are some of the problems as we go along this way. Next week we are going to get into the New Testament heavily because we could play with the Old Testament for the rest of our lives, as a great many people have. The main thing I want to get across to you, as it is quite obvious by now, is that I do not believe that this is a historical textbook for a number of very important reasons. Maybe I should clarify. I know there was a Moses; I've seen him. I know there was Joseph; I've seen him, too. I know that many of these people did exist and they are in spirit or they are off doing their own thing (reincarnated). And many of the things that they said then they do not agree with now. But you have got to remember, things were different at that point in time.

For all of you that are students, remember in the Beginning Lectures I said that like attracts like? So you are thinking, so you will attract around you entities thinking the same way. That is exactly what happened, especially in the case of the Old Testament and Moses. He attracted Jehovah–an archangel, one of those we haven't talked a great deal about, a very "prejudiced" archangel. The so-called chosen people used his power unmercifully against their enemies all through the Old Testament. I won't bother to dig them out now, but I am certain you are aware of a lot of them. For instance, when they went into Canaan, they had to get those people (the Canaanites) out of the way first because that land was given to the chosen people by Moses, and it was going to be the Promised Land. Some of the enemies at that time were Egypt and Assyria, and the people there were wiped out with the power that the priests could wield through the entities and archangels they had around them. They simply won the war and unfortunately they followed a very simple doctrine–they killed mostly. They took a few slaves of course, but they were very strict (as in some of the passages I mentioned here) about taking a non-member of the tribe as your wife. It was a touchy thing to do. So these people forced their way into an area and ended up building Jerusalem, and all of the things with it. Part of the reasoning for this is because of the visions that the prophets beheld and they passed on in the Old Testament; the Old Testament is filled with that.

There is symbology in the Bible. If you want to look at it purely as symbology, look at Moses talking to the burning bush.

It's a classic spiritual communication kind of thing. And the trumpet, you know the trumpet we use in dark circles sometimes? All tabernacles had trumpets through which the voice of the Lord would speak. Of course, it wasn't the Lord in the classic sense. It was not Allah, but it *was* Jehovah, the archangel. These kinds of things simply permeate this book, and make it a very beautiful book.

But I think most people have gotten the wrong idea. It started way back, and I am going to condemn Michelangelo along with it, even though I was one of his students at the time, when he was doing some of the things in sculpture and painting the Sistine Chapel. The Sistine Chapel is the biggest pack of lies, as far as religious truth, that has ever been done. The big classic painting that covers one whole end of the chapel with Jesus casting the enemies into hell–what is hell? Where is hell? Jesus *knew* what it was. Michelangelo should have read the New Testament, a little better! But here again, if you go to the Aramaic, there is the word 'hellfire.' If you do something to me you are going to burn in hellfire. Do you know what it means in the Aramaic? *To blush*, so that everybody knows you are embarrassed. That makes a little different picture! Yet, if you will recall when Jesus was pinned down about heaven in Luke 17:21, he said,

> *'Lo, heaven is neither here nor there. Lo, heaven is within you.'*

So is hell. It's the opposite side. When we get into the New Testament, we are going to talk about these differences and some of the funny religions and why they believe in some things and not in others. Who is Satan? Who is Mephistopheles? Who is this man in the black cape and the red skin and pointed tail and horns running around and doing all of these neat things that only God can do? In the Aramaic, 'someone who deviated.' Someone who sinned. The words are the same. Someone who missed the mark. This automatically brings up the next one. Who is the antichrist? There are thousands of them. There are probably 20,000 of them in the Bible. You can go to the Aramaic to see just exactly what the word says–what is an 'antichrist?'

What is an anti-Nazi? What is an anti-Japanese? Someone who disagrees with the other party. The antichrist and Jesus had many of them. Most of the priests of the Hebrew nation when Jesus was trying to teach, trying to preach, because he was a rabbi–they were anti-Christ. They tried to kill him, they were against him and yet, because of some translations especially in parts of the King James, they even have an elaborate way of identifying the antichrist. They tell when he is going to appear on the earth, take over control, and cast the whole planet into damnation. One of the key points, which I hope you will forgive me, but I think it is kind of interesting–he is going to have cold testicles. Now, I am not just quite sure how you are supposed to prove that point, but why? Because his seed is no good. Even the ancient people knew that temperature had something to do with a man's fertility. We are beginning to relearn that today. But you get all of these innuendos and some of them get far out, like the antichrist and the Second Coming. Christ is going to come again, yes, but he is going to stand right where he is; you are going to go to him. He's not going to come back to the world. He's not going to do things, like he tried to do before. Again, this was added to the scriptures, much later in the game.

Remember, it is so difficult. I mentioned that some of these manuscripts were written as late as 700 AD. They were all handwritten, with stubby little short pieces of quills probably made of reeds. The ink that they used was made of various kinds of things; probably the most stable one that they found was a black stone which they ground up. It was a ferric oxide material and it was very black and of course being a metal, it was permanent. But can you imagine this? Let's take the Torah which is an enormous set of books. The first five books of the Old Testament, can you imagine writing those down? Every synagogue, every temple in every town, and every rabbi that was teaching had a copy of them. Have any of you ever–well you typists, I am sure you have–tried to type a letter quickly without making a mistake? Imagine doing it in longhand, in which the length of the tail or the stroke or the number of dots above or below a word was significant. It gets very hard. But go back even farther. Let's say you were one of the originals who were trying to put it all together. You had a piece of this scroll and a piece of that scroll, and maybe two thirds of this one, and you noticed that they sounded a lot alike, but where are you going to put them in or fit it all together? We'll touch it next time, but did you know that there are a good four chapters in the first four books of the New Testament where that is probably not true at all? Unfortunately, it is the end of it where it is telling some beautiful things about resurrection. That part was actually added much, much later, just like the stoning of the woman who had committed adultery. So as we look at these things, as I have said before when we have had religious discussions, I am thoroughly amazed that any of it survived. Any of it! As much that has gone on–as much change that has gone on–it is really remarkable.

The Old Testament is full of a set of rules and regulations and laws. Some of them are true; some of them are as true today as they were the day that they were written. Some of them are based on superstitions which we now know are no longer valid, like some of the clean and unclean things that you could eat, and the way you treat a woman as she goes through her menstrual cycle. There are things like this that we now understand because we have developed enough of a psychological and scientific basis to see the why. For example, here is a simple one that I think everybody can think of without me saying anything else. Why do you not eat a dead animal that you find lying in the forest or lying on the plain? You don't know how long he has been dead. He might already be spoiled with botulism or something else. So the Mosaic law is, "Thou shalt not eat an animal that is found dead upon the ground for it is unclean." That's simply a safe law. I am sure that the early primitive people didn't know that to begin with. Can't you just see a whole tribe coming upon a dead antelope and eating it and wiping out ninety percent of the tribe with botulism? The ten percent that was left is going to tell everybody that that animal was unclean. Then a little further down the line, someone will do it again and they will figure it out, aha–this is what happened before. So then one of the prophets gets inspired. "Lord Jehovah told me that thou shall not eat unclean animals." And away we go.

You are not supposed to drink blood. Very early in the game when they slaughtered animals they found that they tasted better if you hung them up and bled them. They kept better as well. So how do you make sure that the people take the extra time to do that so that they don't get sick? You make it a law. If you kill an animal for food, you hang it up and allow its blood to run out on the ground like water. For if you drink blood, you are an abomination in the sight of God. The chosen people are going to believe that and it is going to save their lives.

There are some funny laws. You know the one about a man not wearing the clothing of a woman and a woman is not supposed to wear the clothing of a man? The first thing you think of is slacks, jockey shorts, shirts that button on the other side. Wait a minute–they didn't wear those. They wore a dress very similar to those that they wear now in Egypt, mainly the galabiya. I'll bet many times you were not sure if they were a man or a woman until you tested the persons' vibration. It was some of these subtle things–some of the undergarments, some of the trappings, jewelry, or pierced ears. Many religions of today have taken one narrow little piece of scripture and built a whole foundation of belief and superstition on it.

But what to me is the Old Testament? It is a lot of really interesting stories showing the obedience of a people to their God. (As I would interpret it, to the archangel, and a particular one–Jehovah, or Yahweh.) Why was it written the way that it was written? To bring about and to build a very large, very powerful nation. And at one point in time, it was. It was right up there on a par with Babylon, with Egypt, and with all of the other big nations of that time. It crumbled in internal dissension just as almost all other big cultures have done before. Egypt did the same thing.

The New Testament

In the New Testament, the first thing we want to look at is not the harmony in the first four gospels, but the lack of it. I'd like to run down just a few things here for us to consider. It's very easy to do when you have a system like this, the Bible Concordance and reference in both the King James Version and the Lamsa Version, because these are the bible references in which the material we are looking at is mentioned. The books we are looking at are Matthew, Mark, Luke, and John. As you can see on this page of the reference, there are none of the subjects we want to explore that are mentioned in all four books. In other words, none of the subjects listed on this page did all four books tell in common. I won't bother to read the whole thing, or we would be here all night, but for instance–the genealogies, the birth of Jesus at Bethlehem, Mary's visit to Elizabeth, John the Baptist's conception, John the Baptist's birth, the angel appearing to Joseph, the birth of Jesus in Bethlehem, the circumcision of Jesus, the visit of the Magi, the flight into Egypt, the return to Nazareth, Jesus at the age of twelve celebrating the Passover, the preaching of John the Baptist, Christ's baptism in the river, Spirit leading him into the desert, two of John's disciples decide to follow Jesus, Christ returns to Galilee, the first miracle, Christ goes to Jerusalem for the Passover, Nicodemus is conceived, Christ leaves Jerusalem and stays eight months in the Northeast, John the Baptist–none of these are mentioned in all four books. Finally, the commencement of his public ministry in Galilee is mentioned by all four books. Now all the things that I just ran through are rather important. Jesus' birth and all of the scenes and material that surrounded his birth to prove that he was the Messiah are not mentioned by all four authors. So let's just run on down the list. He returns to Galilee, he heals a leper, he calls Matthew, he answers his objections for not fasting, he heals a man with a withered arm, he withdraws to the lake, he heals many, he ascends the hill and offers a prayer all night, he chooses the twelve disciples, the sermon on the Mount, the healing of the Centurion servant, the raising of the widow's son, John the Baptist's mission, and on and on, and then finally, the twelve return to Jesus telling him what they have done. As you know, he sent them out to do some things.

They go to the other side of the Sea of Galilee where he feeds five thousand people. And that is mentioned by all four books.

We go on and on and finally, Jesus re-enters Jerusalem and weeps over the city that is doomed. That is mentioned by all four authors. Beginning at sunset, the two days of Passover (the final Passover where Jesus is going to be crucified shortly thereafter) is mentioned by all four. He indicates his betrayer–in this case, Judas, as you know. That is mentioned by all four. The scattering of the twelve disciples, his foretelling of their scattering, and Peter's problem with Satan–these are told by all four. The agony in Gethsemane, told by all four. (Which really didn't happen... but that's okay.) The betrayal by a kiss is told by all four. Telling Peter about the cock crowing, told by all four. His judgment by Pilate is told by all four. Jesus is mocked by the Romans–told by all four. Jesus partially buries his own cross, is relieved by Simon, and refuses to take the stupefying myrrh-filled wine–reported by all four. Words from the cross, referring not only to the thieves that were crucified beside him, but also the famous one, *'Forgive them for they know not what they do'*–all four. The centurions' testimony about Jesus giving up the ghost or giving up the spirit, told by all four. And the rising from the tomb, told by all four. The women coming to the tomb to prepare the body, told by all four. And that's it.

Now we have just talked about a man's life that should have influenced especially those four people, to an incredible degree. It was a very sad thing, and I could talk all night about my feelings about Jesus the man, and some of the problems that he had with people. It's a sad situation, when you look at the real story. If you forget–because it is simply not true–that Jesus was the anointed son of God, that he was not an immaculate conception. He was a *man* like you and I. A very smart man, no doubt about it, a man who studied a long time. We here at the Chapel and most of you here tonight are students, you are working for your clairvoyance and clairaudience. You are working on trance work, and healing skills. Jesus studied for over twenty years before he did anything. Are you ready? And he was constantly plagued by his disciples not believing him. He would do miracles and it scared them. Then he would turn and tell them that they could do the same thing and it really scared them! You all know the story of Doubting Thomas. After the resurrection of Christ, he had to prove that it was really the risen body of Christ. Doubting Thomas is where we get that term. But all through it, we see a man, beautifully sensitive, beautifully educated in his philosophy and Hebrew tradition, trying very, very hard to do a very, very difficult job. Even his chosen twelve do not believe him, do not follow him, and are afraid of him. In the last night that he spent before his betrayal, as you know, he asked them to go into the garden and pray with him, and they all fell asleep. No one could stay awake and sit by his side as he was going through something that was a big problem. And of course the classic one that you have heard me lecture on many, many times in Luke 8:22, the calming of the storm at sea. All of the disciples were sure they were going to be drowned and he simply stood up and rebuked the wind, commanded the seas to be still, and it was still. And they hid from him in the back of the boat. They said,

> *'O who is this man, who even commands the winds and the waves and the sea to obey him?'*

Now true, he didn't teach them very long, as I mentioned last time. At the most it was eighteen months to two years. As I mentioned also, on the computer it looks like about fourteen months. So he really had very little time to instill into them what was really going on. But it is incredible, how slow they were to realize what the picture really was. Of course a couple of them, Peter and John, went on afterward and did many, many spectacular healings and raised the dead just as he told them they should do. But it is incredible how little impact he had outside of the shock value of the populace who was watching him. Very few people did the major thing that he told them to do. Believe in him, do the things that he did.

> *'Truly, truly, I say to you, He who believes in me shall do the works which I do; and even greater than these things he shall do...'* (John 14:12)

With the exception of the Spiritualist Church, and some of the Holistic Healing groups that are going on now, healing is no longer performed in the church as a standard practice. And yet it is one of those things that was literally a commandment to his chosen disciples.

> *'Heal the sick, cleanse the lepers, cast out demons; freely you have received, freely give.'* (Matthew 10:8)

Go forth and heal. It is things like that, that have made an enormous difference in our so-called Christian churches of today. As I mentioned last time, I think that most Christian churches we have today are really 'Paulist' churches. Not that I don't like Paul; he was kind of a neat guy. But I don't agree with a lot of the things that he taught. I mentioned last time that we would look very quickly at some of those churches. Incidentally, those of you who have had the chance to look at this series of books, they are really quite good. I think there are three or four volumes, this is one on Christianity, and there is one on Islam, one on Buddhism, and one on the Oriental religions. It's quite nice, and the nice thing I like about this is that in the back, here are the major Christian religions, with some of their tenets and beliefs. We will just look at some of these categories. Of course top of the list is Roman Catholic, which of course it should be because it was probably the first founded Christian church, founded by Paul, an apostle of Jesus, so they say. Not quite, because as I told you before, Paul never met Christ. Christ talked to him as a spiritual entity. Spirit communication. Things you are not supposed to do because they are 'evil.' If it were not for spirit communication, Paul would still have been Saul, and would still be running around doing other things. Let's look at some of the Christian churches and what they believe.

Roman Catholic—the base authority of the church is the church. They use the traditional Bible. It is headed by a Pope, who is infallible when defining faith, morals, or concepts. A little difficult... okay? Fundamental theology is the Trinity–God as three persons but one nature–Father, Son, and Holy Spirit. God's Son made man. Redemption is sacrificial death on the cross of Jesus the Christ. Mary, whose Immaculate Conception preserved her from original sin, is revered. Remember when we talked about the Garden of Eden and the beautiful fairy tale going on there about the first sin? Baptism–yes they believe in it by immersion or a flow of water for infants. Concept of salvation and the afterlife–salvation only by the grace of God. The final state of death will be heaven. While you are in purgatory your soul gets purified or you go to hell if you've done something really bad. Man's body will have a resurrection at the second coming of Christ. We will touch on that tonight. And he will judge everyone.

Eastern Orthodox—about the same. Same sacraments, same liturgy, the Trinity of one God, salvation from original sin by breaking God's law in the Garden of Eden. All of you are cursed by something that was supposed to have happened about 4004 BC. At death, the soul goes to heaven or hell or an intermediate state.

The Lutherans—accept the Trinity. Christ as both god and man. The sacraments are baptism, sprinkling of children and adults. Their concept is that man's sins are by disobeying God and salvation is through God's grace. Christ will come to judge all souls; the good will live with him eternally and the not so good will be punished eternally.

The Presbyterians—they are getting much less strict in their concept. They of course use the Bible as the word of God. They emphasize the sovereignty of one god but displayed in three persons, again, Father, Son, and Holy Spirit. They practice the sacrament of baptism. Salvation is a pre-gift of God gained through man's repentance and faith in Christ.

The Anglicans—very similar to the Presbyterians. Now if there are any of these people here, I may get stoned, but they appear to be the same thing.

The Baptists—they use the Bible as the inspired word of God. It is the first and only authority for faith and the way to live. They have no formal creed, except baptism. Their concept of salvation is that sin is not living up to God's law as found in the Bible. Some Baptists accept literally heaven and hell as other places. Others look upon it symbolically. Many accept physical resurrection and the second coming of Christ with the last judgment.

The Methodists—they follow the Bible. Their fundamental belief is that religion is a personal experience and is reflected in the love of God, and more importantly the Methodist is the doctrine. They do not accept the Trinity as a formulative understanding. Most believe in the virgin birth. Salvation is through repentance and faith.

The United Church of Christ—the individual is free to interpret God's word within the Christian Revelations. Interesting. But the congregation acknowledges one God as supreme deity, as revealed by Jesus Christ, his son. Most believe in the trinity, and the virgin birth. They practice baptism. Salvation is through repentance in faith, and a striving to know God's will and living by it. After death the man will live on, either with God or away from God. But every individual interprets what this means.

The Disciples of Christ—the principal doctrine is essentially of the Baptist faith. God, the trinity; many accept virgin birth. But it is not required for their belief. The Disciples believe that a salvation comes through the confession of faith in Christ, who saves men from their sins and allocates their souls to God.

The Latter Day Saints—of course as you know, this is the Mormons. The Bible is used and the Book of the Mormon is used–the Pearl of Great Price. The fundamental theology is that they generally accept the trinity as three distinct persons; Christ is the mediator between God and man; and they acknowledge the virgin birth. Their salvation is through atonement of Christ and obedience to the laws and obedience to the gospel. In the Mormon belief, mankind may be saved; life after death is a state of spiritual progress first in the spirit world and later in a resurrected state where all men are to be judged.

We, as Spiritualists, didn't even make it into this book. But the Adventists did. They stress the eminent end of the world and the second coming of Christ who will destroy all evil and reign over a purified earth.

Church of Christ Scientists—Mary Baker Eddy, as you very well know, holds that God is all there really is. It puts considerable emphasis on spiritual healing. Evil, disease, and death are errors of belief to be overcome by spiritual understanding.

Jehovah's Witnesses—stress one God Jehovah, believing his kingdom is here and now and will replace all earthly governments, and that governments should not be obeyed if they are against the law of God.

Unitarian/Universalist Association—stress freedom of belief. Most hold that God is one. They do not believe in the Trinity. Christ was human and salvation comes from man's efforts, not from the grace of God.

The Friends—which are the Quakers, emphasize the direct experience of God's guiding spirit, the inner light, which is expressed through service to others. They are known as pacifists and often work as mediators.

So that is the rough breakdown of who's who in the Christian religion. It's incredible to me because if you notice, they are all rather similar; they all believe that there is something called God. They all believe that there was a man named Jesus who had something to do with that something called God. And yet they are at each other's throats all the time. It is utterly incredible when you look at "modern Christianity." One often wonders what really did cause the Dark Ages, because those concepts, part of them brought on by some of the teachings of Paul, have bathed the earth in blood. If you stand back and really look at it, it is an extremely bloody religion. Some of their very basic philosophies came over, of course, from some of the early Hebrew traditions that came about in the Old Testament. If someone does not believe in your God, he is a heathen and therefore he can be killed. And it was done. But we can't blame it on the Hebrews. Look at the Crusades. They were a glorious mess. Can you just imagine the Crusader who's heard the devout religious fanatic praying to God for the intercession of Jesus the Christ, and the Crusader standing there sword in hand, and praying to the same God to justify him killing the poor man who's praying to the same God kneeling in front of him? Interesting.

But what did Jesus say? We are going to get into some of that in detail as we begin actually reading the book. I think the thing that makes what he said so difficult, is that it is far too easy. It's far too easy. If he had put some parameters on it and really made us work for something, I mean really sacrifice to do right, it might have made a big difference. But he didn't. Part of the problem, of course, as I mentioned last time, was that the Jewish people called Jesus a prophet. He really wasn't because he did very little prophesying. He prophesied about the fall of the temple and this kind of thing, but not like the old prophets of the Old Testament–Ezekiel or Isaiah. But all through the New Testament, you will find Jesus popping up; simply doing what Isaiah says had to be done to prove that he was the Messiah. There are several sections of this that I really dearly love, and there are some of them that make so much sense. But let's just look at a few of them. Let's start with Matthew, Chapter 1, the Birth of Jesus Christ.

> *'The birth of Jesus was in this manner. While Mary his mother was acquired for a price for Joseph, before they came together, she was found with child of the Holy Spirit. But Joseph her husband was a pious man, and did not wish to make it public; so he was thinking of divorcing her secretly.'* (Matthew 1:18)

Okay, let's stop right there. What does it mean up here in the top when it says before they came together? Yet in the very next verse, Joseph is thinking of divorcing her. How can he divorce her if they have not been married yet?

> *'While he was considering this, the angel of the Lord appeared to him in a dream, and said to him, O, Joseph, son of David, do not be afraid to take your wife Mary, because he that is to be born of her is the Holy Spirit.'*

Mary became pregnant before they got married. Pure and simple. Back in those days that was a capital crime. If he had made it known or if she had made it known, they would have both been stoned. They would have killed both of them. Why did she get pregnant before they were actually married? Why does anybody do it today? We are talking about people. Remember, ordinary people who, and we will assume, were in love with each other. So in order to not have himself or Mary killed, nothing was said. Until the angel stepped in and said go ahead and marry her anyway, and so of course, he did. This angel, in most cases, was Michael. In one case it was Gabriel. As you know, these are archangels, the so-called messengers of the Lord. The whole sanctity of the New Testament is bound up in the three dreams of Joseph: the dream where the angel approves that he go ahead and marry Mary, the dream in which Joseph is told to leave the country so that the baby Jesus would not be killed, and the dream of the same angel telling them to come back and to be registered. If it were not for those directions and if those directions had not been followed, this book would have never been written. But let's look at this concept of the virgin birth. So many people look upon it because of the way it is written. But if you look at it, really look at the way it is written.... Please, if you are reading any bible, King James or especially if you are reading the Lamsa (and I would recommend that you get a copy of the Lamsa Bible) read it carefully. Stop and think about what you have just read.

> *'Behold, a virgin shall conceive and give birth to a son, and they shall call his name Emmanuel...'*

Now, what have I just said? I didn't say that a virgin was going to pop out a baby. I'm being harsh there, but I want you to look at it. I said a virgin will conceive and her firstborn child will be a man. That man will be Emmanuel. Jesus. No way can you look at that and decide that here was a virgin without conception who gave birth. The angel of the Lord himself said, "You will *conceive* and give birth." And yes, she was a virgin before she conceived and gave birth, because it was her first child. So let us not get carried away; look at exactly what it is saying. So you should read carefully as you go into these things.

It is repeated in two of the other gospels, worded slightly differently. Then a lot of things happened after Jesus was born.

Of course you know, we have the beautiful Christmas story, with the Magi (the three Wise Men) of which there were only actually two. But that's beside the point. They were there because they were fine psychics. They knew something was going on and they followed the star to Bethlehem. Okay, now you are not going to fool the shepherds, the camel herders, and anyone else at that time and in that part of the world. You are not going to fool them with a comet. You are not going to fool them with a bright meteor. You are not going to fool them with a crescent moon or the planet Venus. No way! They knew the sky. They knew the sky like you and I know our living rooms because they had no compasses. They knew the sky to find direction; they knew the sky to tell the time of night; they were not ignorant of the things in the heavens. Remember, even at this time, a long time before telescopes or anything else like that, they knew the major planets, and they called them planets. They called them 'wanderers,' because they were stars that wandered around the sky, instead of staying fixed like all the rest of the stars are supposed to. But they knew them.

So what was this light that the Wise Men followed to find where Jesus was laid in the manger? The constant companion of Jesus, as I have mentioned before, was the archangel Michael. If you have ever sensed Michael's vibration around you or if you are ever fortunate enough to see him clairvoyantly, you will notice that he always carries a sword. That sword has a hilt that is the most beautifully jeweled piece of work you have ever seen in your life, and it is brilliant! As you know, one of my minor degrees is in astronomy, and at one time I was trying to figure out what in the devil that star was. About this time I had bumped into Reverend Bradley and we discussed this kind of thing. She knew archangel Michael quite well. One night he simply showed us how to make a star. He came near the house in which we were having our talks and laid his sword down across the house so the handle of the sword came inside. Guess what it looked like? A bright star with four spikes! The bottom one went clear down through the floor of the house. How does the star point out something? With a shaft of light. It mentions it in the Bible. So this is what it was. Jesus' constant companion, the archangel Michael, simply held his sword up to guide those very rare people, who through their own clairvoyance and clairaudience knew that something very important had happened. That's how it came about.

Now for some of the other things that came about. Why were they in the stables? Well, there was no place in the inn. It's a little sketchy here, because we envision the Conrad Hilton sitting on the one side and a cave on the other side full of dirt and sand and straw. There was not quite that big of a contrast, believe me. The inns of those days were not the Conrad Hilton. They were simply a few rooms, most of them just a few extra sleeping rooms in a tavern or a home. And they were just simply full. So it was perfectly natural for Mary, Joseph, and their little donkey to simply stay in the stable. There is the dramatic scene of her laying him in the manger. Where better to put him? Mangers are built up off the floor, so cows could eat alfalfa or whatever they were eating, from them. They filled it with straw and it was soft and comfortable and the baby wouldn't turn over and fall out on his head or something like that. It was a good safe place to put him. So much for the romance of the manger scene. What else happened? Did the cows really talk that night? Did all the animals come around and sing? Did Jesus never cry? He was a baby! He probably cried a good deal, like all the rest of us. When did this happen? Was it really December the 25th when it was below zero degrees outside? No. It appears to have been sometime early in October, as close as we can tell.

But then what happens? We know very little about the child, Jesus. As I say, if we take these four books as representing only at the most, two years of his activity as an adult, we know only some of the things that were going on. Jesus grew up. What was he as he grew up? He was the son of a carpenter. Does this make him a carpenter? No. I'm the son of a carpenter. My dad was a carpenter, and I decided not to learn how to build houses. Jesus was probably busy about something else, too. We know from other sources, not these two books, what he was up to and I don't want to get into a lot of this spiritual stuff that we know, but I want to stick to stuff that you can read and verify on your own. We know that at about the age of ten or twelve, he was doing some remarkable things. As you recall, he went to the temple and was teaching. Remember, this is pure Hebrew conceptual kinds of things. He was part of the chosen house of Israel and this is who Jesus was talking to. So he went to the synagogue and he could understand the teachings of the Old Testament. As you recall, he stayed there too late and his mother and father came to get him. He said, "Leave me alone; I must be about my Father's work." So even as a young boy, he was probably very difficult to get along with. Very difficult. He had a temper and we know of a couple of instances where he used it.

But then somewhere at about the age of twelve or thirteen, Jesus disappeared from the scene. It's very difficult, without using non-textbook kinds of things, to figure out what he was doing and where he went. All of the information that we have got so far, that can be verified in literature, is that he was studying with the Essenes at an Essene community along the Dead Sea–probably the northeastern part of the Dead Sea. Who was he studying with? Well, we have some funny little references to some of the teachers at those various monasteries of the time, and one set of descriptions keeps coming up time and time again–the Teacher of Light. We find it in all variations and forms of the word. So Jesus disappeared from the scene and he studied with the Teacher of Light, like I say, for something like twenty years. It was a good amount of time. But what was he studying? First of all, of course, he was studying the Aramaic of the Old Testament and wouldn't we love to have had some of those scrolls right now! We could see precisely what he was studying. When did he decide that he was the Messiah? When did he decide that he was going to go on ahead and live his life to prove to be the Chosen One? It undoubtedly occurred on Spirit side before his incarnation into Mary, because all of those things that were around Mary had to be fulfilled as well. He had to be a direct lineage of the House of David, as we talked about last time. As for the Virgin Birth, he doesn't believe it himself, so it undoubtedly has come about in mistakes in reading. But as he studied, he undoubtedly studied Isaiah extensively, because in Isaiah and a couple of places in the Psalms, all of the detailed information about his life that he would be living is foretold. It is a prophecy. Probably he and Isaiah on the Spirit side, got their heads together and said, "Hey, it's about time, let's meet and put this game into play," and so he incarnated. I sometimes think that part way through the game, he thought he'd bitten off more than he could chew. We'll get to some of those things as we go along.

But then of course to get to things rolling, John the Baptist comes on the scene and roams around the country. He must have been quite a character! Dressed in, well, rags–in reality, probably animal skins. (Oh yes, now I see it; thank you, Padre.)

> *'Now this was John's clothes, they were made of camel's hair, and he had leather belts around his waist, and his food was locust and wild honey.'* (Matthew 3:4)

Wild honey I can see everyone agrees with. The locust–hmm, try it, you might like it. I have eaten fried locusts and they are really not bad. A little crunchy–you have to break their big legs off because the stickers on them are awfully sharp. But it's not bad. Intriguingly enough, that would be an almost perfectly balanced diet. Honey of course is the beautiful side of the carbohydrates and such, and locusts–and all insects–are superb food. You should all eat a cup of eeny-meeny bugs every day. Okay, so here was this man roaming around, screaming, yelling, scaring everybody, and ranting and raving about them not following the teachings of the Old Testament, not following the law. Remember, none of the New Testament is here yet. So he is talking about the old law and he is making everybody mad. He made everybody furious. And there are several things that happen. Jesus comes on the scene and he wants to be baptized by John, and of course, here again, we've got to read very carefully. We have got to look at things as they are said, and not the way Hollywood and some of the other books have portrayed it.

> *'Then Jesus came from Galilee to the Jordan to John, to be baptized by him. But John tried to stop him, saying I need to be baptized by you, and yet you have*

> *come to me? So Jesus answered and said to him, Permit it now, for this is necessary for us so that all righteousness may be fulfilled; and then he permitted him.'* And so he was baptized. Then what happened? *'When Jesus was baptized, he immediately went up out of the water; and the heavens were opened to him, and he saw the Spirit of God descending like a dove, and coming upon him; And behold , a voice from heaven which said, This is my beloved Son, with whom I am pleased.'* (Matthew 3:13)

Who heard that? The other people standing on the bank of the river waiting to be baptized? Who saw that? Those other people? Did John the Baptist see or hear it? No. Again, listen. Please forget Metro Goldwyn Mayer, and all the studios. Again listen to what it says–when Jesus was baptized, he immediately went up out of the water and the heavens were open to *him*. And *he* saw the spirit of God descending like a dove and coming upon him. And behold a voice from heaven said, "This is my beloved Son, with whom I am well pleased." Now that would make a magnificent theatrical presentation, which has been done in every religious presentation of the life of Christ. But ladies and gentlemen, it did not happen the way you have seen it. This is pure clairvoyance, pure clairaudience. Jesus was communicating with God or Spirit. Remember, any place in this book that we see the word God or Father, you can substitute the word Spirit. And this is exactly what happened. So here was kind of like a key, a clue or message to Jesus–bang–I'm on the right track, I've got it. So he went into the desert and fasted for forty days and forty nights. It ends up it was a little over a week. Here again we've got one of these exaggerations and amplification kind of things. It might have seemed like forty days and forty nights. And the devil tempted him. "If you are the son of God, command these stones to become bread...etc." These are all symbolic. He answered with one of these famous quotes that we always hear.

> *'It is written that it is not by bread alone that man can live, but by every word which proceeds from the mouth of God.'*

> *'And again it is written that you shall not tempt the Lord your God.'* (Matthew 4:4)

Now, remember this is Matthew writing. Finally, Jesus says,

> *'Get away, Satan, for it is written, You shall worship the Lord your God and him only shall you serve.'* (Matthew 4:4)

How did Matthew find out? Matthew doesn't come on the scene for quite a while. We will assume that Jesus told him that that's what happened. Like I say, that is the unfortunate part, because Jesus told him; he told someone; and he told someone; and he told someone and they wrote it down two and a half, maybe three, generations later. The first part of Matthew is probably one of the most important books to study. Jesus comes back from the wilderness, he starts going from place to place, and Jesus began to preach a very important concept.

> *'Repent for the kingdom of heaven is coming near.'* (Matthew 4:17)

Then he starts picking out a few of his disciples. Let's see, the first are Simon called Peter, and Andrew. I used to have them memorized, but he picked four. Here again, you have got to read carefully. For instance, the Sermon on the Mount, which is all of chapters 5 and 6 (we will touch that in just a little bit), when Jesus saw the crowds, he went up on the mountain, and when he sat down his disciples drew near to him. Every picture you see, every movie that you see, every radio script you have ever heard of, shows all twelve of them... but there were only four at that point in time. Jesus had only picked his first four: Peter, Andrew, James, and John. So many times we see it in a lot of the literature, Jesus talking to the multitudes and delivering the Sermon on the Mount, when it is simply not that way. Let's go to Matthew 4:25.

> *'And great crowds followed him from Galilee and from the ten cities and from Jerusalem and from Judea and from across the Jordan. When Jesus saw the crowds,*

> *he went up to the mountain; and as he sat down, his disciples drew near him. And he opened his mouth and taught them saying…'*

Then follows the Beatitudes and the Sermon on the Mount. *If* there was anyone else around, there would be very, very few because he deliberately walked away from them. He could have simply sat down right there and had his multitudes around him to deliver that address. One of the things that you will notice, if you will read any of the Bibles, but especially the Lamsa Bible–and read it carefully–you will notice that we know very little about what Jesus really taught the disciples. In this case, we *do* because it is the foundation of some of his basic teachings. But in many, many areas he will give a parable if there are other people around. He will give a parable, and then something else will happen, *'And he took his disciples aside and taught them.'* We have no idea what that was. I wish that we did! Because it would answer some questions.

Let me just touch a couple of these teachings to his disciples that we do know about. You remember the Beatitudes?

'Blessed are the humble, for theirs is the kingdom of heaven.' What's humble? It's an easy translation for that word, 'poor in spirit' or 'unassuming.' Theirs is the kingdom of heaven.

'Blessed are they that mourn, for they shall be comforted.' Straightforward.

'Blessed are the meek, for they shall inherit the earth.' Okay, now what does this sound like? In our days of the macho men of today, what in the devil is the significance about being meek? Meek in the classic sense means to not resist, to bend, to flow, to be able to bend like a reed in the wind.

> *'Blessed are those who hunger and thirst for justice, for they shall be satisfied. Blessed are the merciful, for they shall have mercy. Blessed are the pure of heart, for they shall see God. Blessed are the peacemakers, for they shall be called sons of God. Blessed are those who are persecuted for the sake of justice, for theirs is the kingdom of heaven. Blessed are you…'* (the disciples?)

'...when men reproach you and persecute you and speak against you every kind of evil, falsely, for my sake.'

I want to go over the Lord's Prayer with you. From the Aramaic it is such a beautiful thing. As I mentioned, Jesus asks his disciples to pray in this manner.

'...Our Father in heaven, hallowed be thy name. Thy Kingdom come. Thy will be done, as in heaven so on earth. Give us bread for our needs from day to day. And forgive us our offences, as we have forgiven our offenders. And do not let us enter into temptation, but deliver us from evil. For thine is the kingdom and the power and the glory forever and ever. Amen.' (Matthew 6:9)

And of course, look at the footnote that 'evil' is error.

One thing that I would be very tempted to do would be to read from the King James and then the Lamsa, the King James and then the Lamsa, and we would be here all night, contrasting and comparing even just the first few chapters of Matthew. But there are a few places where I am going to do this because it will help, I think, to show you how different ideas have arrived from the same basic teachings. But as part of this Sermon on the Mount are some very, very beautiful warnings. For instance in Matthew 6:1,

'Be careful concerning your alms, not to do them in the presence of men, merely that they may see them; otherwise you have no reward with your Father in heaven. Therefore when you give alms, do not blow a trumpet before you, just as the hypocrites do in the synagogues and in the market places, so that they may be glorified by men. Truly I say to you that they have already received their reward.'

There's a very beautiful and very heavy psychological thing going on here. If you have to stand up and proclaim your righteousness, if you have to stand up and proclaim your beauty so that everybody else hears it, it means you don't really believe that you have it yourself. You are trying to get verification from those around you. And hence he says that they have already received their reward.

> *'But when you give alms, let not your left hand know what your right hand is doing. So that your alms may be done secretly, and your Father who sees in secret, shall himself reward you openly.'*

So what are alms? Not only gifts to a church but your activities to other people: your acts of compassion, your acts of love, your acts of helping. Don't broadcast them. Keep them just to you. Let not even your right hand know what your left hand is doing. This is simply a way of saying, as we would say here at Chapel, don't sit around and mind screw about it. Did I do the best thing? Was it really good? Does that make me better? Leave it alone. Do it and forget it.

Another one that we often hear a great deal about and we are all guilty of this–we worry. That seems to be one of the best things we do.

> *'For this reason, I say to you, Do not worry for your life, what you will eat and what you will drink, nor for your body, what you will wear, Behold, is not life much more important than food, and the body than clothing? Observe the birds of the sky, for they do not sow, neither do they harvest nor gather into barns, and yet your Father in heaven feeds them. Are you not much more important than they? Who is among you who by worrying can add one cubit to his stature? Why do you worry about clothing? Observe the wild flowers, how they grow; they do not get tired out [worn out] nor do they spin. But I say to you that not even Solomon with all of his glory was arrayed like one of them.'* (Matthew 6:25)

Then he punctuates as chapter 6 ends, *'Therefore do not worry about tomorrow; for tomorrow will look after itself. Sufficient for each day is its own trouble.'*

If we could learn just that one little teaching it could make our daily lives much, much smoother. As you have heard me talk, especially during Sunday lectures, we get all upset about what's going to happen tomorrow. There is nothing we can do about it. There is an excellent chance that what we are worrying about won't happen anyway. So we worry ourselves sick about it. Take each day in stride. As it has been said by some of the great poets, live today as if it were the last day of your life; as if when you go to sleep tonight, you are not going to wake in the morning. Did you live your life today exactly in a way that you felt was right and you felt good about doing? If you didn't, make sure you do it tomorrow morning.

Let's look at another beautiful one, this thing about judging others.

> *'Why do you see the splinter which is in your brother's eye, and do not feel the beam which is in your own eye?'* (Matthew 7:3)

Isn't that a goody? And aren't we good at that one?

> *'How can you say to your brother, Let me take out the splinter from your eye, and behold there is a beam in your own eye? O hypocrites, first take out the beam from your own eye and then you will see clearly to get out the splinter from your brother's eye.'*

'Do not give holy things to dogs.' In this case, non-circumcised people–in other words, non- Jews. Remember he was teaching to the chosen House of Israel, not the gentiles. At that point in time, the gentiles were not circumcised, which was of course Hebraic Law. When the word 'dog' is used in all but I think two places in the Bible, it is referring to persons not chosen of the House of Israel; not to puppy dogs running around in the yard.

'And do not throw your pearls before swine...' (pearls in this case meaning your wisdom) *'...for they might tread upon them with their feet, and then turn and rend you.'* And any of you who have tried to discuss your philosophy here at the Chapel with other people, know how that can happen.

> *'Ask, and it shall be given to you; seek and you shall find; knock and it shall be opened to you. For whosoever*

asks, receives; and he who seeks, will find; and to him who knocks, the door is opened.'

A little further down is a teaching that lots of people chatter about but very few people do well.

'Whatever you wish men to do for you do likewise also for them; for this is the law of the prophets.'

This is the Golden Rule, the classic teaching. Do unto others.

One of the teachings I wanted to discuss as a direct comparison between the King James and the Lamsa paints quite a picture. I am sure that those of you who were raised in Sunday school will have bumped into it. Let's go to the King James first. We are in Matthew.

'And when he was to come to the other side into the country of the Gergesenes, there met him two possessed with devils, coming out of the tombs, exceeding fierce, so that no man might pass by that way. And, behold, they cried out, saying, What have we to do with thee, Jesus, thou son of God? Art thou come hither to torment us before the time? And there was a good way off from them a herd of many swine feeding. So the devils besought him, saying, If thou cast us out, suffer us to go away into the herd of swine. And he said unto them, Go. And when they were come out, they went into the herd of swine; and, behold, the whole herd of swine ran violently down a steep place into the sea, and perished in the waters.' (Matthew 8:28)

That paints quite a picture doesn't it? Now, let's read the same passage from the Lamsa Bible.

'And when Jesus came to the port on the other side, to the country of the Gadarenes, he was met by two lunatics, who were just coming out of the cemetery. They were exceedingly vicious so that no man would dare to travel that road. And they cried aloud saying, What business have we together, Jesus, son of God? Have you

come here to torment us before the time? Now there was nearby them a large herd of swine feeding. And the lunatics kept asking him, saying, If you are going to heal us, permit us to attack the herd of swine. Jesus said to them, Go. And immediately they left and attacked the swine, and the whole herd went straight over the cliff and fell into the sea and were drowned in the water. And they who fed them ran away and went to the city, and reported everything that happened, and told about the lunatics. So all the city went out to meet Jesus; and when they saw him, they urged him to depart from their borders.'

A question... did Jesus heal them? What's this thing about casting devils into swine? You notice that the Aramaic did not mention 'devils.' Lunatics, crazy people, possessed by a devil, possessed by an evil spirit? No. That is the King James interpretation. More importantly, and it would be an interesting assignment to ask the question I just asked–did Jesus heal them? But as you are searching through the next three chapters to find that answer, remember–what did they consider more important? Let's go play with the pigs, instead of letting you heal us. And he granted their wish. Go play with the pigs. And they did. Did he get a hold of them later and heal them? A good question. Look it up, do some reading.

I want to touch on a couple of little things that have upset people. It upsets a lot of people! It is the whole thing of crucifixions. Here again, you have to read Isaiah and read it carefully to see why crucifixion. Our modern Christianity has got the wrong picture of it! Jesus died for our sins and we are washed in his blood and purified... *no.* The only reason for the crucifixion was that he was living up to and fulfilling the prophecy of Isaiah who said that he would be condemned, would be crucified, and raised on the third day. It's as simple as that. He was the Messiah.

Then there are the words that Jesus spoke from the cross. '*My God, my God, why hast thou forsaken me?*' Can you imagine the man Jesus saying that? Even if we substitute Spirit for God, "Spirit, Spirit, why have you forsaken me?" A man who spent twenty years of studying, very likely Isaiah, and then all of his adult life, at least within his ministry, living up to Isaiah's prophecy, and is now going to question what is happening? Very fortunately, we have a very beautiful answer to this question. As you know, when he was crucified, they put a sign above his head on the cross that read, "This is Jesus, king of the Jews." It was written both in ancient Hebrew and in the Aramaic.

Who was there, incidentally? All of the disciples? No, not at all. Mary, Mary Magdalene, and John were the only ones there. There is an implication that Peter might have been standing off on the sidelines looking over a bush, but remember he was trying to avoid being associated with Jesus so that they wouldn't crucify him too. Do you remember when we were reading all of the agreements that were in the four gospels, those places where each of the four authors agreed that the same thing happened or didn't happen? They don't agree on a lot of this.

How about the bandits that were hanging beside him? There is a very beautiful verse from the story that has to do with simply the positioning of a comma. In the King James, it reads,

'And Jesus said unto him, Verily I say unto thee, today shall thou be with me in paradise.' (Luke 23:43)

Or was it, as it is in some Bibles, *'Verily, verily I say unto you, today. You will be with me in paradise.'* In the Aramaic it is just that point blank. *'Jesus said to him, Truly I say to you Today, you will be with me in Paradise.'* The reason that many of the churches don't like this is exactly what I read to you earlier this evening: you have to go to purgatory, and you've got to be weighed in the check and balance. Incidentally, this is pure Egyptian–the Scale of Thoth weighing your heart, to see if you are worthy to go to heaven or to hell. Let's just substitute a few things and put an angel there instead of an Ibis-headed god, and let's change the scales to the rules of feathers, and we have the Hebrew concept of being weighed in purgatory. In fact there are several Christian sects that believe that Jesus died on the cross and went to Purgatory, and then came back to his tomb. The Bible doesn't say anything about that. Not at all. In the Lamsa Bible,

> *'Now from the sixth hour there was darkness all over the land until the ninth hour. And about the ninth hour,*

Jesus cried out with a loud voice and said My God, my God, for this I was spared.' (Matthew 27:45)

The 'spared' can be reinterpreted more directly as meaning 'my destiny.' *'My God, my God, for this is my destiny.'* That is probably exactly what he said. Because that is exactly what he meant. He had lived, up to this point, almost to the last line of Isaiah's prophecy. He was, of course, sold out by Judas. He was condemned by Pilate and the rest of the group, although Pilate had nothing to do with the crucifixion. But he had to be crucified to live up to the concept of the Messiah. And for that he was spared.

A little earlier, in Gethsemane, he was there with his disciples and he asked them to stay with him. He cried. He cried because he probably saw what he had failed to do. His chosen disciples did not believe him. How could he expect the rest of the people to believe him? Jesus cried many times. He was very emotional man. And finally, after these comments to Spirit or to God, whichever you want, they offered him a sponge with vinegar to drink as he hung on the cross. This is not verified in all four books, but let's assume that they did.

'But Jesus again cried out with a loud voice and gave up his spirit.' (Matthew 27:50)

He died. And then follows in the next four verses, some of the most incredible things that have not been verified, but if they had occurred, I am certain would have been verified some place outside of the Holy Scriptures. Remember, when they decided to kill this man, there were some people who weren't quite sure what he really was. Some of them, in fact, were not quite sure that he could be killed. They had tried it several times before. They tried to throw him over the cliff; they had tried to throw rocks and stone him to death. He always got away. But, was he going to get away from this? I think that's why they (the Jewish rulers) pulled in the Roman guards, the whole concept of Rome. Certainly Rome was not going to goof it up. So Jesus dies on the cross. This is from Matthew 27:51.

> *'And immediately the curtains at the door of the temple were torn in two, from the top to the bottom; and the earth quaked and rocks split; and tombs were opened; and the bodies of a great many saints who were sleeping in death rose up and went out; and after his resurrection, they entered into the holy city and appeared to a great many.'*

That would have been quite a phenomenon, to say the least! But Matthew is the only one who mentions it. Can we say that Matthew was just a little overcome by everything that happened? He wasn't there. In fact, he probably wasn't even in the same province, because they scattered when Jesus was arrested. They ran and hid because they did not want to be associated with this whole thing.

Who was at the crucifixion? They are mentioned here. What about the body of Christ? As you know, they took it and laid it in a new tomb that was not of course built for him. Because this was Friday afternoon, or Friday evening, they had to go the next morning to anoint the body with oils and so on and so forth, and wrap it in wrappings and all of the paraphernalia of the tomb and of a rabbi. Remember, Jesus was a rabbi. And then, what happened? Well, he missed the prophecy of Isaiah, because he died late Friday afternoon. He stayed in the tomb Saturday and he rose Sunday morning. No way can you make that three days. No way! A day and a half at the most. But even the writers themselves, Matthew, Mark, Luke, and John, or whoever wrote these books, referred to that three day period. We know that he died on Friday because of the reference to the Passover Feast, and we know where in the week that activity was. He apparently spent Saturday in the tomb and he rose Sunday morning. As you know, he disassociated his body when he rose, so that again, he could live up to the prophecy, this particular one which is found in the Psalms. So that his body would not undergo decay. It would not be defiled.

There are several beautiful things having to do with who came to the tomb. As you know, Mary Magdalene and the other Mary came to the tomb and of course they found it empty. Here again, we have a difference in definition. In a couple of the books the stone was rolled aside, in the other books the stone was fractured into pieces. The guards that were placed at the tomb by Pilate had gone to sleep. The political authorities of the time were sure that someone was going to steal the body to *make* this event live up to Isaiah's writings. So, they posted centurions at the tomb. The centurions who were there guarding the tomb, simply went to sleep.

> *'And behold, a great earthquake took place; for the angel of the Lord came down from heaven, and went up and rolled away the stone from the door, and sat on it.'* (Matthew 28:2)

The stone was rolled away from the opening to the tomb, and Jesus' body was gone. Jesus came out of the tomb, and he was seen by several people. Mary Magdalene did not recognize him at first. She loved him very, very much. Why she did not recognize him is a very good question. As you know, he went to appear to his disciples many times, and as in the doubting Thomas kind of thing, they did not believe him. They couldn't understand what this was all about. Then of course he gave what to many of us are some of the most important teachings of his whole career. From the King James, you know he appeared to them at the Sea of Galilee and asked them if they had any food. He built a fire and sat down and cooked fish, and ate with them, as only a fully materialized spirit could do. Then as he was about ready to leave, he said to them,

> *'All power is given unto me in heaven and in earth. Go ye, therefore, and teach all nations, baptizing them in the name of the Father, and of the Son, and of the Holy Ghost: Teaching them to observe all things whatsoever I have commanded you; and, lo, I am with you always, even unto the end of the world.'* (Matthew 28:18)

This is the point. He is asking them to teach "whatsoever I have commanded of you."

What did he teach? What were his commandments? Remember when I first started this evening, I said the problem with the life of

Christ is that what he was teaching was too simple. The only commandment that he gave was that you should love one another. The only instructions that he gave them was that you should believe upon the works that he did and *do* them, and do them even greater.

Then we have a great host of people who are chattering about this second coming. You hear it all the time. Our born again Christian friends, I believe, are just running around holding their breath until it occurs. Ummm… he's already here! What did I just read to you? *'Lo, I am with you always, even unto the end of the world'* Does that sound like someone who is planning to come back and do something? *No*. He's already here working from his side to us. What is this second coming thing based on? Some very interesting little quotations. One is in Matthew 24:27,

> *'For as the lightning cometh out of the east, and shineth even unto the west; so shall also the coming of the son of man be.'*

What on earth does that mean? It simply means exactly what Jesus did. He did come on the scene like lightning. And boy, didn't it reflect into the west? Not something he was going to do, but something he already did.

Let's go over to John, and this is a famous one that you hear all the time.

> *'In my Father's house are many mansions; if it were not so, I would have told you. I go to prepare a place for you. And if I go and prepare a place for you, I will come again, and receive you unto myself; that where I am, there ye may be also.'* (John 14:2)

What is he talking about? If you go back up a couple of verses, he's talking about when they die, when they cross over. Yes, he's going to come to them, yes he's going to meet them, and he's going to meet them as spirit to spirit. Precisely that and nothing more. Remember that he is talking to his disciples. Certainly not to us humble gentiles who pay a little more attention to what he was teaching than anyone else on the planet, it looks like.

Finally, over in the Acts of the Apostles 1:11,

> *'Ye men of Galilee, why stand ye gazing up into heaven? This same Jesus, who is taken up from you into heaven, shall so come in like manner as ye have seen him go into heaven.'*

Is this the second coming? They carry it a long ways, as I am sure you know. They've got it that he is going to come and rule the world. He's going to judge. Even *that* you must wonder about. What did he say about judging? *'Judge not lest ye be judged.'* But he's going to be judging and he's going to straighten the world up? I kind of doubt it.

I have several things marked here. As I have mentioned to you, I am a great one for marking up my Bibles. So if I go to hell, I'll give you a call. I may very well go to hell, but I won't go to hell because of what I've done to this book!

There were very few things that he actually prophesied. One, of course, was this thing of the son of man:

> *'While they were traveling through Galilee, Jesus said to them, The son of man will shortly be delivered into the hands of men; And they will kill him, and on the third day he will rise up; And they were very much grieved.'* (Matthew 17:22) Of course they were!

Probably one of the most beautiful ones, from our standpoint, is when Jesus is sitting around just talking with the group.

> *'He said unto them, Who do you say that I am? Simon Peter answered, saying, You are the Christ, the son of the living God. Jesus answered, saying to him, Blessed are you, Simon Bar-Jona (Son of Jona) for flesh and blood did not reveal it to you, but my Father in heaven. I tell you also that you are the stone, and upon this stone I will build my church; and the doors of Sheol (hell) shall not shut upon it. I will give you the keys of the kingdom of heaven; and whatever you bind on earth shall be bound in heaven; and whatever you loose on earth shall be loosed in heaven.'* (Matthew 16:15)

What is the stone? Peter when it is translated from Hebrew means rock. But what is he talking about here? He's not talking about Peter. What is this cornerstone, what is this stone upon which he is going to build his church? It is the fact that flesh and blood did not reveal to him who Jesus was, but *Spirit* did.

> *'For flesh and blood did not reveal it to you but my Father in heaven and I tell you all so upon this stone, I will build my church.'*

His church is a spiritual church. His teachings were spiritual teachings. Where is heaven? It is within you. Where is hell? It is in the dark corners of your psychotic imagination. What is right and wrong? You *know* what is right and wrong.

Read the first four books of the New Testament. I am prejudiced and I am sorry, but read the first four. Paul had some drawbacks. All you ladies, I am sure, don't like Paul at all. He didn't think much of you at all. You weren't allowed in church–if you had any questions you could sit out on the steps and if your husband wanted to tell you the answers when he came out, great, but if he didn't want to, too bad. Women had that position; we talked about it last time. Remember the New Testament era, the time in which the New Testament took place, is a short time before the birth of Christ and about thirty years after that. If we just use ordinary dates and believe them, we've got around 30-32 AD. Thirty years. Customs had not changed at all. And this is what got Jesus in trouble: he was healing on the Sabbath. On the Sabbath you are supposed to do nothing but rest. Don't do any works. This is the kind of thing that eventually got him in trouble with the priests and Sadducees. He was pointing out to them that what they believed was no longer true. It was simply no longer valid. About the only place that he agreed directly with them was in regards to the Ten Commandments. His remarks about adultery–if you look after a woman in lust, you have committed adultery in your heart already. It makes no difference. Gina Lollobridgida was probably the most recent source of the most sin in the North American continent!

It is the simplicity of his teachings. When they asked him point blank, "Why are you here? Why have you come?"

> *'I have come that you would have life and have it more abundantly.'*

That's not sackcloth and ashes! That's not crawling around on your knees and begging for forgiveness. Let's take just that premise. There is absolutely nothing in the New Testament that should spur anyone to build a church. Where was all of his teaching done? When he taught in the synagogues, he was simply reading and discussing the Torah. He was simply reading to them the things of the Old Testament and how they should be looked at. Apparently that made the other rabbis very angry. But when he taught his people, when he taught his disciples, he did it outside. He did it out under the sky–under the stars if it was night, or under the sun if it was out in the hot desert.

He was a very human man. He cried. He got angry. As you know he tore up the front end of a temple because of the money changers. He killed a fig tree just on a mental command because he and his disciples were hungry. They came upon the fig tree that had no fruit on it, and so he cursed it because it was barren. It was the wrong time of the year for the poor fig tree. The poor fig tree couldn't do anything about it. But it made him mad and he cursed it and it withered up and died in front of them. Power–yes. Absolute power. Anything he wanted to bring about, he could have, but the fig tree got in the way and his temper flared. He destroyed it to make a point.

Let's look at the concept of the Last Supper. Here again, some of our famous artists have ruined our picture of that. Da Vinci's "The Last Supper"–oh, what a spread! You know, the big table with the heavy legs, and the table cloth, and the whole bit–no. If there was a table, there was probably a little, low circular table sitting in the middle of the room. They were seated on the floor, or maybe on cushions. Remember he was a rabbi, and so were his disciples. So they were all wearing their head coverings. They sat around in a room and as it got dark they probably lit it with oil lamps. He had a few chosen. He loved

Peter. We have the beautiful questioning between Jesus and Peter. Jesus asks Peter, "Do you love me?" If you go back to the original text you will notice that the three loves that he uses are the three major kinds of love. The first one is the kind of love like respect, the second one is the kind of love like father to son, and the third one is love like the love we think about when we talk about being in love. He pins Peter down. "Do you love me this way? Do you love me that way? Do you love me that way?" Peter answers affirmative to all of them. And Jesus ends his comments with, "Feed my flock, feed my sheep, feed my ewes." Because that is the order in which someone pays attention to a flock of sheep. Of course, he was referring to the people who he had already introduced to the new concepts that he had been trying to get across.

There was a question that I will have to answer because we are almost out of time. A lady asked me, "Did Jesus have any lovers?" Well, that depends on what you mean by lovers. If we are talking about going to bed with someone out of wedlock–no, of course not. It would be against his law. It would be against Hebraic law. If you had to pick a woman that he loved, it would undoubtedly be Mary Magdalene, because she was with him quite often, the *only* woman to be with him very often. As you recall she anointed his feet with oil, she took care of him when he was tired, she rubbed his brow as he was falling to sleep, this kind of thing. So if you had to pick someone that he loved very, very much, it would be her for the women. If you were to pick the men that he loved, and he loved everybody, but if we are going to more specific, he loved Peter. As I mentioned, the comment about love–yes, on all three levels. And he loved John, which is amazing. John is the one who was written about in only small sections in the Bible that really tell us very little about him. But John was very close to Jesus. He was there at the crucifixion. He was there at all of the appearances of Jesus. He walked with Jesus. In fact there is a little fight between the resurrected Jesus and Peter, because John is there following them along. Jesus reprimands Peter for implying that this other person ought to leave. No–not at all.

At the Last Supper, as you recall in the story about the betrayal, Jesus announces that someone at this table is going to betray him. John is lying on his breast, lying on Jesus' breast. Remember they are sitting on the floor, so he is laid up against Jesus and Peter pulls him aside. Peter apparently was sitting just to the other side of John. So Peter says, "Hey, John, ask the master who's going to be this person who does that?" Peter doesn't have enough guts to ask him himself. So he asks John to ask Jesus. John lies back over towards Jesus and whispers in his ear, "Who's going to do this?' and as you know they are eating. They are dipping bread into some kind of who knows what goop, to sup. So Jesus dips his bread in and hands it, of course, to the one who is going to betray him, Judas.

Who did Jesus love? Everyone. Was Jesus *in* love with anyone? If we look at it in the etheric way, yes. Certainly, Mary Magdalene, certainly John, very likely Peter. If we look at it in a sexual way, we have no idea, but I doubt it very much, because Jesus would not break his own law. Remember, he was a rabbi. He could not have gone to bed with Mary Magdalene and lived up to Judaic law. He could not have gone to bed with John or with Peter and lived up to the very law that he was trying to straighten out.

Was Jesus a happy man? I don't know. If you take it just as the four gospels are written, you would almost have to say no because they are too serious. He cries too much. He's disappointed too much. He was reaching for an impossible goal. In the few months that he had allotted himself to be a light unto the world, he didn't make it. And unfortunately, today, Christianity in its ordinary sense is probably one of the most widely spread religions on the face of the planet. Yet if we take each of them in their own way and look at them as individuals, how many of them are truly Christlike? I am afraid that the percentage is going to be small. One of the reasons why is because someone who is Christlike is not going to stand on the street corner and scream that he is. He is not going to prove it by going to a Sunday church once a week. He is going to prove it by doing what Jesus said to do: believe in him and do the things that he did.

And you can do those things and even greater! Above all, love ye one another. To use his own words,

'Love ye one another, as I have loved you.'

Please take the time to read the Bible. Preferably read the Lamsa Bible, and the New Testament, especially. We have touched on just a very few verses, mostly in Matthew. Read all of it; read carefully. Don't jump to conclusions. Look at the footnotes. The footnotes are beautifully prepared. A few of those are so beautiful that if you will take the time to read them, I think you will enjoy it. To read and understand the King James Version of the Bible, I would recommend that if you are really going to do it, read the Clark's Commentary, all five volumes of it. It gives you a hint of what's really going on. But I think in the Lamsa Bible, we have the closest thing to what actually was going on. I can say that because as you all know, I am a Spiritualist. I am a medium, and I have talked to a great many of these people. I know some of these disciples or apostles rather well. You'd be surprised at some of the things that they have said. I've talked to Jesus, and I am sure all of you have or will experience his presence. He said he would be there. He would be there for everyone. Not just the chosen people of Israel. He would go to everyone.

'And Lo, I am with you always.'

He meant that!

CPSIA information can be obtained
at www.ICGtesting.com
Printed in the USA
BVOW08s1447301117
501366BV00002B/90/P

9 781609 766917